DT
DS

DELTA TEACHER DEVELOPMENT SERIES

Series editors Mike Burghall and Lindsay Clandfield

Jo Blackwell

Teaching Lexically

Principles and practice

Hugh Dellar and Andrew Walkley

DELTA PUBLISHING

Published by
DELTA PUBLISHING
Quince Cottage
Hoe Lane
Peaslake
Surrey GU5 9SW
England

www.deltapublishing.co.uk

ISBN 978-1-909-78322-5

Edited by Mike Burghall
Designed by Christine Cox
Cover photo © Tom Franks/Shutterstock.com
Printed by CPI Antony Rowe, United Kingdom

Acknowledgements

First and foremost, we would both like to thank everyone at Delta for believing in this project from the start, and for their hard work and commitment to ensuring it sees the light of day.

Secondly, we would like to thank colleagues past and present from both the teaching and the publishing realms. Without the constant discussions, debates, arguments and interactions over the years, we would not have been able to develop our ideas as fully as we have.

Despite the inevitability of such a list failing to mention all concerned, we feel it only proper to mention in passing Leo Selivan, Ivor Timmis, Nick Barrett, Rebecca Sewell, Luis Pedreira, Margot Van Der Doelen, Karen Spiller, Chris Wenger, Dennis Hogan, Gavin McLean, John McHugh, Bryan Fletcher, Richard Cauldwell, Mark Powell, Chris Gough, Jon Wright, Julian Savage, Andrew Fairhurst, Sally Dalzell, John Smith, Maud Dunkeld and Philip Kerr.

Thirdly, we are both eternally grateful to our wives and children, for indulging us during the long hours of writing that this project required of us.

And finally, we would like to thank Michael Lewis and Jimmie Hill – for lighting the flame for us back in the mid-1990s, and for subsequently encouraging us to kindle it.

From the authors

Hugh's story

The seeds for this book were planted in the early 1990s. I had qualified as a teacher and was living in Jakarta, Indonesia. When I started trying to teach myself Indonesian, I was unconsciously using a 'grammar + words' approach, memorising single words and studying grammar forms and rules. The results were mixed, to say the least!

It took me a while to realise that a sentence like *anjing itu menggonggong* – 'the dog is barking' – wasn't a good example of how the present continuous was generally used, nor was it representative of what is said about dogs or barking. In short, it was a sentence I'd learned to somehow get to grips with the language, yet which had no real utility. At the same time, what was helping me was learning repertoires of relatively fixed questions and answers (often featuring grammatical structures I'd not yet studied, but was able to use within limited contexts), common phrases I heard a lot, and so on. Of course, there was also lots of repetition and practice.

When I read *The Lexical Approach* (1993) by Michael Lewis, I found my language learning experiences had inadvertently brought me to a lexical view of language – and his book provided me with a clearer way of thinking about this. I later came to understand that Lewis was simply one writer working within a long tradition of lexically-oriented thinking.

However, while my initial reading of *The Lexical Approach* energised me, it also confounded me as I felt many of its ideas about putting this way of seeing language to practical use weren't as developed as they might have been. The activities suggested often seemed tokenistic, and didn't amount to a thorough reconstruction of practical pedagogy.

In the years that followed – through my classroom practice, my writing of classroom material, and my conversations with students, colleagues and other EFL professionals – I came to the ideas laid out in this book: our attempt to make lexical teaching more accessible and more widespread!

Hugh

Andrew's story

My route to a lexical way of teaching probably started with my failed attempts to learn French at school. It was only after I started teaching in Spain that I had any real success in speaking a foreign language – a success that stemmed far more from using the language than from studying grammar rules.

I started out with no training, but my main approach was to not do to others what my teachers had done to me! Instead, I mainly chatted to my students and told them some words when they asked about them. We listened to songs and watched videos.

Grammar finally came back into view when I did my CELTA course. I learnt how you could present grammar via dialogues, and how it could be related to real-life communication. I also discovered the *Collins Cobuild English Course* (1988), which based its syllabus around frequent words, and *Conversation Gambits*, from the same year, which contained chunks for conversation.

These experiences primed me to receive *The Lexical Approach* when I read it on my Diploma course. However, I was also taking on other (sometimes contradictory!) ideas – such as teaching skills, and teaching grammar through comparing sentences and discussing differences in meaning.

When I first met Hugh, we were both beginning to wonder about where a lexical approach might go: what would the syllabus be? What should materials and classes be like? We continued to be influenced by other writers, our classroom experience and discussions with colleagues. Getting involved in writing and teacher training brought this into focus, because, when you're paid to share materials and practice, you want to be clear about your own beliefs and principles.

So for me, this book is an outline of where we have both got to so far in determining our beliefs, how these inform our own practice and how we can explore and share that practice. It's *a* lexical approach, rather than *the* lexical approach, *a good way* of teaching, rather than *the only way* of teaching – and we hope it helps you on your own journey.

Andrew

Contents

Contents

'What is a teacher? A teacher is someone who has what you need and knows how to give it to you.'

Christopher Ross, 2001

'By far the greatest obstacle to good reading is insufficient number of words in the learner's lexicon. [In research studies] lexis was found to be the best predictor of success in reading, better than syntax or general reading ability.'

Bhatia Laufer, 1997

'Word meanings are like stretchy pullovers, whose outline contour is visible, but whose detailed shape varies with use.'

Jean Aitchison, 1996

'The teacher's main responsibility is response-ability.'

Peter Wilberg, 1988

'In most of our utterances, we are creatures of habit, immensely predictable, rehearsing the same old platitudes and the same old clichés in almost everything we say. If it were not so, ordinary language would become unworkable. Humankind cannot bear very much creativity.'

Patrick Hanks, 2013

'After Elementary level, the largest part of a language learner's task is to build up an adequate stock of high-priority words and lexicalised phrases, including both knowledge of their forms and an awareness of their more important meanings, the major collocational and syntactic constraints on their use, and so on.'

Michael Swan, 1996

A

Teaching lexically

There have been many thousands of pages written about how people learn languages, yet we would suggest they can all be neatly summarised in a very small number of principles.

Principles of how people learn

Essentially, to learn any given item of language, people need to carry out the following steps:

1 Understand the meaning of the item.
2 Hear/see an example of the item in context.
3 Approximate the sounds of the item.
4 Pay attention to the item and notice its features.
5 Do something with the item – use it in some way.
6 Repeat these steps over time, when encountering the item again in other contexts.

Principles of why people learn

The second area of principle that we think is uncontroversial, but that is worth spelling out, is why people want to learn foreign languages. The Council of Europe, which published the Common European Framework of Reference for languages (CEFR), suggests people learn for the following reasons:

- To deal with the business of everyday life in another country, and to help foreigners staying in their own country to do so.
- To exchange information and ideas with young people and adults who speak a different language, and to communicate thoughts and feelings to them.
- To achieve a wider and deeper understanding of the ways of life and forms of thought of other peoples, and of their cultural heritage.

One underlying assumption that the CEFR makes is that students will be taking classes, as part of their efforts to learn languages. It is perhaps worth questioning why this might be. After all, many people learn languages without ever participating in formal study. It seems to us that one of the fundamental reasons students take classes is that this allows them to set aside some time for study. A lot of people have neither the time nor the discipline to study on their own. While it is clearly true that the best language learners do a lot outside of class, we believe that teachers should recognise that, for what is probably the majority of learners, class time is basically all they may have spare for language study.

Bibliography
We cite other authors and resources throughout the book and the full reference can be found in the bibliography on pages 145-146.

Glossary
A glossary of terms as we are using them can be found on pages 147-150. The first instance of their use in the book is marked with an asterisk *.

That has implications for the pace of progress and for level, but it also emphasises how vital it is that what happens in class meets the main linguistic wants and needs of learners; chiefly:

- To be able to do things with their language.
- To be able to chat to others.
- To learn to understand other cultures better.

Teaching and learning choices

Most of the principles outlined above are relatively undisputed, but the thousands of pages written about such limited principles are testament to the fact that debates do remain. In particular, there is much disagreement about the following:

- The very nature of language itself.
- What language to teach.
- Whether you can actually teach and learn languages – or whether they are simply acquired.
- The order in which to teach the language you choose.
- Practical ways in which each principle of how to learn language is realised.
- The relative importance of each principle.

Debates often revolve around the speed of the learning process, and how easily the learner will be able to take in the items of language taught and use them effectively in the world outside the classroom. There is also much discussion about how the process can be made more – or less –motivating for learners.

The choices teachers make with regard to these issues may be informed by research and the consideration of evidence, but it is also fair to say that reliable research and evidence can be hard to come by. As such, teachers will inevitably base some – or all – of their decisions on beliefs, arguments and previous experiences as both teachers and language learners.

Choices are also likely to be at least partially the product of the attitudes and beliefs of the time and place that teachers are living in, and, as such, may also perhaps be a reaction to what has come before. For example, one might see the current argument against fun activities and games – and the move towards more correction and intervention (as exemplified in the recent emergence of the Demand High concept) – as being a reaction to the free-spending, debt-creating economy of the 1990s and 2000s! The move in language teaching towards such practices could be seen as a reflection of the contemporary discourse that claims that what people want now is something more controlled and austere.

To recognise and acknowledge this is simply to state that, as teachers, trainers and materials writers ourselves, we are no different when it comes to our principles and our choice of exercises that we feel best realise the principles described earlier. As such, in the pages of Part A that follow, we would like to explore our beliefs and principles in more depth, so that you can see how they fit with the exercises and practices that will follow in Part B of *Teaching Lexically*.

One view of language

Grammar plus words plus skills

Traditionally, the most dominant view in English Language Teaching is probably that grammar + words = productive language.

In other words, there has long been a belief that language can be reduced to a list of grammar structures that you can drop single words into. You may perhaps have seen this described as something along the lines of 'grammar providing the order into which you slot words'.

This is a view of language that we disagree with.

There are a number of implications that follow from this more traditional view of language – some of which may sometimes be explicitly voiced by teachers, and some which may not. Firstly, grammar is seen as being the most important area of language. If words are there to slot into the spaces which grammar presents, then it is grammar which must come first, and it is grammar which will help students do all the things that they want to do. It also follows that the examples used to illustrate grammar rules are relatively unimportant.

Seen from this perspective, these examples don't necessarily have to represent what is actually said because understanding the rule will enable students to create all the sentences they could ever possibly want – in accordance with the rule. It therefore doesn't matter if an example used to illustrate a rule could not easily (or ever) be used in daily life.

Similarly, if words are to fit in the slots provided by grammar, it follows that learning lists of single words is all that is required, and that any word can effectively be used if it fits a particular slot. Seen from this point of view, *Dracula didn't/doesn't/couldn't/mustn't/won't live in Brazil/Spain/the UK* are all equally possible and grammatically correct, as are *I'm studying English, I'm not studying English* and *Am I studying English?*

Naturalness, or the probable usage of vocabulary, is basically regarded as an irrelevance; students just need to grasp core meanings. At the same time, synonyms* – words that have very similar meanings – such as *murder* and *assassinate* – are seen as being more or less interchangeable and, if on occasion they are not, then this is a choice based purely on subtle shades of difference in meaning rather than anything else.

In addition to this, an associated belief has developed: that grammar is acquired in a particular order – the so-called 'building blocks' approach that sees students start by attempting to master what are seen as more basic structures, before moving on to more advanced ones. When following this approach, students do not get to see, let alone use, a structure before they have been formally taught it. For this reason, beginner- and elementary-level coursebooks do not generally have any past or future forms in the first half of the book, and may exclude other common tenses and grammatical structures altogether.

The section on teaching young learners on page 138 stresses further the importance of exposure at lower levels.

Finally, over the last thirty years, another layer has been added to this view of learning. This looks to address skills – speaking, listening, reading and writing. If content is essentially catered for by the presentation of grammar rules plus words, then where there is a deficit in fluency or writing or reading, the claim is that this may be connected to a lack of appropriate skills.

These skills are seen as existing independently of language, and a lack of them is thought to result in such problems as not being sufficiently confident, not planning, not making use of clues such as pictures to deduce meaning, not thinking about the context of a conversation, and so on.

As a result, many courses will claim to teach these skills, and you will typically find coursebooks with sections on grammar, sections on vocabulary, and then sections labelled as speaking, listening, writing or reading. The prevailing formula might then read: 'grammar + words + skills = productive language'.

A lexical view of language

From words with words to grammar

In some sectors, the 'grammar + words + skills = productive language' view is presented as the only option, but in fact there are countries and institutions which organise their language syllabuses differently, and there is also an alternative view of how language itself works that is supported by research, observation of language and logical arguments.

This alternative view is one we both share.

If we return to the principle that learners want to be able to do things with their language and to communicate, then communication almost always depends more on vocabulary than on grammar, even if we assume the 'grammar + words' model. For example, take the sentence 'I've been wanting to see that film for ages'. Saying *want see film* is more likely to achieve the intended communicative message in a conversation than only using what can be regarded as the grammar and function words: 'I've been *-ing* to that for'.

From this point of view, we should see words as more valuable. This does not entirely exclude the 'grammar + words' model, but it does undermine it. Would the message be less clear if the order of those words were changed? Not dramatically:

film want see   *see want film*
see film want   *want film see*

For an exercise on the limits of grammar – see page 61.

Actually, the division between vocabulary and grammar is rarely clear-cut; instead, it is rather fuzzy. Grammar is restricted by the words we use, and vice versa. In daily life, there are not infinite variations of each and every structure, and we don't accept synonyms in all cases. For example, we may say *I've been wanting to see that for ages*, but not *I've been fancying seeing that for ages*. Similarly, we may say *it's a high/tall building*, but not a *high man* or a *tall temperature*.

Furthermore, we often make use of phrases, or chunks* of language, which appear to be stored and recalled as wholes, rather than constructed from an underlying knowledge of grammar + single words. To put it another way, we consistently choose one particular way of saying something grammatical, rather than any of the many other possibilities.

In their seminal 1983 article – 'Two puzzles for linguistic theory: native-like selection and native-like fluency' – Pawley and Syder cite the way we tell the time as an example of this. All of the following are grammatically possible, yet most are not chosen by fluent speakers:

It's six less twenty.   *It's two thirds past five.*
It's forty past five.   *It exceeds five by forty.*
It's a third to six.   *It's ten after half five.*

Most competent users of English – including you, almost certainly – tend to opt for either *It's twenty to six* or *It's five forty*. There are thousands of similar instances, and it was these ideas, among others, that led Michael Lewis to declare in *The Lexical Approach* (1993) that language was 'grammaticalised lexis*' rather than 'lexicalised grammar'. As a result, he rejected the idea that we should continue with a syllabus based on neatly ordered grammar structures and, instead, advocated syllabuses, materials and teaching centred around collocation* and chunks alongside large amounts of input from texts.

From this input, a grasp of grammar 'rules' and correct usage would emerge, especially if the input were mediated by the guidance of teachers helping students to notice forms and meanings.

More recently, Michael Hoey has given theoretical support for this approach. In his book *Lexical Priming* (2005), he shows how words which are apparently synonymous – such as *result* and *consequence* – typically function in quite different ways. Statistically, one is more common than the other in most situations, and often these differences are very marked.

For more on some of the problems caused by focusing on synonyms – and how to tackle them – see page 54.

The way synonyms are used differs not only in terms of the other words immediately around them that they collocate with, but also in terms of the words that co-occur in the wider surrounding text. Near-synonyms may also occur in different parts of sentences or in different genres*, or may be followed by different grammatical patterns.

Hoey argues that these statistical differences must come about because, when we first encounter these words (he calls such encounters 'primings*'), our brains somehow subconsciously record some or all of this kind of information about the way the words are used. Our next encounter may reaffirm – or possibly contradict – this initial priming, as will the next encounter, and the one after that – and so on.

If this was not the case, then *result* and *consequence* would be equally prevalent in all cases, or one would be used more consistently in all contexts. Hoey suggests that many of what we might think of as being our grammatical choices are actually determined by the words themselves and by our experience of how they are used – and the patterns that attach themselves to the words – rather than by any underlying knowledge of grammar rules and an ability to then slot in words.

Hoey has also cited evidence from psycholinguistic studies to support his claims about such processes, and to help explain why language use works in this way. One experiment he mentions shows how words are recognised quicker when they are related in use than when they are not. So, for example, once a test subject has been given the word *cow*, the words *milk* or *field* might then be recognised more quickly than, say, the word *airport*.

In another experiment, unrelated pairs of words such as *scarlet onion* were taught. After a day during which the test subjects were exposed to a lot more language, participants were then tested on recognition of words based on prompt words. When the prompt word was *onion* – the word *scarlet* was recalled more quickly than other words.

These experiments suggest, firstly, that we do indeed remember words in pairings and in groups, and that doing so allows for quicker and more accurate processing of the language we hear and want to produce. Quicker, that is, than constantly constructing new and creative sentences.

If you accept this, then it's not too great a leap to believe that spoken fluency, the speed at which we read and the ease and accuracy with which we listen may all develop as a result of language users being more familiar with groupings of words. This certainly seems to be a more likely source of development than relying on constructing sentences from the bottom up, using grammar and words.

Seen like this, problems connected to skills essentially come back to being more about

The sections on teaching EAP (page 139) and exam classes (page 140) emphasise how essential it is for students to broaden their lexicons.

problems with language: students not only don't know enough words, but they also lack experience of how words are used or how they might sound in a group of words.

Some academics, such as Nick Ellis (2013), have suggested that what allows us to acquire new language is our encounters with vocabulary intimately intertwined with grammar. Ellis gives the example of the sentence *He mandubled across the floor*. We can work out what *mandubled* might mean, more or less, because we know many other 'x + verb *across the floor*' patterns (*walk across the floor*, *stroll across the floor*, *go across the floor*, *slither across the floor*, *crawl across the floor*, and so on).

Of all these possible examples, the vast majority of actual uses will consist of a very small number of words, with *go across the floor* and *walk across the floor* being the most probable. Ellis argues that it is repeated hearings of the frequent combinations that establish these base patterns in the mind and that, once we have these patterns, we are then able to understand and to slot in new words.

This shows how patterns can be generative. It also shows how grammar can work, but we need to be very clear that this isn't the kind of grammar which is generally taught in coursebooks. Instead, it is what we could call 'lexico-grammatical' patterns.

Now, for the sake of clarity, let us state that, in keeping with these ideas, we believe that:

- words have more value than grammar.
- language is essentially lexically driven, and words generally come with their own connected grammar.
- our own usage is determined by our experience of how language is used.
- there's a huge number of patterns that can be generative to at least some degree (and this includes the traditional grammar patterns taught in ELT).
- the vast majority of the examples of any one pattern will be made up of a small percentage of all the possible words that could be used with the pattern.
- collocations and patterns will be primed to go with other collocations and patterns in similarly limited ways.

A lexical view of teaching

Towards a practical lexical pedagogy

See page 7 for the list of principles.

Setting out these principles about language is one thing. There still remains the issue of choosing what to teach, the order things might be taught in, and how we can guide students through the six steps necessary for learning that we outlined at the beginning of Part A.

Over the last thirty years, some researchers who have seen flaws in the 'grammar + words + skills' model have argued that what learners learn, and the order they learn it in, can only be determined by the learners themselves. They have also suggested that the conscious teaching/learning of grammar is useless, or at best of only marginal benefit.

Stephen Krashen's and Tracy Terrell's *The Natural Approach* (1982) and other methods based on extensive reading* have emphasised the hearing/seeing stage. According to these perspectives, students do not explicitly learn language; rather, they are thought to acquire the language by seeing or hearing things which are comprehensible, but which contain linguistic features just beyond what they are capable of producing themselves.

The order in which this acquisition occurs is seen as being fairly fixed. From this point of view, instruction – particularly at lower levels – has very little purpose, apart from to provide comprehensible input, though it is claimed that, at later stages, some instruction about rules may help with noticing and may help learners to monitor what they are saying for errors.

There are other models that also take the idea that language can't be pre-taught as such, but can only be taken on board when students are ready to receive it. These approaches have tended to focus on the stage at which learners use language, when participants are also able to learn through hearing other speakers' language, comprehending it and incorporating it into their own usage.

This idea is at the heart of Task-Based Learning (TBL) and Michael Long's Interaction Hypothesis (1996), which suggests that new language is learnt through interaction with, and input from, others at the point that communication breaks down. Long and other TBL advocates have increasingly recognised that teachers may have a role to play when it comes to helping students notice forms as they arise during the process of doing tasks*, provided this is not based on a pre-set grammar syllabus of the type usually found in coursebooks.

For more on ways of working with spontaneous speech – see page 80.

More recently, so-called Dogme teachers (see *Teaching Unplugged* (2009) in the Delta Teacher Development series) have advocated a similar process – with a somewhat stronger teacher role that involves identifying and working with what has been dubbed 'emergent language' from student conversations. This may lead to a spontaneous teaching focus on – and practice of – a structure or structures as well as of vocabulary. This approach emphasises conversation over task, but again strongly rejects a pre-set syllabus applied to a whole class, and is (sometimes vehemently) opposed to coursebook use.

All these approaches to the practices of teaching can be seen as responses to observations that all teachers must surely have made at one time or another:

- We teach a structure.
- Students practise it, and seem to understand and be able to use it in controlled conditions.
- Then, in freer, more meaning-focused communication, the students revert to making mistakes with the very same structure.

These approaches also have roots in influential research that suggested that foreign language students acquire structures in a similar order to native speakers, and that this order can't be changed – so there is no point teaching grammar if students are not ready for it.

This line of thought was then reinforced by the logical argument that students in any one class will all be at different states of readiness, so teaching the same thing to everyone, without knowing whether they are ready, will not optimise classroom teaching. Finally, there is the belief that we learn best from experience and from our own mistakes.

However, there is also an irony here. These theories have emerged from a questioning of the traditional grammar syllabus, but the validity of the new theories is effectively based on how successfully grammar is learnt! This is then generalised out to all language. It is claimed that lots of reading or listening is the most efficient way to acquire all language, because that's the way grammar seems to be acquired. Here are some similar diktats that seem to have emerged from all of this:

- Don't pre-set any part of the syllabus, because grammar isn't acquired block by block and students are all individuals.
- Don't explain or teach anything, because students can't make active use of explicit grammar teaching.
- Don't use any coursebooks, because grammar can't be cut up into the kind of nuggets that most books offer up and, anyway, coursebooks stop proper interaction.

It is obviously worth asking if this is really true for lexis in the way that it is supposedly true for grammar. We believe words clearly can be learnt consciously – and can be learnt very efficiently. For example, there have been several experiments looking at the use of flashcards to learn words, with one side of the card being in the target language and the other side containing a mother tongue translation. These tests have shown that students using such an approach are able to acquire and retain large amounts of vocabulary, especially when these words are revisited over time.

We would suggest that this is likely to be equally true if those words were collocations or grammaticalised chunks, such as *Have you been here before?*, instead of just single words. Of course, we're not suggesting that if students were to learn such chunks, they would then be able to use the present perfect tense more generally. They may adapt the chunk incorrectly, saying *Have you been here yesterday?* for example, but in the greater scheme of things, we feel this is a relatively minor problem.

The section on teaching low-level learners on page 137 gives further guidance on presenting grammar as chunks.

One major problem with the 'grammar plus words' building block model is that, as students adhering to it set out to learn the language, they are not even permitted to *see* a sentence such as *Have you been here before?* for weeks or even months, as mastery of the basics is demanded first.

However, the answer to the very real problem of learners not being able to take on board structures in one or two lessons should not be to simply wait around for things to somehow come up in class and then be acquired, because here's the thing: most studies suggest that extensive reading (and, we must assume, extensive listening also) is actually a very slow and inefficient way of acquiring new vocabulary, when compared to active study.

And if vocabulary can be efficiently learnt through study, we might then consider why we shouldn't also pre-set a vocabulary syllabus in courses and materials. When students have a particular task to do, or a conversation to take part in, we can predict a good part of what might be said. Thornbury and Meddings say as much in their book *Teaching Unplugged*:

'The activities in Teaching Unplugged aren't designed to generate specific exponents, but you can ask yourself what language areas are likely to be generated. Revise these in advance if it helps you feel more confident – but be prepared for all the other language that will emerge.'

For them, this predicting of language is a way for teachers to give better post-conversation feedback – and we certainly wouldn't disagree that this is a good thing to do. Note, though, that they refer to language areas, which, while they may not intend it to, suggests 'grammar + words' (in lexical sets). If this is what is implied by the phrase 'language areas', we would obviously see this as unhelpful. Instead:

The chapter on speaking – and in particular the focus on cheating (page 76) – explores ways of predicting what students might say.

- We would urge teachers to think of whole phrases, sentences or even 'texts' that students might want to say when attempting a particular task or conversation.
- We would then argue that at least some of those lexical items are learnable, and some of that learning could be done with the assistance of materials before students try to have particular kinds of conversation.

Conversations or tasks then become not only an opportunity for teachers to develop emergent language, but also serve as a rehearsal space for previously studied items.

Finally, we would absolutely agree that, while students are talking, teachers should listen to them and be prepared to help them with the new things they want to say. For us, the study of potentially new items, and the teacher providing help towards better communication, can come before, during and after conversation and, as we shall see, coursebook materials can play a vital role in all of this.

Teaching lexically: some problems

The difficulty of thinking fast

In a way, the above comment by Thornbury and Meddings highlights a very important and practical problem inherent in any approach that requires teachers to react to what learners are saying, and to then notice emergent language, focus on form, and possibly get the students practising any new input that arises out of this. The truth is, it's very difficult to do all these things simultaneously in the heat of the classroom – let alone to do them well and to do them consistently!

Just think for a moment about what is involved. To react and then teach, teachers have to:

- hear what students say.
- understand what they say.
- notice problems or gaps as they speak.
- decide what the new or emergent language is.
- make judgements about the students' level, the frequency or usefulness of any possible new language and whether or not the students are ready for it.
- note the language, or write it on the board.
- remember the context for the new language to be explained.
- (ideally) be prepared to give other examples.
- (ideally) have questions ready that check and expand on the students' knowledge of the new language – or that relate to other connected items of language.
- (ideally) think of some kind of further practice.
- keep a record of new language, so that it can be revised or referred to again in future lessons.

At all stages of this process, teachers' judgements may be affected by what Daniel Kahneman (2011) has described as 'biases in our decision-making'. For example, a teacher's interpretation of what is a mistake or a gap in the students' language – and of how it may best be corrected or improved on – may be governed less by what is relevant to that student and more by the teacher having been encouraged during their training to notice particular kinds of errors. Following on from this, whether the teacher then decides to develop a perceived mistake into a focus on form may depend on whether or not they have successfully taught that particular form before.

In terms of deciding what vocabulary needs to be taught at any given moment, teachers may also have an 'availability' or 'representational' bias.

The availability bias may make teachers prioritise less frequent words simply because mental images of them are more readily available. So, for example, we may think the words *blonde* or *banana* are far more common than *arise* or *whereby*, because we can picture the former words, and can think of many people who are blonde or imagine eating bananas. However, in their overall usage, as measured by corpora such as the British National Corpus, *blonde* is actually around nine times less common than *arise*, and *whereby* twice as frequent as *banana*!

The tasks on page 36 aim to develop the way you think about frequency.

We may also be influenced here by the most basic representative sentences of English grammar. Very simple sentences are of the 'noun … is … adjective' or 'subject … does … object' variety. Words such as *arise* and *whereby* do not fit into these simple representations, and this may contribute to them being ignored or under-taught in the classroom.

Similarly, the examples of new language that we come up with in class are more likely to reflect this relatively straightforward representational nature than actual common usage.

For instance, when asked to give an example of the word *rise*, people may well produce simple sentences such as *The sun rises* or *A balloon rises*, rather than *I saw an article the other day which said that directors' pay had risen ten times faster than everyone else's.*

The tasks on pages 40–43 will help you think more about how to provide good examples.

Now consider the fact that, often, this kind of decision-making has to be done while paying attention to individuals within a potentially very large class, and you begin to see some serious flaws in the practice of approaches such as Task-Based Learning or Dogme, however much you may sympathise with their underlying principles and views of language.

Kahneman suggests that some of the biases that come to the fore in what he describes as 'fast thinking' – the kind of on-the-spot thinking that teachers engage in in class – can be overcome through slower, more analytical thought, and that large amounts of practice can lead to more successful spontaneous judgments. He cites the example of chess grand masters, who become capable of creative, spontaneous and successful moves only through hours and hours of analysis and the practice of particular gambits.

To apply this analogy to the classroom, if teachers want to get better at drawing attention to the most frequent language, then they need to practise noticing language.

We think examples such as *I saw an article the other day which said that directors' pay had risen ten times faster than everyone else's* or *We got up at five to go and see the sun rise* are better than *The sun rises*, because they are a more realistic reflection of how the word 'rise' is actually used. They also show other grammar patterns: *I saw an article the other day which said, said that … had risen, risen x times faster than …; get up at x to … see the sun rise.*

The tasks on pages 56 and 58 will help you get better at noticing patterns.

However, most teachers (native and non-native) are unlikely to be able to produce such examples, or draw attention to such patterns, without a considerable amount of planning and study.

In order to plan efficiently, most teachers need coursebooks or other materials.

We would suggest, then, that coursebooks can play an important role, not only in presenting language to students but also in enabling teachers to become better lexical practitioners and, in the long run, perhaps better spontaneous and reactive teachers in a Dogme or Task-Based Learning mould. The question you may then want to ask is: What kind of coursebooks?

Teaching lexically: some practicalities

Pragmatism in a grammar-dominated world

Most coursebooks that are produced for a global audience are organised according to the 'grammar + words + skills' approach. There are certainly some books which incorporate more aspects of a lexical view than others. They may contain more lexis, have a greater focus on collocation and chunks, but few, if any, break the building block taboo: the unspoken rule that you can't expose students to aspects of grammar that have not already been presented and practised remains.

Current coursebooks almost never present phrases such as *What are you doing later?* simply as chunks where the grammar is left unanalysed. As writers, we have made an effort to change this through our own General English series *Innovations* and, more recently, *Outcomes*, but these books have been written against a backdrop of pressure from all sides. Publishers continue to offer teachers and schools books based on the unpacking

The section on assessing materials (page 135) gives examples of the kinds of questions you can use to critically evaluate your classroom material.

of discrete grammatical structures. Frequently, feedback from users then picks up on the desire for more grammar – and a vicious circle of expectation and fulfillment develops.

Naturally, we would like to see this change, and we hope that we might make some small kind of progress towards this goal by influencing you, the readers of *Teaching Lexically*. Part of this change could come from teachers and other decision-makers within their institutions taking a more lexical view of language and looking more critically at coursebooks.

Teachers themselves can also, of course, write more lexical materials or take more Dogme-like approaches, but the reality is that most teachers just don't have enough time – and aren't paid enough – to do this. Plus, as we have seen, Dogme lessons can end up, at least in part, simply being materials-free replays of old lessons which teachers have delivered before with the use of coursebooks.

For this reason, what we hope to show you is how you can apply a lexical view of language to any coursebook. All books contain plenty of language, plenty of collocations, chunks and non-tense-focused grammar, but much of this may not be highlighted by the book because of its 'grammar + words + skills' focus. Even where, for example, single words dominate, there is still real potential for lexical teaching in your preparation and in the interaction between you and your learners.

However, to get to this stage, you will need to approach coursebook materials in a different way, perhaps plan differently, and, above all, you will need to think about language lexically, and ask new and different questions about the language you're planning to teach.

As such, Part A will present a brief overview of vocabulary and grammar, as seen from a lexical point of view, and consider how we might lead students through the aforementioned six stages of learning new language.

Then, in Part B, you will find:

- tasks to train yourself to notice language in your coursebook in this lexical way.
- tasks to train yourself to predict language the students might use.
- tasks to develop teaching techniques.
- tasks to develop ways of applying these techniques to exercises* you will see in coursebooks.
- tasks to deal with correction.
- tasks to build up repertoires of 'spontaneous' teaching within your class.
- a limited number of activities to revise and practise language.

In other words, *Teaching Lexically*, the book, is less about recipes and activities for lessons, and more about training for preparing lexical lessons with whatever materials you are using. It is less about changing or replacing materials with something new, and more about the better exploitation of what is there already. To this degree:

- For those who have read *The Lexical Approach*, to which we are much indebted, we hope you will find something new and useful here.
- For those of you who are more 'grammar + words' inclined, we hope you will like the rigorous focus on language.
- For those who are TBLers or Dogmeticians, we hope you will appreciate the importance placed on the role of the student, and find the focus on planning for language valuable.

So before you apply the tasks found in *Teaching Lexically* to your own coursebook, let's just consider in more detail, and from a lexical point of view:

- what vocabulary is; what grammar is; what skills are.

Vocabulary: a lexical view

Units of meaning

Asking what vocabulary is may seem rather strange. Surely vocabulary is just words and their meanings:

- We can match the word *table* to the thing, or call up a picture in our heads.
- The word *pull* can go with the action of pulling, or on a sign on a door.
- The word *out* can be dealt with using a visual of an arrow coming out of a box, or a sign giving directions.
- The word *absolutely* has a simple definition of 'very' or 'completely'.

However, what are the 'words' in *They pulled out of the deal?* Here, *pulled* and *out* are part of the same unit of meaning*, even though they are two separate words. And what about *He pulled out without looking?* Again, *pulled out* is one unit of meaning, but its meaning here is different to the example above.

In each of these cases, we must then say that 'deal' and 'without looking' – what we can describe as collocates* of *pull out* – are also contributing to the meaning. Collocations are pairs or groups of words which commonly go together – eg *a long day*, *score twice*, *go home*. The extent to which a collocate determines the meaning of its partner will vary, but it is especially true of the most common verbs like *have* or *take*. In many languages, combinations such as *have dinner*, *have a rest*, *take it easy* or *take advantage of* may be translated with just one word in each case.

And what if someone tells you to *lay your cards on the table?* With idioms like this, we have six words, but really only one meaning: 'show me your position or what you're thinking'. Furthermore, changing what we often think of as the 'grammar' words within this idiom would change the meaning. Saying either 'lay *a* card on the table' or 'lay your cards on *a* table' would suggest that you're really playing cards, while 'lay *some* card on the table' would change the meaning of *card*. In other words, collocation and connected patterns allow us to distinguish different meanings of the same form of a word (*card*/*lay*).

For tasks to help you think in more depth about units of meaning, see page 35.

So when we think about vocabulary, we may want to first think in terms of 'units of meaning' – rather than individual words.

Paul Nation (1993, 2001) suggests that, in most cases, the simplest way to get to meaning is through translation. However, if this is not an option, then we may resort to explanations, drawings and the like. The key is to keep things simple, because, from a lexical teaching point of view, meaning is almost the least of a learner's problems if they want to use an item well!

Once we have established meaning, we should be aware of the other connections to those words that allow us to use them or to recognise meaning accurately and quickly. For example, with any item we are comfortable with, we know about its:

- co-text* (other words that are likely to occur within a text containing the item).
- register* (appropriate levels of formality or politeness).
- genre (the kind of text the item will generally be used in).
- contextual opposites (antonyms*).
- other words in related lexical sets.
- word form and related words within the same word family.
- function and pragmatic use (how the item can be used to do different things in discourse*).
- connotation* (negative or positive shades of meaning).

- synonyms (words of the same or similar meaning).
- other words in a connected group (hyponymy*).

We will now explore a number of connected areas in more detail.

• How words work with other words and with grammar

Let's take the word *argument*. If you think of collocations, you might come up with *have an argument* or *present an argument*.

Most of us would think of *having an argument* as being connected to angry' words', while *presenting an argument* gives a different meaning of *argument* as a series of connected ideas or evidence. Now think of the grammar connected to these two units of meaning. You are more likely to 'have an argument' *with* someone *about* something, but 'present an argument' *to* someone *for* or *against* something.

Some would characterise this as collocation, rather than grammar.

For tasks to help you get better at asking the kinds of questions that draw attention to specific grammatical features, see pages 68–70.

Other features might be that a word/collocation may more commonly occur in one grammatical structure than another. So *present an argument* might be more common as a passive than *have an argument*, say, and less common in the present continuous.

We can ask questions to draw attention to these grammatical features, such as 'What preposition follows *have an argument?*'

• Collocation

We might then recognise that if you have an argument about something, it's likely that this something will be different to the something that you might present an argument for or against. This difference extends to the use of pronouns, as 'presenting an argument for *it* or against *him*' are both unusual. We might say:

- **have an argument about** *it/him/something stupid/money/her spending so much time out*
- **present an argument for** *a change (in the law)/a (adjective) approach/using the CEFR as a basis for course design*

We can also look at the collocations and grammar that might precede each chunk. For example, we are more likely to say '*want to present* an argument' than to say '*want to have* an argument'.

The adjective collocates are also likely to be different:

- have a *terrible/furious* argument
- present a *convincing/compelling* argument

We can also draw students' attention to collocation by asking questions. The answers may vary quite considerably. Some may even be meant as jokes by students, and they might not always be correct, in which case you may need to change or correct them. We could ask, for instance:

- *What verbs can go with argument?* (have)
- *Who has an argument?* (girlfriend/boyfriend, husband/wife, footballers, countries)
- *What might a husband and wife have an argument about?* (money / having an affair / drinking too much)

You can plan the examples that you want to give in class by thinking about collocation in this way. Thinking like this before teaching can also make it easier for you to respond to, and to use, student answers to the questions above. You might end up with an example like this one:

- *My friend Maria had a terrible argument with her boyfriend last night.*
  or
- *My friend Maria had a terrible argument with her boyfriend last night about his drinking.*

• Co-text

With an example like the one above, you might also start to think about how the whole sentence might be used in a conversation. Alongside the sentence about Maria's terrible argument with her boyfriend, we might also expect to hear things such as *What about? She phoned me, she was really upset, calm down, came round to my house, crying, floods of tears, screaming at her/each other* … and so on. This is the co-text. There may also be words connected to the reason for the argument – perhaps *alcoholic, out of control, drunk*, etc.

Of course, when we think about *present an argument*, the co-text would be quite different. We might expect, for example, things like *suggest, go on, question, show, conclude*, etc.

Again, we can ask students questions to access some of this language. For instance:

- *How might you feel if you have an argument?*
- *And when you have an argument, what might you do?*
- *And what might happen afterwards?*
- *What might you say – or ask – if someone tells you that they had an argument with their boyfriend last night?*

For more on how to ask questions that allow exploration of co-text, see page 48.

• Genre and register

The different kinds of co-text that will occur with the different collocations featuring *arguments* also reflect the kinds of texts we are likely to meet these collocations in.

Have an argument is far more common in spoken texts than *present an argument* is, so we might also expect to hear responses from a listener in a conversation such as *Really?* or *That's awful*. We might expect to find *present an argument* more commonly used in academic texts, and perhaps even in the introductions or abstracts for academic articles – ie within very specific genres.

Some words, such as *sir* or *crap*, might be seen as belonging to a formal culture or to a very colloquial one (ie to different registers). We might ask our students questions about this kind of thing, in order to find out how aware of register they are. We could ask what kind of texts you *present an argument* in. However, note that while these kinds of questions do allow a brief focus on register, they are not very productive in terms of getting at connected *language*.

You may think of other questions that are more useful.

• Lexical sets

The chunk *have an argument* could be seen as belonging to a lexical set of different 'kinds of talk' – *chat, talk, exchange, disagreement, gossip, discussion, laugh, row, speech, interview, conflab*, and so on. However, *argument*, in *present an argument*, might be seen as belonging to a different lexical set, that of 'kinds of statement' – *suggestion, explanation, advice, opinion, apology*, etc.

Some words in lexical sets might occur as co-text. For instance:
We were just having a chat and I mentioned that she could've done things differently, and we ended up having an argument.

However, note that not all words in any given lexical set will be of equal frequency (*conflab*, for instance, is very infrequently used) nor are they all likely to occur in the same text (*have an argument*, for example, is not very likely to be used in the same conversation as *have an interview*).

This is also true for more familiar lexical sets: *cat, dog, giraffe, elephant* and *aardvark* may form part of the lexical set 'kinds of animals', but some are far more common and not all would normally feature in the same conversation or text.

We might explore other words in lexical sets by asking *What other kinds of talk can you think of?* To be honest, though, for *have an argument* this is perhaps not the best question. Students may not immediately be able to think of other examples in the way they would if they were asked *What other kinds of animal can you think of?* This is something to bear in mind.

For more on what kind of questions best explore which aspects of word knowledge, see page 46.

Not all questions about aspects of word knowledge work for all words. Some will generate a lot of language, and others will not. Learning to be selective about which questions to ask when takes time – and requires plenty of both forward planning and retrospective reflection.

● Antonyms

We most commonly think of opposites in terms of adjectives or certain verbs: *strong/weak*; *lose/win*, etc. However, when we think about collocations, we can see that opposites of single words often vary, so:

- The opposite of a *strong cheese* might be a *mild cheese*, while the opposite of a *strong wind* might be a *light wind* (or even a *light breeze*).
- Similarly, the opposite of *lose weight* is *gain/put on weight*, but the opposite of *lose your keys* is *find your keys*.

This means that, rather than thinking of opposites as being connected to single words, we would be better off thinking of them in terms of the contexts they're being used in. These contextual opposites are known as antonyms.

However, we might also consider less common opposites, such as in the case of *have an argument* and *present an argument*. Again, the opposites will vary:

have an argument	*have a chat / have a laugh*
present an argument	*challenge / respond to an argument*
have a terrible argument	*have a little argument / a slight disagreement*
present a compelling argument	*present a weak / unconvincing argument*

Furthermore, the opposites of individual words change when we put them in new collocations:

have terrible weather	*have great weather*
present an award	*receive an award*

Obviously, there may also be other alternatives to the opposites above. These things aren't fixed and, on occasion, the opposites we opt for may be determined by our own experience of language – or simply on what we see as the opposite at the time. For instance:

- You could quite easily see the opposite of *present an award* not as *receive an award* but, rather, as *give a punishment*.
- In the same way, you could see the opposite of *have an argument* as *not say anything*.

Sometimes, there just won't be any fixed direct opposites, but this doesn't mean the idea of opposites should not still be of interest.

Opposites will also often occur within texts. For example:
What were you two arguing about?
>*We weren't having an argument. We were just having a laugh.*

● Word form

As we saw in the last example, we may also use different forms of a word within conversations and texts (*argue/argument*). Sometimes, different words that could be seen as derived from one root word will have different meanings, and will be used in different contexts.

For example, *argumentative* is associated with *have an argument*, but the adjective *arguable* and the adverb *arguably* are more connected with *present an argument*. The verb *argue* will be used in quite different contexts, depending on the meaning of *argument*:

- With *have an argument*, we might expect the co-text to include phrases such as *we're/they're always arguing, we/they never argue, we/they argue a lot.*
- With *present an argument*, we're more likely to see things such as *I/he argue(s) that ...*, *he goes on to argue*, or *it is argued that ...* in the co-text.

In class, you might ask the students:
What's the verb form of 'argument'? And the adjective form?
Once they have provided the answers, you may then also want to give extra examples and ask extra questions about collocations that are connected to these different forms – because these will all be used differently.

• Pragmatic meanings

Sometimes, using a phrase such as *The kettle's boiled* (in the UK at least) has the additional meaning of a request 'to make tea'. It's easier to imagine a pragmatic/functional meaning for *have an argument* than for *present an argument*. For example, we could imagine someone waiting outside an office when another person appears and is about to knock. The waiting person says:
They're having an argument.
Clearly, this is not a simple description. Pragmatically speaking, it's an explanation of why they are waiting, and advice to the other person not to knock. So we might then expect a response such as:
Oh right. Thanks. I'll come back later.

For most people, these leaps of understanding are clear, and we don't really need to teach such aspects of the language. However, there may be some common phrases which are more culturally bound, where we might want to emphasise this aspect. We could test this in class by asking for different responses to the statement, which might elicit* something like this:

A: *They're having an argument.*
B: *What about?*

A: *They're having an argument.*
B *Why?*

A: *They're having an argument.*
B: *Again!*

A: *They're having an argument.*
B: *I'll come back later.*

For tasks to help you explore what might come before and after particular items of language, see page 57.

• Synonyms

Finally, we may know synonyms of words. This is one of the most familiar features of word knowledge.

In class, many teachers often use synonyms as a way to give meaning. However, we have left it till last because, when things are viewed lexically, you come to realise that there are very few, if any, complete synonyms. We might see that *row* is a synonym of *argument* in *have an argument*, but not *present an argument*. When we think of the meaning in *have an argument*, *row* may share some collocations, but not others, so someone is much more likely to be *at the centre of a growing row* than *at the centre of a growing argument*.

Row may also be more common with certain genres, such as political journalism. It is also used by native speakers far less frequently than *argument*, and so, in class with students who have a limited amount of time, rather than asking 'What's another way of saying *have an argument*?' – a question which might generate words with similar (but slightly different) meanings, we would probably be better off teaching something different and more frequent – or else simply exploring the word they have just learnt in more detail.

Grammar: a lexical view

A broader, more nuanced perspective

One of the most common misconceptions about teaching grammar from a lexical perspective is that it somehow means a ban on the use of grammar terms such as noun, verb, preposition, the present continuous, and so on – or, worse, that it means no explicit focus on grammar whatsoever.

Certainly, there are plenty of people who have acquired a second language without having learned this kind of meta-language*, but we believe that if students are familiar with these terms, it makes it easier for teachers to draw attention to language and to encourage the students to notice salient features. We have already seen one small example of this earlier, when we looked at how we might expand on students' knowledge of words that are part of the same word family.

We have also seen that a central part of the process of learning has to be noticing, and many theorists – even those like Krashen and Long, who emphasise a more 'natural' kind of acquisition that mirrors the way children acquire their own first language – suggest that some knowledge of rules may contribute to the learning process.

For more on concept checking, see the tasks on page 62 – and those on page 63 for more on explanation.

We very firmly believe that the kind of basics that you might have learned on initial training courses, such as explaining rules and checking concepts with questions, are good things to have in your repertoire.

However, as we have already seen, taking a lexical view of language means realising that what can be described as 'grammar' is much broader than traditional ELT coursebooks suggest:

- A traditional coursebook will typically have between 20–30 grammar points, many of which will be repeated and expanded upon at different levels. This means probably no more than about a hundred items altogether.
- In contrast, a lexical view of language might reveal, and make explicit to learners, several hundred patterns – if not thousands.

At the same time, though, having a lexical view of language also means seeing the restrictions on creativity and the limitations on variations that occur within patterns, because, as mentioned earlier, a small number of possible words tend to dominate in any given pattern.

When tackling the meaning of verb tenses (which still tend to dominate courses), a lexical teacher might not want to spend much more time on them than they would on teaching a comparable number of words. For example, the meaning of present tenses is essentially *now / the future* – the present simple signifies one of the following: *habit / at a particular moment / timetabled / fact / always*; while the present continuous form simply means *temporary / in progress / incomplete* or *emphasis*.

Now, it would clearly be wrong to spend hour after hour teaching and re-teaching these words. Yet when we spend hour upon hour of precious classroom time going over and over the meanings of these structures, that is, unfortunately, all that we are really doing – in the sense that this repetition of these rules adds nothing extra to students' ability to communicate more fluently.

Teaching grammar lexically is, then, about teaching a greater variety of patterns and exploring them in more limited ways. Limited, but not limiting, because the other key thing about teaching grammar from a lexical view is that we pay attention to actual usage – and this also means thinking more about usage beyond the sentence level.

• Chunks as grammar and in discourse

At lower levels in particular, it may well be best to restrict students' exposure to some grammar structures. Single phrases – or chunks, if you prefer – such as *Have you ever been to* + place? – can be presented and learned as individual items, rather than being treated as examples of a particular structure (in this instance, the present perfect simple) that then has to be taught in its entirety – with examples of positive sentences, negatives and question forms, all filled with a wide range of different verbs.

It's worth pointing out here that '*Have you ever been to* + place?' is a generative pattern, just as '*have + subject + past participle*' is. It may be less 'creative' and limited, but it is also grounded in common usage. Furthermore, when looking at such a pattern, the lexical teacher might focus more on exploring language that might be used alongside it – and less on the many different possible ways that the structure itself could be lexicalised.

We might be less concerned, for example, with using auxiliaries in short answers (*Yes, I have / No, I haven't*) and more concerned with what follows a particular structure in everyday conversation. This might means considering the range of possible responses to the question above:

- *Yes.*
- *No.*
- *No never. Have you?*
- *No, never, but I'd love to.*
- *Yeah, quite a few times, actually.*
- *No, but I'm thinking of going there this summer, actually.*

  And so on.

In other words, we would focus more on discourse than on trying to 'cover' all aspects of the grammar in one go.

For more on exploring natural usage, see the tasks on page 66

At higher levels, we would obviously expand on the range of different ways a structure can be lexicalised (*Have you ever seen it? / Have you ever tried it? / Have you ever fallen off?* etc), but we would still maybe focus more on the most common verbs used within the structure, and continue to look at how discourse around examples of the structure can be explored.

In this way, a lexically-oriented teacher will perhaps tend to show a structure's interaction with other grammatical structures more often, and will more frequently recycle structures that students have already met.

• Words defining grammar: usage over rules

The lexical teacher may also understand that some traditional rules (for example, those often taught about *some* and *any*, or about countability) are over-simplified, and they may well sometimes feel the need to give extra examples that clarify such matters for students.

In addition, teaching grammar lexically means acknowledging that grammar structures are often restricted by lexis or by meaning. For example, we don't use the present perfect when we also use *ago* in a time phrase, while the contextual meanings of certain nouns and verbs necessitate the use or non-use of articles (*Would you like a coffee?* but *I don't drink coffee*) or the use of either simple or continuous forms – *I don't see it like that. I see it differently* (= I have different opinions/ideas) but *She's seeing someone at the moment* (= She's dating them).

Lexical teachers will also be aware of the fact that individual words and items tend to be frequently used with particular grammatical patterns – the phenomenon known as colligation* – and that this has more impact on discourse than has perhaps been generally realised. This means we need to be aware of grammatical features such as the patterns around verbs. Take these sentences, for example:

I expected it to be quicker.
I didn't expect it to take so long.

When we use 'expect' to recount surprise or disappointment, we could say that in positive sentences it tends to colligate with comparative forms, while in negative sentences it often colligates with *so* (or *such*).

For more on how to draw students' attention to syntax, see pages 56 and 58.

A lexical view of language might mean limiting the amount of time we devote to tense-based grammar, but increasing the amount of time spent on the grammar around words, with more attention being paid to areas such as noun phrases* and to what might be described as syntax* and discourse.

• Grammar is all around

Finally, teaching lexically means we will often focus on all the language that's present in exercises, and on everything that the students are trying to say. This means that in grammar exercises, we may draw attention to vocabulary, but also that we may draw attention to grammar – both 'traditional' and 'lexical' – in vocabulary exercises.

It may also mean that we sometimes correct and draw attention to grammatical structures that students are trying to produce, before they have been formally taught them via their traditional grammar syllabus.

Finally, teaching lexically may involve a conscious decision not to devote whole lessons to any one particular grammar structure, but it may also mean that we end up providing the students with many more encounters with grammar and many more opportunities to notice patterns than traditional approaches – where grammar and vocabulary are generally parceled up and separated – allow for.

Skills: a lexical view

The central importance of language

We noted earlier that, over recent decades, there had been a trend in ELT towards treating reading and listening as skills that are somehow separate from language, but that the insights of lexical views of language suggest that poor skills are largely the result of language problems:

- Essentially for those who can already read in their own first language, the vast majority of problems they have when trying to read in English are due to the fact that they do not know enough language, and they do not know enough common combinations of words.

For exercises on sound shapes and hearing language – see Chapter 5.

- When listening in English, there will be the additional problems of not being able to hear sounds, or not recognising words they already know when they are used in connected speech.
- If their studies have predominantly focused on written forms of the language, students may also just not know about more spoken forms.

Conversations are organised differently to written texts and can have differing grammar and lexis. It may also be that learners do not know a sufficient number of the kind of native-like choices that Pawley and Syder refer to, such as *It's twenty to three.*

Speaking like some kind of idealised native speaker will not be necessary in most situations that students will encounter, but native-speaker usage is still something to consider where students may be listening to or reading native-user texts, whether they be newspapers and academic articles, or films or songs in English.

Listening and reading

We have already argued that simply doing lots of extensive reading and listening is an inefficient way of learning new lexis, and that vocabulary can be consciously learned. It therefore follows that learning more lexis in combination with other words and grammar will help improve reading and listening.

If that lexis is based on things learners may need to say while going about the business of everyday life, or while expressing their thoughts and feelings, then there is a better chance it will improve speaking as well as listening.

Given this, we see the way we approach all language tasks in Part B of *Teaching Lexically* as an important – albeit covert, on occasion – way of improving skills. However, we do also see a role for the kind of stages and activities that most coursebooks include in their skills lessons. We just believe they need to include a greater focus on language.

• Pre-reading/listening

Typically, pre-text tasks are based on the idea of activating schemata*: that is, the idea that if we somehow spark the reader's or listener's existing knowledge of a subject or language, they will then be better able to interpret the text.

Seen from a skills perspective, such activation is enough – so, for example, if we had a text about crime, we might get the students to think about connected ideas and language. This could be things like *bad, dangerous, stealing, murder, police, court, prison*, etc. The argument is that doing this would then allow the students to better process a text such as this one:

A: *Did I tell you about having my bag stolen?*
B: *No. What happened?*
A: *Well, I was er hanging about outside college waiting for a friend … you know Jean?*
B: *Yeah.*
A: *It was his birthday and we were going for a drink.*
B: *Oh right. How old was he?*
A: *23.*
B: *Really? How come he's only in his first year, then?*
A: *Oh, he … Oh, just various things. It's a long story. Anyway, I was, I was waiting for him outside college, just in the street, yeah, and, and this guy came up to me and asked me for directions. He had this big map …*
B: *Oh God! Yeah, I've heard this kind of …*
A: *Really?*

B: *Yeah. They have the map to distract you and then someone else comes up and grabs your bag.*

A: *Exactly, exactly. God, I feel like such an idiot. I like put my bag down to look properly and show him, and he makes this big show of thanking me … and then he runs off!*

B: *Oh no!*

A: *Exactly. And I'm like that's odd and I look down and my bag's gone.*

B: *What a bastard!*

A: *And it was all just done in a couple of seconds, you know. I just hesitated, but he was gone.*

B: *Did you tell the police?*

A: *Nah. It's not worth it. They can't do anything.*

B: *True. Sad … but true.*

A: *And even if they did catch them, they probably wouldn't do much. It doesn't even go to court half the time.*

B: *They should string them up if you ask me!*

The conversation is about stealing and crime. The situation was obviously bad, and might be seen as dangerous. They even mention 'court' at some point. However, we would argue that knowing all of these words does not allow you to genuinely understand the text. To do that, what you need is to understand and be able to hear much more of the language and the forms used in the conversation.

For more on how to ensure language from texts comes up during prediction activities, see page 87.

Given this, at a simple level, we would say that teachers need to 'push' language more during these pre-text stages and effectively pre-teach more, so, instead of simply accepting the word *stealing* when students suggest it, we might then ask what people might steal from you, and say/write something like *I had my bag stolen* or *Did I tell you I had my bag stolen?*

We might also ask where and how you might have your bag stolen and (knowing the content of the listening that's to come) guide the students to, for example, *He grabbed my bag in the street*. In other words, lexical teachers will tend to see pre-listening tasks primarily as language teaching opportunities.

• Comprehension-checking tasks

While they read or listen, students are typically asked to try to find the answers to comprehension questions. Often, this involves first tackling a simpler gist* task, such as one that asks what crime happened. This may then be followed by a second task, with more detailed questions (eg *Where was he? Why was he there? How many people carried out the robbery?* and so on).

We see nothing wrong with such questions, but worry that the skills-focused teacher will tend to mainly be concerned just with meaning. As such, in this case, the following answers may be seen as sufficient: *stole a bag / (outside) college / to meet a friend / two.*

As lexical teachers, we see meaning as just a starting point. Learners need to notice and, over time, remember the actual word combinations that were used to express meanings, and so we might elicit answers from the students such as those above, but then rephrase them as:

He had his bag stolen / He was hanging around outside the college, waiting for a friend / He was meeting a friend to go for a drink / two – one who distracted him with the map and another one who grabbed his bag.

For more on how to focus on language when checking the answers to comprehension tasks, see page 89.

This way, students hear the key lexis with the grammar it was used with again. Of course, it may be the case that many of you already do this kind of more thorough focus on whole sentences when checking answers.

● Language focus

After comprehension has been checked in some way, there will then often be some kind of focus on language used in the text. Obviously, in many cases, this will be a grammar point (in this case, perhaps that might be *have something done*) or a lexical set (maybe different kinds of crime) that the text has partially exemplified. However, there may also be an exercise looking at words in the text:

- The 'grammar + words' teacher is likely to ask students to match single words with meanings.
- The skills teacher might also pick out unusual words or more idiomatic items, such as *string them up*, and encourage the students to guess meanings from context.

From a lexical point of view, the problem with this is that, in asking students to guess unusual words, paradoxically more time and energy is spent on infrequent language that learners may never hear again – when it could be used to explore something more useful!

For more on the way words sound different when spoken in isolation and in streams of speech, see page 101.

This is also often the case with matching words to meanings, which has the additional problem of not drawing attention to the combinations that words are often used in. Finally, insufficient time might be spent on how the words sounded in context, when rapid speech might change what Richard Cauldwell (2013) has called their 'sound shape'.

Lexical teaching tasks that focus on language are, therefore, more concerned with frequent words and how they work in context, reusable chunks and the sounds of words in chunks.

● Post-text talk

A skills view of reading or listening may actually lead to little interaction between students, because the lesson is seen to be about reading or listening. Where there is a speaking task, it will often be about the reading, or simply some kind of further comprehension check.

A lexical view of texts would involve thinking about how texts are talked about, which would encourage the teaching of language that the students could use to talk about texts. It also suggests that texts should be used to encourage the students to talk about their thoughts and feelings, and to understand more about culture.

For more on ways of deepening the connections that students have with key lexis in texts, see pages 93 and 94.

However, because the use of texts in the classroom is also about learning language, we need to get students to do something with that language. In this case, it might be a good idea to get the students to do some post-text speaking, based on some of the language from the text that may already have been focused on.

Speaking

The 'grammar + words' view has tended to view speaking in class as a chance to practise words and grammar, but has also led to the creation of a distinct and separate class of functional tasks, which might allow for the teaching of some chunks that help learners do particular things – advise, complain, request, and so on. Added to this, the skills view of speaking has tended to distinguish between accuracy and fluency activities:

- Accuracy is focused on getting students to produce particular language – words or grammar – and correcting the way they try to use them, particularly in terms of form or pronunciation.
- With fluency, the idea is to focus on meaning or on a task, and not to worry too much about mistakes. As such, teachers are encouraged not to interrupt or correct students during fluency-oriented activities.

With the exception of functional roleplays, it has often been the case that there's little or no connection between the tasks done in class and the kinds of conversations the students will have outside of class. Nor has there necessarily been much emphasis on explicitly pre-teaching much language that may be useful during fluency activities.

Taking a more lexical view would mean seeing fluency as generally coming from knowing, and being able to recall, appropriate language automatically. Ideally, this would involve doing more to provide students with models* of conversations that are closer to the kinds of discourse they may actually wish to participate in.

Unfortunately, in coursebooks that are based on a 'grammar + words' view of language, listening texts in particular are often either thinly-disguised grammar presentations, or else interviews/lectures that are there just to give the students practice in listening.

As a result, lexical teachers need to be more aware of other opportunities for showing how conversation works. One way is to consider how conversations develop vertically* and horizontally*:

- **Vertical development** can be seen in the way in which a sentence such as *I'm going to the States next month* might then develop as an A-B-A-B conversation. If a sentence such as this is present in classroom materials, teachers can explore this kind of development by asking students for examples of typical questions or comments they might come up with in response to it – things such as:
  Really? / Why? / Where exactly? / How long are you going for? / That'll be nice, and so on.
- **Horizontal development** involves exploring the variety of ways we might add to a comment or answer. Imagine that the following sentence appears in classroom materials: *I'm just fed up with my job.* To develop this horizontally, we could elicit ideas on what might be said next, to expand upon this statement – and then accept or reformulate* student offerings in order to come up with things like:
  It's not going anywhere / It's the same thing every day / My boss is awful / The atmosphere at work is just terrible, and so on.

Each of these different comments may then lead to a different kind of A-B-A-B vertical development. There are many opportunities for this kind of work outside of formal speaking activities, and these can lead to students practising similar conversations, even when not doing an explicit speaking lesson or task.

For more on how to take advantage of opportunities for speaking, see pages 72 and 73.

A lexical view would also see all speaking activities, including casual conversations with students and warmers, as opportunities for teaching. This means all classroom speaking moments should result in the teacher engaging in some kind of correction or focus on form or reformulating language.

In this sense, we share a lot with Dogme or Task-Based Learning approaches but, as we have already suggested, we differ in that we're suggesting that some of the language the students will need should be explicitly pre-taught – and not just anticipated.

Writing

Writing, from a skills perspective, primarily involves processes that good writers may go through. For example, in a writing lesson, there is often an emphasis on some or all of the following:

- brainstorming ideas.
- planning what to write.
- drafting, reading and editing.
- getting comments from others and then redrafting.
- (possibly) starting from scratch again!

Working through these processes is often seen as being separate from the teaching of new language, with even correction being done through a system of codes aimed at getting students to work with their existing resources in order to create a better text.

As with other skills, we would say that teaching writing lexically has less to do with abandoning these processes, and more to do with ensuring that at each stage we are also teaching and highlighting language:

- When students are attempting a particular kind of writing, they need to see models of that kind of writing. We can then highlight and draw attention to lexis and patterns within the models.
- When brainstorming ideas, we need to try to provide phrases the students might use, rather than just single words that summarise ideas.
- When correcting students' work, we might reformulate and show new language that will help them express their feelings and ideas more succinctly. We might ask them to rewrite a text, as a way of doing something with this new language.

Finally, in this last respect, writing also has a more general role to play in lexical teaching. Students need to do something with the language they encounter, and this may include writing. Traditional teaching has often involved getting students to write their own examples of new grammar structures or of words. We would diverge from this, in that we tend more towards getting students to write examples based on collocations, phrases or lexical patterns. We would also suggest the kind of texting* activities described by George Woollard in his excellent work *Messaging* (2013), where students think about – and write – what goes before and after sentences.

For more on the value of non-genre-based approaches to writing, see page 123.

A practical pedagogy for teaching and learning

Naturalness, priming and non-native speakers

In terms of why and what students learn, teaching lexically means thinking about the naturalness of what we might teach, and always teaching words with other words. It is important to note that we talk about 'naturalness' – not 'correctness' or 'native-like language'.

Focusing on naturalness involves thinking about the reasons students learn – the aforementioned needs to deal with the business of everyday life, and to express thoughts and feelings. As such, it also involves thinking about why we would say something, who to and when – or about where we would read something, or what we might write before and after a phrase, etc.

This kind of thinking means that lexical teachers are more likely to generate additional language that could be useful to students than to offer up rules or single words or examples that suggest no co-text or use. Examples, therefore, may well be 'natural' without being exactly 'correct', in terms of what we or other native speakers might say.

This is in keeping with theories such as Lexical Priming. If our language is primed by our experience of how language is used, by definition everyone's experience is unique and so everyone's English is unique: native and non-native alike.

How far you want to experience native-speaker primings (including pronunciation) and converge with native-speaker usage is basically up to you and your students. We would simply remind you that all students want to express real meanings connected to their own lives.

To summarise, then, lexical teaching is much more to do with how we think about what to teach and what to notice than it is about activities or techniques that are right or wrong.

The process

Of the six stages we started with, a lexical teacher will place the greatest emphasis on paying attention and noticing – and on repeated encounters. However, all six steps might be summarised like this:

1 Understand meaning.

Meaning is a relatively small part of priming or how words are used, and grammar meanings are generally quite limited and basic, so it's best to tackle meanings in the quickest and simplest way possible. That is almost always translation, if it is a possible option in your context. The key thing is to translate the whole unit of meaning, rather than just single words.

2 Hear/see examples of the language in context.

Lots of input is vital. Learners need to hear and see longer examples, which may well mean teachers saying examples or providing words in context and in anecdotes; extensive reading and listening can be good, but it needs to be combined with noticing and conscious learning.

3 Approximate the sounds of the language.

Lexical teachers will get students to repeat language in chunks or collocations, where sound shapes might change. We will also primarily drill* things that we think the students may hear or may want to say.

4 Pay attention to the language and notice its features.

Students need to be trained to look beyond single words. This means, as teachers:

- We need to ask questions to generate related words.
- We need to get students to underline or highlight words that go together.
- We need to highlight and drill variations of chunks.
- We need to encourage conscious memorisation of collocations and phrases.
- We need to correct and reformulate spoken and written output, in such a way that students become more aware of the language.

5 Do something with the new language – use it in some way.

Lexical teachers working in the General English field tend towards emphasising speaking, as most of our students will have that as their main goal, but practice of new items could mean drills, extended writing, the writing of dialogues, inventing examples, and so on; and students doing something with the new language may also occur when answering teacher-led questions.

For activities to revise language – see Chapter 7.

6 Repeat these steps over time when encountering the item again in other contexts.

We can help to ensure this happens:

- by giving more grammaticalised and natural examples.
- by asking about co-text and other aspects of word knowledge.
- by drawing attention to grammar outside grammar lessons.
- by encouraging conscious memorising and learning.
- by repeating speaking tasks you have done in previous classes.
- by revisiting texts you have read before.
- by regularly doing revision activities in class.

Progress

Obviously, in writing this book, we are advocating a way of teaching that we see as quicker, that learners can more easily put to use, and that is also more motivating! However, we need to be clear that we are not claiming this is a magic bullet!

• The learner

The reality of becoming a language user, whether fluent or not, is that it takes time – years, if learners want to achieve anything above an A1 level! It also inevitably requires a certain amount of somewhat boring work, particularly if accuracy is a goal – so while we think you will see a positive change in your own classroom practice if you switch to a more lexical style of teaching, don't expect miracles!

• The teacher

In a similar way, we mustn't expect the change in teaching practice to be that easy, or to lead to a new perfection. In his book on motivation, Zoltán Dörnyei (2001) looks to the model of the 'good enough' parent, which psychologists suggest makes for a happier family. He argues that for a happier working life and classroom, we too should aim to be 'good enough' teachers.

You may sometimes find yourself short of preparation time and fall back on old ways. We all have off-days! Maybe it's best to try to apply one new principle every week, or every other week, rather than every day.

You may start to notice all the things you aren't teaching. Don't beat yourself up about it! None of us can teach everything. Focus on one new thing that you did teach. After a lesson, you may sometimes think that you gave an example which was a bit weird – or just plain wrong. It doesn't matter: we all do it. Just think about what would be better for next time.

Many of you will be using a coursebook which is not completely geared towards a lexical approach, and so you may sometimes feel that your opportunities to apply the principles we present in Part B of *Teaching Lexically* are somewhat limited. This might be frustrating.

We hope that this might lead you to reassess the materials you are using, and maybe seek out something different. However, we are also realistic, and we recognise that many of you will not have that choice. If that's the case, just try to put a different principle into practice: you don't have to do them all!

And remember that, in the end, a small change may be good enough!

B

Variety out of regularity

This section is intended less as a recipe book of activities and more as a way to develop lexical approaches to commonly used exercises and tasks.

For us, interest comes less from using a wide variety of tasks or teaching techniques and more from the language, and the variety of students. Using the same material and asking the same questions can often result in quite different responses from different students. Following those responses can lead to more unexpected language, which may, in turn, lead to new teaching, new questions … and variety!

Organisation

The chapters that follow are organised according to traditional divisions of language and skills. There's then a final extra chapter on recycling and revision. Each chapter consists of a set of key principles, and each page follows a three-part structure: *Principle*, *Practising the principle* and *Applying the principle*.

Principle

The principles often recap points made in Part A and add some thoughts related to particular aspects of language, or typical exercise types and tasks.

Both the chapters and principles build on each other. We aim to cater for a variety of teachers and you may find some are too basic. We have, therefore, also tried to present principles so that they can be looked at in a different order, allowing you to reference related exercises in Part B in case you want to skip to what is most relevant to you.

Practising the principle

Here, you have a task to help you think more about the principle in question, and to discuss how it may affect your teaching. The reading, listening and writing sections are accompanied by texts in an appendix. These allow us to give examples in the *Principle* section, while also giving you a new text to practise with.

There is no answer key to this section. There are often many possibilities – and no definitive right answers. We want you to explore what the principles mean to you and to decide whether they suit you and your teaching context.

Applying the principle

This often repeats the task in *Practising the principle*, but encourages you to apply it to your own teaching. In addition, it may provide comments on when to try applying particular principles in class, alongside some teaching tips and techniques.

While we often refer to materials, these do not have to be published materials. As you will see in Part C, we strongly believe that writing materials is great for teacher development.

Although the task itself applies to *one* lesson, we hope you will incorporate some principles as an everyday part of your teaching. It's up to you how this works. You might:

- Take one principle and apply it until you're comfortable with it – or decide it's not for you!
- Try each principle in turn and see what works best for you, before applying the best ones more consistently.
- Only try principles that sound more relevant to your teaching context.
- Randomly try out a principle and work from that to other principles that are referred to. Ultimately, you will find that all the tasks are interrelated.

An exception to the rule

You will find an exception to the three-part approach in the chapter on recycling and revision. Here, there are a small number of activities that we regularly use to revise language.

Chapter One

Teaching vocabulary lexically

What's the 'word'?

Identifying units of meaning

Principle

As teachers, we need to give meanings of words to students, but first we need to decide what the 'word' or 'unit of meaning' actually is. Obviously, we can confidently translate or explain some single words like *garlic* or *dolphin*. However, as we saw on page 19, word meanings are often dependent on the other surrounding words. Despite this, we often focus on single words because of:

- the word lists for a unit in a book.
- vocabulary exercises that are based on single words.
- students asking about single words.

So, for instance, in one Pre-intermediate word list we have the words: *charity, close, coach, gang, train* and *shake*. In the contexts below, we might consider the underlined parts as the whole 'unit of meaning' – which will be relevant when translating or explaining these words:

- *<u>run</u> a marathon <u>for charity</u>*
- *my <u>closest friend</u>*
- *I'm going to <u>meet John and the gang</u>*
- *I <u>shook his hand</u>*
- *<u>train for the marathon</u>*

Whereas, here, we might consider the units of meaning as follows – which may result in different translations of the keywords:

- *I <u>work for a charity</u>.*
- *Our <u>companies have a close relationship</u>.*
- *He <u>got involved with a gang</u>.*
- *<u>Shake the box</u> and guess what's inside.*
- *I'm <u>training to become</u> a teacher*

By only focusing on single words, our translations or explanations can, at worst, provide the wrong meaning. We also feel this practice discourages our students from noticing connected words and discourages teachers from giving good further examples for students to build on.

Practising the principle

- How would you normally respond to students who ask what the items below mean?

apply	*dog*	*harm*	*come across*
crash	*ice*	*queue*	*miserable*

- Now look at the pairs of examples below. Decide:
  - what 'unit of meaning' you would include for each translation or explanation.
  - if you think the meaning or translation of each keyword is different to what you suggested above.

1a He's applied for several jobs without success.
1b You need to apply the principle to your context.

2a There was a car crash on the motorway.
2b She was injured quite badly in a crash.

3a There's no harm asking if you can go as well.
3b I think too much TV can cause harm to children.

4a The weather's been miserable for the last week.
4b He was miserable all weekend because they lost.

5a I had to queue for ages in the bank.
5b Sorry. Are you in the queue?

6a She came across as quite weak in her interview.
6b We came across it when we were walking round the town.

7a I usually take the dog for a walk in the evening.
7b Can you feed the dog?

8a I could really do with an ice-cold drink.
8b Careful you don't slip on the ice.

Applying the principle

- Look at the word list for the next unit you are going to teach, and choose ten words you think the students may want to know.
- Look through the unit. Find the context each word is used in. Then decide the best unit of meaning for each of the words – and how you'd explain or translate them.
- Think of one more example you could give the students that shows the same meaning of the 'word'. Alternatively, do the same for vocabulary in one or two exercises in the coursebook you are teaching.

Choosing words to teach

Considering frequency

Principle

Any material will include some words that are not very frequent in corpora of general usage. Students may need to know these less frequent words because:

- they're important to a particular topic.
- they're needed for comprehension of a story or text.
- they just happen to come up in conversation – they're what a student wants to say at a particular moment.

However, it makes sense to prioritise the teaching of more frequent words where we can, because the students are more likely to encounter and need these words outside the class. Over time, we may also want to:

- test more than just the meaning.
- ensure the students see a range of examples.
- explore the grammar and connected language.

Nevertheless, as we saw in Part A, writers, teachers and students may be poor judges of frequency (see page 15).

We may *overestimate* the frequency of words that:

- we can easily picture/recall, but which are actually used in fairly narrow ways.
- fit into an easy 'X is Y' pattern.

We may *underestimate* the frequency of words that:

- are a bit more abstract and less easily 'pictured'.
- don't fall into neat lexical sets.
- are typically used in more complex sentences and in writing.

More frequent words will also tend to:

- be applicable in a wide variety of settings and topics.
- have multiple meanings.

We also need to be aware that when words have multiple meanings, some meanings will be relatively infrequent. We will look at how we might deal with this in our explanations on page 39. However, for the moment, let's just focus on a simple measure of frequency.

Practising the principle

- Decide which word in each pair below is more frequent:

1 *government / apple*
2 *fun / serious*
3 *store / supermarket*
4 *kilo / weight*
5 *photography / perspective*
6 *sweat / dispose*
7 *million / football*
8 *regime / nest*

- Check your ideas by looking up each word in a good online learner's dictionary. For example:

  The Macmillan Dictionary:
  http://www.macmillandictionary.com/ uses a star system:
  *** words are the most common 2,500 words in the language.
  ** words are the next most common (2,500–5,000).
  * words are the next most common (5,000–7,500).

  The British National Corpus:
  http://www.phrasesinenglish.org/searchBNC.html
  Match 'search the word/phrase' and match by 'same lemma' (this counts all examples: singular and plural, past and present, etc). This will give a frequency per million. Anything with over about 40 matches per million would usually be a three-starred word in the Macmillan dictionary mentioned above.

Applying the principle

- Choose ten words from the word list of a unit or a vocabulary exercise that you are going to teach.
- Try to put the words in order of frequency and then check your ideas.
- Challenge an interested colleague with queries about frequency, and keep a record of who wins!
- You can also test yourself online, using the Macmillan dictionary's red word game: *http://www.macmillandictionary.com/red-word-game/*

Giving explanations 1

Using the target language

Principle

When you provide the meaning of a word, be clear about the context you're dealing with. (See the activity 'What's the 'word'?' on page 35.)

As discussed in Part A, the most effective way of getting basic meaning across is translation. However, if translation isn't possible in your context, it's worth thinking about other ways to explain each item.

When planning explanations, learner dictionaries are a great aid, because the definitions use fairly simple words. The *Collins Cobuild Advanced Dictionary* (2006) has a particularly interesting way of giving definitions, as it often uses the target word with its most common collocations or grammar. Definitions like those below may encourage students to notice usage. For example, within the entry for **fine**,we have:

*When the weather is **fine**, the sun is shining and it is not raining.*

*A **fine** is a punishment in which a person is ordered to pay a sum of money because they have done something illegal or broken a rule.*

*If someone **is fined**, they are punished by being ordered to pay a sum of money because they have done something illegal or broken a rule.*

As a teacher, you can improve these definitions by:

- making use of the context of the material you are using, or what a student has said.
- further simplifying the definition – depending on the level of your students.
- giving an additional example.

For example:

If it's going to be a fine day, then the weather is going to be nice. No rain, sunny, not too hot.

*If a company is fined, they have to pay a lot of money because they broke some rules or a law. For example, some UK banks **have been fined millions** for selling products to people who didn't need them.*

Practising the principle

- Look at the examples from classroom material below, and imagine a student asks *What does … mean?* about the words in **bold**.
- Decide the full units of meaning for each of the words in **bold**.
- Write explanations in the 'Cobuild' style we used earlier.
- Think of additional examples to clarify things, if you think they are relevant or needed.

1 We met through a **mutual** friend.

2 They were **accused** of stealing paintings worth over £2 million.

3 Your clothes **stink** of smoke.

4 We got **ripped** off by a taxi driver, coming in from the airport.

5 There's no **point** worrying about it now.

6 It's just another example of people **poking** their noses into things that have nothing **whatsoever** to do with them!

7 He's **training** to become a teacher.

8 I **applied** for 30 jobs before I got an interview.

Applying the principle

- Choose 8–10 items of vocabulary that you are going to teach. They could be from:
  - the word list for the next unit in your coursebook.
  - a vocabulary exercise you plan to use.
  - a text you plan to use.
- Decide the full unit of meaning for each of the words you have chosen. If the words are taken from a word list, you'll need to find the examples in the unit.
- Write explanations, in the style of the *Collins Cobuild* dictionary.
- Think of an additional example that matches the context you would explain each word in.

Giving explanations 2

Different ways of conveying meaning

Principle

Remember that when you're conveying meaning to your students:

- the most efficient way is generally to translate the word or chunk in the context in which the students are seeing it.
- If this is not possible, a simple explanation based on the context in which the students have encountered the word is the next best option.

However, some language can be hard to explain through formal definitions, because the words in the definitions will also be unknown to the student, or will be insufficiently precise. For example:
*She **smiled** at me*
*a **chair***
*He **left me in the lurch***
***Mackerel**'s very good for you*

In these cases, it would be better to:

- **draw** the word. (*smile / chair*)
- **mime** the word. (*smile*)
- **point** at or show the thing. (*chair*)
- show a photo from the internet. (*mackerel*)
- **tell a (short) story** or example to explain. (*left me in the lurch*)

Note that:

- We can include the mime as part of the kind of explanation we suggested on page 37:
  If you smile at someone, you do this (mime).
- If the internet isn't available and the word is too difficult to draw, settle for a more basic explanation:
  Mackerel? It's a sea fish. It has strong taste. It's this shape (draw).
- An example story for **left in the lurch** might be:
  *I had to go to an important meeting one evening, and a friend said he'd look after my three-year-old boy, because my wife is away. The meeting was at 7 and at 6.45 he phoned to say he couldn't come. I had no time to find anyone else. He really **left me in the lurch**.*

Practising the principle

- Look at the examples from classroom material below, and imagine a student asks what the words in **bold** mean.
- Decide the best units of meaning for each of the words in **bold**:
  - Which ones would you just give a definition for?
  - Write your explanations for each.
- For the ones you wouldn't explain in this way, how would you convey meaning?
  - Use the ideas outlined earlier.

1 They **postponed** the meeting until the following week.
2 Did you have to **fill in** an application form before you started?
3 You should never **click** your fingers if you want to attract the attention of the bar staff.
4 We rented a lovely little **cottage** out in the countryside.
5 He was **stabbed** in a fight.
6 They offered me a strange drink made from **avocado** juice and chocolate.
7 It's a **no-win** situation.
8 I usually wear fairly **casual** clothes.

Applying the principle

- Choose 8–10 items of vocabulary that you are going to teach. These could be from:
  - the word list for the next unit in your coursebook.
  - a vocabulary exercise you plan to use.
  - a text you plan to use.
- Decide the full unit of meaning for each of the words you have chosen. If the words are taken from a word list, you'll need to find the examples in the unit:
  - Which of the items would you just explain?
  - Which could be more easily drawn/mimed/pointed to/shown in a photo/exemplified through a story?
- Think of an additional example that matches the context you would explain each word in.

Giving explanations 3

Going beyond the immediate context

Principle

So far, we have suggested that explanations or translations should focus on the examples the students are dealing with at that time. This usually ensures that meaning is conveyed more clearly. However, there are times when you may go beyond this immediate context. For instance, if:

- the word form your students encounter is less frequent than another form in the same word family.
- the usage of the frequent word they encounter is less usual than another usage.
- different uses of a word are clearly and closely related, even though the dictionary presents them as separate meanings.
- you think your students will know another meaning of the word, and you want to link them.

Look at these situations in class:
Text: *You eat the **core**! Don't you find it a bit tough?*
Student: *What does **core** mean?*

Text: *Hattie analysed 60,000 studies …*
Student: *What does **analyse** mean?*

The following explanations go beyond the initial context,but clearly connect the different uses.

The core is this (draws). *It's the central, most important part – because it has the seed* (draws in). *We often use **core** to talk about the central, most important thing. For example, we talk about **their core business** or **the core ideas** or **your core values**.*

*When you **analyse** things or **do an analysis**, you do maths or a test to find information to explain a situation. So if you **analyse studies**, you might do some maths. You might **do a statistical analysis** to see if a drug or policy is effective. If you **analyse blood**, the **analysis might** show what's causing a disease.*

However, if don't you feel a single, simple connected meaning is possible, then stick to the immediate context. Simplicity remains the key when conveying meaning. A grasp of complexity and subtlety will come with exposure to words in context over time.

Practising the principle

- Look at the pairs of sentences below, and decide how closely the words in **bold** are connected in meaning.
- Decide which is the more frequent use (see page 36).
- If the meanings are suitably close, think of an explanation that clearly links the two forms or uses.
- If you think the words aren't connected closely enough, just think of two separate explanations.

1a The country **consumes** over 50% of the world's aluminium.
1b After his death, I was **consumed** by guilt.

2a He's clearly very **ambitious** and keen to get on.
2b They've unveiled an **ambitious** new plan for the north of the country.

3a I **bet** you were angry when you heard.
3b I'll **bet** you £20 they lose.

4a They need to act fast if they want to **restore** confidence in the police.
4b She's **restoring** one of my old paintings at the moment.

5a The whole administration is totally **corrupt** and needs to go.
5c I don't let them watch TV. It **corrupts** kids' minds!

6a I'm the **manager** of three gyms in the centre of town.
6b Don't worry about me. I'll **manage**.

7a The whole project was a **miserable** failure.
7b The city was great, but the weather was **miserable**!

Applying the principle

- Look at a word list for the unit you are going to study next – or a vocabulary exercise you plan to use.
- Find three words that have multiple meanings, and then find collocations that illustrate them.
- Find three words that have other common forms, and then find collocations that illustrate them.
- Think how you could give explanations that can link meanings or forms.

Giving good examples 1

From words to collocations

Principle

We have already suggested that after you give an explanation, it may help the students if you provide a further example in order to:

- reinforce the meaning.
- develop the students' awareness of other aspects of word knowledge.

This is especially important if you are working from a word list, or have a vocabulary exercise that's based on single words. A good starting point in these situations is to provide some collocations.

You may find it helpful to look in an online learner's dictionary or a specialist collocation dictionary.

For instance, using these sources, we might give some of these collocations for the word 'efficient':

an efficient ***service***
an efficient ***way***
efficient ***methods***
extremely *efficient*
an efficient ***use of***

Note that dictionaries often only present collocations that *strongly* associate with another word, such as those on the left below, and exclude words that 'collocate with everything' – such as those on the right. However, this second set is actually more frequent, and certainly more useful at lower levels:

violent *storm*	***a big*** *storm*
storm ***brews***	***there [be]*** *a storm*
storm ***blows***	***hear*** *the storm*
storm ***lashes s.t.***	***be damaged in*** *the storm*

Finally, note that the list of collocations we come up with may affect the explanation we give, because we may want to provide a very general meaning of an item to cover all uses (see page 39). Here, for instance, 'ambitious' shows these things really want success – or need effort to make them successful.

an ambitious	***politician***
	plan
	project

Practising the principle

- Write down six common collocations for each of the words in the box below.
- To get ideas, you could do a Google search:
  - Put the keyword and a * for the collocate within quotation marks. For example: "I * a crash" or "our core *".
- Check your ideas by looking in a dictionary – or a collocation dictionary if you have one.
  - Did you miss any obvious collocates?
- Try and find out which collocations are more frequent, by:
  - doing a Google search, where you now put the actual collocation in quotation marks. For example, "have a crash" vs "cause a crash" vs "cause *the* crash".
  - using *www.phrasesinenglish.org*, or a different online corpus or concordance. If you match by 'same lemma' rather than 'exact word', it will count all forms of the words.

1 *a crash*	**5** *formal*
2 *core*	**6** *government*
3 *provide*	**7** *restore*
4 *adjust*	**8** *virus*

Applying the principle

- Choose six keywords you are going to teach in your next lesson.
- Think of some collocations for each keyword.
- Try to show the students some of these collocations in your lesson. You might do this orally, or by writing them on the board:
  - while students are doing exercises.
  - when you're going through the answers.
  - when you explain a word that the students ask the meaning of.

You might also incorporate collocations in a 'frequency challenge' that you do with an interested colleague (see page 36).

Giving good examples 2

Collocates of collocations

Principle

Many exercises in coursebooks now teach pairs of words as collocations. This is good, but, as lexical teachers, our aim should ideally be to give examples that go *beyond* simple collocations. As we saw in Part A, a collocational pair of words can be seen to have collocates themselves. So if we take the collocation *efficient service*, we could add to it the collocates:

***provide** an efficient service*
***have an extremely** efficient service*
***introduce a more** efficient service*

The examples above build on an adjective-noun collocation. Look at these other kinds of collocations:

senior staff	(adjective-noun)
a car crash	(noun-noun)
blissfully happy	(adverb-adjective)
drive dangerously	(adverb-verb)
raise taxes	(verb-noun)
the economy grows	(noun-verb)

We can add to these collocations, by thinking about collocates to the left and right of the collocation:

***retain** senior staff*
*senior staff **take responsibility for***
***be involved in** a **serious** car crash*
***be fined for** driving dangerously*
*raise **airport** taxes*
***The government** raises taxes*
*the **French** economy grows **fast***

Once you have thought of your additions, you might turn them into an example sentence. To make these sound natural, you may have to:

- change the tense.
- add to the verb phrases.

You might then end up with sentences like these:
We retain senior staff well.
We're struggling to retain senior staff.
The French economy has grown dramatically in the last year.

Practising the principle

- Look at the basic collocations that focus on two-word combinations:
  - Think of two more collocates for each collocation.
  - Think of collocates that are used on the left and the right of the collocation.
- Write a sentence based on each collocational phrase that you come up with.
- Check your sentences sound natural, in the sense that you can imagine when, why and by whom they might be used – or ask a colleague what they think.

1 *deep depression*	**5** *take a photo*
2 *ceasefire agreement*	**6** *plants grow*
3 *bitterly disappointed*	**7** *burst into tears*
4 *flatly refuse*	**8** *come to terms with*

Applying the principle

- Find an exercise based on collocations that you are going to teach.
- Try to think of at least one collocate for each collocation:
  - Some may not have any obvious or useful ones, in which case leave them as they are.
- Think about how you could present these on the board. This could be:
  - by using an infinitive (eg *retain senior staff*).
  - as a fully grammaticalised sentence.
- Try to show the students some of these collocations and sentences in your lesson. You might do this orally, or by writing them on the board:
  - while the students are doing exercises.
  - when you're going through the answers.
  - when you explain a word that the students ask the meaning of.

You might also write an additional exercise to focus on these other collocates, either for use in the same lesson or for use as revision in a later lesson.

Giving good examples 3

Stories and co-text

Principle

In Part A, we saw that when keywords are used within texts, they will not only have direct collocates, but may often also be more loosely associated with other words. We termed these words 'co-text'. We can access and draw attention to co-text by thinking of 'stories' based on the key collocations. These stories may be true for you, or things that happened in the news, or they may simply be imagined.

For instance, for the collocation *efficient service*, we might follow our translation/explanation with an example from our own experience. We might tell the students (depending on their level) something like this:

The other day, I went to a government office to register as a self-employed person and I expected it to take ages, but in fact they were ***really efficient****. I was given a ticket and told to wait in a queue, but I only had to wait ten minutes and then the registration took five minutes. It was great.*

Through this story, the students may:
- see how *efficient* is used about a service.
- revise other language they (half) know.
- hear new language.
- make associations between the old and new.
- be better prepared to tell/understand similar stories.

In terms of how you highlight some of this language for the students, you might:
- just tell the story at a natural speed.
- tell the story, and emphasise bits by raising your voice and talking more slowly.
- write a reduced part of the story on the board.

Here are some possibilities of what you might write:
I expected it to take ages, but they were very efficient.
The service was very efficient. I only had to wait 10 minutes.
The service was very efficient. You get a ticket instead of having to stand in a queue.
It's very efficient now to register as a self-employed person. It only takes five minutes.

See also page 57: 'Horizontal and vertical development'.

Practising the principle

- Look below at the collocations from various exercises.
- Think of an experience you have had that's connected to each of these collocations.
- Write or record how you would tell each anecdote:
  - They shouldn't be more than four of five lines each – or take more than 30 seconds to say.
- Write shorter one- or two-line examples from each anecdote that you might write on the board.

1 *give a hand*	**5** *a training course*
2 *go on a diet*	**6** *feel guilty*
3 *waste money*	**7** *let someone down*
4 *a bunch of flowers*	**8** *overlook the river*

Applying the principle

- Look at an exercise you are going to teach, and choose two or three words that you can think of an anecdote for – and that you think the students might have stories about.
- Think about how you will tell your anecdotes.
- For each word or collocation, write an example with some co-text that comes out of your story.
- Tell your anecdotes to the class. You could do this:
  - when pre-teaching the words before an exercise/text (see page 85).
  - when you get to these words, while you're checking the answers to the exercise.
  - as a model, before you ask the students to share their own experiences based on the words/collocations.
- Try to write at least one of your examples on the board as you tell the anecdote, or immediately afterwards.

Giving good examples 4

Words in conversation

Principle

Words and collocations are often used differently in conversation and in texts. For example, in a text or a vocabulary exercise, you might see something like this:
lose the match
Sweden lost the match 3–0.

In conversation, the same item might be expressed like this:
A: *How was **the match**?*
B: *Oh, **we lost 3–0**!*

Here, the collocation is spread across the exchange. We don't say which match, and we replace the team the person supports with a pronoun (*we/you*) because in real conversation these things are usually known.

One way to get to examples that are more typical of spoken language is to think about paired exchanges. Think about:

- when you would say something.
- who you'd say it to.
- why you'd say it.
- how the other person might respond.

Even for words that aren't obviously 'conversational', like *whale* or *take notes*, we can still encourage the students to think about how conversations around them might work. There are obviously many possible examples, but here are two:
A: *We went whale watching one day.*
B: *Really? Did you see any?*

A: *Did you go to class yesterday?*
B: *Yeah. I took some notes. Do you want to see them?*

Ask the students how they would reply:

- You might just listen to their replies.
- You can correct their ideas and write them up.
- You can write several possible replies.

If a keyword is in the first part of your dialogue, you might only write the first line on the board:
A: *We went whale watching one day.*

See also page 57: 'Horizontal and vertical development'.

Practising the principle

- Look at the words in the box below.
  - Think of typical two-line examples, showing how they are each used in spoken language.
- In the case of a collocation, remember:
  - you don't have to use all the words together.
  - the collocates may be split across the exchange.
  - you may even replace one with a pronoun.

1 *the economy*	**5** *sort out a problem*
2 *efficient*	**6** *restore an old motorbike*
3 *injure*	**7** *take sides*
4 *a blissfully happy couple*	**8** *pick your brain*

Applying the principle

- Look at a vocabulary exercises in the next unit of your coursebook:
  - Are there examples given?
  - Are they ones that might be used in conversation?
- Choose three or four words from the exercise,and write your own two-line examples following the principles outlined earlier.
- Write these examples on the board when you teach the words to the students.
- Try to involve your students, in some cases by writing a first line that contains the keyword and then asking them for possible responses.
- You could write one or more of these responses on the board – or just listen to the students' ideas.

Asking questions about words 1

Why some questions go further than others

Principle

As we have seen, if students are to be able to use a word fluently, they need to know far more than just the pronunciation, spelling and meaning. Once you have explained and exemplified a word, a key skill is to then ask questions about the vocabulary item being looked at. In essence, you can't really know how much the students are already aware of without asking questions. Questions can:

- test students' awareness of these aspects.
- provide opportunities for you to teach more about an item.
- involve the students more in the learning process.
- create space for student stories, queries, jokes, and so on.

Learning to ask good questions about vocabulary items takes time – and the next activities are dedicated to the development of this skill. Some possible questions about an item are better than others, as they 'go further' in class:

- Open questions* are usually better than closed* ones that can be answered with a simple yes or no.
- Open questions also often allow for a degree of surprise, in terms of the ways they can be answered.

Good questions for checking what students know/understand about vocabulary:

- usually include the keyword(s).
- are impersonal and can potentially be answered by all the students in the class.
- aren't about personal experiences (based on the words) the students may have had.
- ask about possibility, and about the most typical usage and co-text.
- explore different aspects of word knowledge.
- generate connected language.
- elicit feedback that allows you to extend learning.

Practising the principle

- Look at five possible questions you could ask about the vocabulary items in **bold** below. Decide:
  - which are more open, and which are more closed.
  - what answers you imagine each question would generally elicit.
  - which questions would elicit the largest amount of connected language.
  - which ones only students with specific experience could answer.

The bus drivers are all **on strike** at the moment, so you'd better get a taxi to the airport.

A If you are *on strike*, are you happy with your job?

B Have you ever been *on strike*?

C Can you think of three different reasons why people might sometimes go *on strike*?

D If you are *on strike*, do you go to work or not?

E How might things end when workers go *on strike*?

We have years of experience in managing and **resolving conflicts**.

A What do you think is involved in the process of *resolving conflicts*?

B Are any of you any good at *resolving conflicts*?

C Can you think of three different situations in which it might be necessary to *resolve a conflict*?

D If you need to *resolve a conflict*, does it mean there's a problem?

E What kind of skills might you have, if you're good at *resolving conflicts*?

Applying the principle

- Look at the next vocabulary exercise you're going to teach. Try to think of one question you could ask about each item in the answers.
- When you teach the lesson, try asking your questions. Record yourself and your students if you can.
- Afterwards, think about which questions worked best, in terms of generating connected language – and why.

Asking questions about words 2

Matching questions to purposes

Principle

As we saw on page 44, asking questions about the vocabulary we're looking at can make our lessons more interactive, and gives us the chance to see how much our students already know about particular items. It also allows us to then add to that knowledge, either by working with ideas that the class come up with or else by simply giving extra information.

Certain kinds of questions can be used time and time again, in order to explore certain aspects of word knowledge. We can find out about:

- Word class*
  What kind of word is X here?
- Word family/word formation
  Do you know the verb / noun / adjective form of X?
- Word grammar/verb patterns
  Which preposition goes with X here?
  What kind of verb form is X followed by?
  Can you see any particular pattern connected to X?
- Collocation
  Which verb/adjective/noun/adverb goes with X here?
- Synonyms
  Can you think of another way of saying X here?
- Antonyms
  What do you think the opposite of X is in this context?
- Homophones*/pronunciation
  How do you pronounce X in this context?
- Connotation
  Does X have a positive meaning, or a negative one?
  Is X a good thing or a bad thing?
- Register
  Is X formal or informal here?
  What's a more/less formal way of saying X?
- Co-hyponyms*
  Can you think of any other (vehicles/ways of looking, etc)?
- Co-text
  What does X involve?
  Can you think of three different reasons why you might X?

Practising the principle

- Look at the questions that a teacher might ask about each item in **bold** below.
- Decide which aspect/s of word knowledge each question is testing/exploring (eg: collocation, pronunciation, antonyms, synonyms, homonyms*, homophones, word class, register, connotation, co-text, etc).

1 Is **safety** an adjective or a noun?
2 So what other things can you **break**?
3 What other word could we use instead of **go up** here?
4 What's the opposite of **losing** your key? And **losing** a match?
5 So is **skinny** a positive or negative thing to say about someone?
6 Would you usually say **moreover**? What might we say instead, then?
7 How could you finish this sentence? **She's just popped out to** ...
8 So this noun here – **river bank**. Anything to do with money, do you think?

Applying the principle

- Next time you use a vocabulary exercise in class, try to record yourself. If you have a smartphone, this should be easy to do.
- Later, listen to the way you go through the answers.
  - Did you ask questions as you were checking the answers?
  - What kind?
  - Which aspects of word knowledge are the questions you asked testing?
- Look again at the exercise you taught.
  - Can you now see any other questions you could have asked?

Asking questions about words 3

Exploring different aspects of word knowledge

Principle

As we saw on page 45, one of the key skills a lexical teacher needs to develop is the ability to ask good questions about vocabulary. Most typically, this will be done whilst checking answers to vocabulary exercises – possibly as you elicit each answer from the group. It can also be done after you've explained, and maybe given an extra example of, any particularly problematic items.

For example, if we have the collocation *heavy suitcase* in an exercise, we might ask some of the questions below. Possible answers are given in brackets:

What's the opposite of a *heavy suitcase*?
(a light suitcase / a light bag)

Why other things might be *heavy*?
(a bag / a book(s) / a box)

How else can you describe a *suitcase*?
(big / small / light / nice / strong)

Why might a suitcase be *heavy*?
(It's very big / It has a lot in it)

What might be the problem if you have a *heavy suitcase*?
(You can't carry it / You have to pay for excess baggage)

What might you ask someone if you have a *heavy suitcase*?
(Could you help me with this? It's very heavy)

What do you have to do with a *suitcase*?
(pack it / check it in / carry it)

These questions explore antonyms, collocations and co-text. For other words, we might explore aspects such as word form and so on.

Practising the principle

- Think of a suitable question to ask about each item in **bold** below.
- Write questions that test/explore how much the students know about the aspects of word knowledge mentioned in brackets after each example.
- Think of the answers you'd expect to each question.

For example:
Can I get a glass of **dry** white wine, please? (antonym)
What's the opposite of *dry white wine*?
Expected answer: *sweet white wine.*

1 They're going to **elect** a new leader. (word family / word formation)
2 He's **accused** of murdering seven people. (word grammar / verb pattern)
3 Many experts **contend** that being fit and fat is the exception, not the rule. (register)
4 They're a very **talkative** class. (connotation)
5 We **fell out** last year and haven't spoken since. (co-text)
6 How much money does she **make**? (synonym)
7 I've **read** it three times. (homophones / pronunciation)
8 The criticism **dented** my confidence. (collocation)
9 Put the bag in the **boot** of the car. (co-hyponyms)
10 It's not **like** him to say a thing like that. (word class)

Applying the principle

- Find a vocabulary exercise you're going to use in class.
- Decide what aspects of word knowledge it focuses on.
- Decide which aspects are neglected, and think of three or four questions that you could ask about some of the items in the exercise:
  - The questions should test/explore some of these neglected aspects.
- When you teach the exercise, try to ask these questions while you're checking the answers.

Asking questions about words 4

Asking extra questions about useful items

Principle

If an item of vocabulary is worth exploring, it's often good to ask more than one question about it. A lexical teacher will sometimes ask connected strings of two or three questions, in order to fully explore the way in which an item is usually used.

For example, imagine you have elicited the answer shown in **bold** below:

I did my degree in **Finance** and Marketing at Newcastle University.

You might first ask:
*What's the adjective form of **finance**?*

Once you have the word ***financial***, you could then ask:
*Which nouns go with the adjective **financial**?*

Listen to the ideas that the students come up with:

- Accept the ones you think are correct.
- Reject the ones that aren't – and, if you can, explain why they're wrong, by giving better ways of saying the meanings that the students have tried to express.

You may then want to add one or two extra noun collocates yourself – and maybe write them on the board like this:

financial	aid
	support
	adviser
	scandal
	difficulties
	problems

You can plan for this kind of thing, by checking possible collocations in a good dictionary.

Practising the principle

- Look at the items of vocabulary in **bold** below and the examples in *italics* that the teacher wrote on the board, after asking connected questions about each item.
- Decide which questions were asked to produce each example.

1. He's very **fit**. He goes running every day.
   I'm really unfit at the moment. I get out of breath just walking upstairs.
2. It was the toughest **decision** I've ever made.
   I'm so indecisive. I can never make up my mind what to buy or wear!
3. I **took out** a loan to buy a horse for my daughter.
   I'm still paying off my mortgage. I've got twelve more years to go.
4. He was **kicked out** of the team because he was always late for training.
   He was kicked out of the house after his wife found out he'd been cheating on her!
5. My dad was **operated on** four days ago, but he's already back on his feet.
   She's suing the plastic surgeon who carried out the operation.
6. I don't really enjoy listening to recorded music on CDs. I prefer **live** music.
   I saw them live in Sofia last year. It was a great concert. The support band were really good as well.

Applying the principle

- Look at a vocabulary exercise you plan to use.
- Choose two items that you think are worth exploring. This might be:
  - because there's predictable connected co-text.
  - because other forms of the word collocate widely.
  - because synonyms/antonyms work in slightly different ways to the items themselves.
- Once you've decided on two items, think of two or three connected questions to ask about each.
- Predict the answers you'd expect, and what you might write on the board as a result.

Asking questions about words 5

Digging deeper into co-text

Principle

On page 43, we saw that thinking about who you might use an item of vocabulary with, when and why you might use it, and what you might say with it can help you to think of better examples of language in normal use.

Another reason why it's important to consider usage, co-text and typical examples is that it helps you to plan the questions you'll then ask as you're teaching. Imagine, for instance, you were teaching the word 'mortgage'.

Here are some questions you could ask – and, in brackets, the answers you would expect to elicit/teach.

- *So what's the verb you do to a mortgage? You go to the bank and say that you want to MMM MMM a mortgage? Anyone?*
  (take out)
- *And once you've taken out a mortgage, what do you have to do every month?*
  (pay the mortgage / make your mortgage payments)
- *And it's not just what you borrowed, but you also have to pay something extra on top. You have to pay …?*
  (interest)
- *And what's the rate at the moment? Anyone know?*
- *So what happens if you don't pay your mortgage? What might happen?*
  (the bank repossesses your property)

Asking questions like these allows stronger students to show what they know, and also gives the teacher the chance to take these offerings and use them to teach more to the weaker students in the group – maybe while also slightly improving the language suggested.

From all these questions, you might then write an example like this on the board:

They missed their mortgage payments for six months in a row and, in the end, the bank repossessed their house.

Practising the principle

- Think of three or four questions you could ask about each of the items of vocabulary below, in order to get at the co-text that's often used with them.
- Then decide what you might write on the board, to show some of this co-text in action.

1. *put me off*
2. *have an affair*
3. *a scar*
4. *to faint*
5. *discrimination*
6. *nuclear power station*
7. *not make out anything at all*
8. *get sponsored*
9. *humanitarian*
10. *chaos*

Applying the principle

- Look at a vocabulary exercise in the coursebook you're using.
- Decide which two items are most worth exploring, in terms of the co-text that's commonly used with them.
- Think of questions to ask about each item.
- Decide what you might write on the board.

Asking questions about words 6

Ensuring your planning adds to student priming

Principle

When planning, look at the vocabulary exercises you are going to teach. Think about which items will be most difficult for your students – and which will be most worth exploring, in terms of usage and co-text. Once you have decided this, you can decide how you'll explain these items, and what extra examples you might give. You can also decide what questions you will ask, and what co-text– extra language around the items – you might then teach as well.

Obviously, you won't have time to teach everything that the students will need to know about all the items. This is why it's important to be selective, and to focus on the items which go furthest in terms of being open to exploration.

It's also wise not to worry too much about not being able to cover everything. Remember, one of the ideas at the heart of the lexical priming theory is that knowledge is always provisional – and can only develop over time and as a result of repeated exposure.

If you can, write explanations, extra examples and questions to ask on the actual pages of the book that you're using – or on copies of the material. This will help you to remember what you planned to do, and will allow you to get some examples up on the board that you can then explore in more detail, when you're checking answers and giving feedback.

The best time to get your boardwork up is while the students are trying to do vocabulary exercises on their own.

Practising the principle

- Choose the two or three items from this Intermediate level exercise (about work and training) that you think are most worth spending time on.
- For each item, write explanations, extra examples and questions to ask.

1. I sometimes have to **work shifts**.
2. It's not very **well-paid**.
3. You have to have good **people skills** to do it.
4. I have a lot of **responsibility**.
5. You get special **training** as part of the job.
6. It can be very **stressful** sometimes.
7. It's very **physically demanding**.
8. There are plenty of **opportunities**.
9. I basically sit at a desk all day **doing paperwork**.
10. He gets £60,000 a year and a **bonus** at Xmas.

Applying the principle

- Look at a vocabulary exercise in the coursebook you're using.
- Choose the two or three items that you think are most worth spending time on.
- For each item, write explanations, extra examples and questions to ask.

Using vocabulary exercises 1

Purpose and procedures

Principle

Writers of material with a stated level make judgements about what vocabulary they think:

- students know, and can use in a variety of ways.
- students may partially know (perhaps the students will know meanings, but few other aspects of word knowledge).
- what students won't know at all.

The material should contain all these levels of vocabulary knowledge. However, even then, different students will have picked up different words, and, while all the students may know the meaning of some words, they will use them with varying abilities.

One of our fundamental jobs as teachers, then, is to find out the limits of students' word knowledge, so we don't waste time simply re-teaching things the students already know. We can do this by:

- setting speaking or writing tasks, and noticing where communication breaks down.
- setting reading tasks, and noticing what the students underline or check
- setting listening or reading tasks, and noticing which parts students misunderstand.
- setting vocabulary exercises, and noticing the words that students check and the items they get wrong.
- asking questions about vocabulary, such as those we explored on pages 44–49.
- providing fuller examples, which may in turn generate new language or new meanings.
- allowing the students themselves to ask us questions about language.

We will look in more detail at the first three techniques listed above in later chapters. In the rest of this chapter, the focus is on exploiting formal vocabulary exercises.

We will look at different kinds of vocabulary exercises, because different exercises allow you to find out different aspects of the students' word knowledge.

Practising the principle

- Bearing in mind the principle outlined opposite, think about why you might not do each of the following things, when running a vocabulary exercise:

1. Spend 10 minutes introducing the exercise, and/or eliciting words connected with the vocabulary area.
2. Explain all the words in the exercise before students do it.
3. Ask different individual students to answer each question in the exercise in turn.
4. Sit at your desk while the students do the exercise.
5. Tell the students **not** to use a dictionary.
6. Make the students do the whole exercise individually, and not allow any work in pairs or groups.
7. Elicit or give each answer, and then move on to the next task in the lesson.
8. Not bother doing the further practice exercise in the book.

- Are there any circumstances where you think it would be good to do any of these things? Why?

Applying the principle

Next time you use a vocabulary exercise in class, do one of the following – from when you first introduce the vocabulary exercise to when you start the next task:

- record yourself.
- get a colleague to observe you.

After the lesson, think about:

- what words or aspects of word knowledge your students didn't know, and how you found out.
- how much you taught that was new to the students.
- whether each and every student in the class was taught something new.
- how long the whole exercise took.
- things you think were effective, and things you'd do differently – and why.

Using vocabulary exercises 2

Providing extra support

Principle

Essentially, vocabulary exercises are written as tests to find out what students know – and don't know – about words (see page 50: 'Purpose and procedures').

If teachers explain all the words in an exercise *before* the students do the exercise, they run the risk of spending valuable time telling some or all of their students things that they already know.

However, as you get to know a group, there may be times that you feel that some vocabulary exercises have so many new words in them that it will make the exercise difficult or very slow for the students to do.

One option is, of course, not to do the exercise at all, in which case you need to:

- think about how this impacts on other tasks.
- focus on other language in the texts in the book (see chapters 4 and 5).
- choose some other language focus, based on your students' needs or wants.

However, if you feel the language is useful, or for institutional reasons you have to teach the content of the exercise, you will need to provide help such as:

- pre-teaching some words.
- encouraging the students to work together, to share knowledge.
- allowing them additional time, so that they can use dictionaries.

As you go through the answers, you may also limit:

- the words you focus on in detail (see page 49).
- the aspects of word knowledge you explore beyond the basic meanings (eg only focus on collocation).

Practising the principle

- Look at the possible ways to support the students with difficult exercises below. These are alternatives to simply explaining the task and getting the students to do it individually. In each case, decide:
  - how much extra support the technique provides.
  - how much extra time it will take.
  - how easy it would be to set up and do in your context.

1 Ask the students to do the tasks in pairs or groups.

2 Explain each word in turn, and give an example. Then ask the students to do the task on their own.

3 Demonstrate the task with the group. Give two examples for the words you think the students won't know. Give the answers if they don't know them! Then get them to do the rest on their own.

4 Put the students in groups, and tell them to find words in the exercise that *none* of them know – and then look up the meanings in a dictionary.

5 Tell the students you're going to say the words and their translations. They should note any they didn't know. Then set the task for them to do on their own.

6 The students do as much as they can do, and then compare their ideas in pairs.

7 Ask the students to mark words in the exercise with a 1 (*I know and use*), 2 (*I think I know*), 3 (*I don't know*). Get them to compare ideas. See which words are mainly 3s. Explain those words only. Then set the task.

8 Set a speaking task connected to the vocabulary. During feedback, pre-teach some of the vocabulary in the exercise through correction.

Applying the principle

- If you often use the techniques in *Practising the principle*, next time try going straight into the exercise without pre-teaching/support Explain the task, and then get the students to do it on their own.
- If you generally just go straight into an exercise:
  - Choose a different technique from the list – and try it.
- After class, consider how things went, compared to other lessons, and if you will repeat what you did.

Using vocabulary exercises 3

Questions to practise vocabulary

Principle

You will often find that vocabulary exercises – whether in a coursebook or from other sources – don't provide students with an opportunity to integrate the new language with their existing knowledge. As we saw in Part A, this is an essential part of learning language, and will have to take place at some point.

We have also suggested that freer tasks – whether directly connected to a vocabulary exercise or not – offer you the chance to get feedback from the students on the limits of their knowledge, so you can then teach something new (see page 50: 'Procedures and purpose').

For both of these reasons, after a vocabulary exercise it is good to provide some kind of freer further practice, where the students make use of the vocabulary in some meaningful way.

One of the easiest ways to do this is to write questions containing words from the exercise, in order to generate a personal response. When doing this, bear in mind these principles:

- Make the questions open or have a follow-up question, so the students don't just say *yes* or *no*.
- For very frequent words, you could base several questions on different collocations of the word.
- Have several questions, so everyone is able to answer at least one. Don't expect all questions to work with every student in every class.
- Try to make the questions about people's experiences, thoughts or feelings – or allow them to talk about their culture (see 'Principles of why people learn' on page 7).
- If you think the questions may be too sensitive or that your students won't have sufficient life experience to answer them, use starters* such as
  - *Do you know anyone who ...?*
  - *Have you heard of stories in the news where ...?*
- If a word is too specific – such as 'a whale' – give the students an option or follow-up question that allows them to talk about co-hyponyms (in this case,'other animals')

Practising the principle

- Look at the practice questions below, based on the words in **bold**. The words are at a variety of levels.
- Try to answer them, either with a colleague or just by thinking about what you'd say in response to each one.
- Then decide:
  - how much language each produces.
  - if they follow the criteria in *Principle*.
  - if you could improve any of the questions in any way – or think of completely different questions that would be more productive.

1 Do you often **put** things **off**?
2 Do you know anyone who **could do better for themselves**? In what way?
3 What **improvements** could be **made** in your education system? Explain why and how.
4 When did you last see a **play**?
5 Have you ever given a **presentation**? Where? Who to? What about? How did it go?
6 Have you ever been treated by a **paramedic**? What happened?
7 When did your favourite team last **win**?
8 Do you think sending people to prison is always the best **punishment** for crimes? Why? / Why not?

Applying the principle

- Either choose a vocabulary exercise from your coursebook, or choose 8 words from a unit word list.
- Write questions to help the students practise the language.
- Do them in class. You can:
  - write them on a IWB/Powerpoint before class.
  - copy the questions, and hand them out in class.
  - dictate the questions to the students in class.

Using vocabulary exercises 4

Other simple ways to practise

Principle

We have already seen that getting students to discuss questions is one way to practise vocabulary in a personal, meaningful way. There may be more, but we personally use a limited number in our teaching. We often ask students:

- To say which of the things in the exercise they do/use.
- To use the words to talk about, for example, cuisine in their country or an accident they had.
- Which of the things in the exercise are good/bad. Why?
- Which they like/don't like. Why?
- Which of the things in the exercise have happened to them.
- To give real examples of the things in the exercise – and say something more about each.
- To write examples sentences that are true for them.
- To describe X with these words. Their partners should guess what X is – or draw it.
- To roleplay one or more particular situations, using the phrases.
- To look at the statements using the vocabulary, and say if they agree/disagree.

Whatever practice activity you choose, check:

- you can do it yourself!
- what specific words are being focused on – or which items you think will generate more language.
- what other language is being generated.

This should give you a better idea about what words to spend more time on during the feedback. For example, if the exercise is 'names of foods' and the practice is to 'talk about foods you like or dislike', you might ask 'concept-checking questions*' such as '*Why might someone not eat pork?*' or '*Why might someone like oranges?*' or give examples such as '*I love oranges – I love anything sweet*'. These will support the students when they do the practice and talk about themselves.

Thinking about what language you would use in the practice activity will also help prepare you to give feedback on what your students actually say (see the chapter on 'Teaching speaking lexically' on pages 71–81).

Practising the principle

- Look at the words and phrases in the box below. Choose two different activities you might set to practise them (including asking practice questions – see page 52).
- Try to do the task you thought of yourself – either in your head or with a colleague – to check it works.
- Note what additional language is generated.
- Think about the concept-checking questions and/or examples you might use during feedback on the exercise that presents this language (see pages 44–49).

competitive	*have responsibility*
be under pressure	*creative*
rewarding	*work in a team*
do paperwork	*dull*
insecure	*be involved in planning*

Applying the principle

- Look at the next vocabulary exercise that you are going to use.
- Decide if you will use the follow-up practice task, if there is one, or, alternatively, if you'll write your own (see the questions on page 52, or choose a task from this page).
- Think about the language that might be generated.
- When you do the feedback to the initial exercise, try to ask two or three questions or give examples that will help your students to do the practice.

Single-word exercises

Going beyond meaning

Principle

Coursebooks often feature exercises that focus on single words. For example:

- Match the word to the definition/translation.
- Match the word to a picture (or label the picture).
- Sort the words into different groups (eg transport or clothes).
- Decide if the words are X or Y (eg for men or women/positive or negative).
- Choose the odd word out in each group.
- Change the verbs into nouns (or some variation on word-building or word families).
- Match the words to synonyms.
- Match the words to their opposites.

The majority of these exercises only focus on meaning. Even where exercises do focus on other aspects of word knowledge, the students don't get to see examples of usage and, in the case of opposites and synonyms, they may not realise these will vary, depending on collocations, and context (see page 21). As the old joke puts it:

I bought a new thesaurus the other day. It's OK, but nothing to write house about!

As we have seen in Part A, there's a lot more to knowing a word than the meaning, so single-word exercises require more work from the teacher!

When checking answers to single word exercises, you will want to at least give some collocations. You may also want to:

- ask checking questions (see pages 44–49).
- give examples (see pages 40–43).

As we mentioned in 'Other simple ways to practise' (page 53), when going through answers, you might spend more time on words that come up again in any follow-up practice activity. Alternatively, if time is short, you may focus on the most frequent items, or on the ones that you think are most useful to your students.

Practising the principle

- Look at the single-word exercise below. It's aimed at Pre-Intermediate/A2 students.
- Plan the extra information you would write on the board for each item:
  - Which items can you list collocations for?
  - Which can you write a whole sentence for?
  - Which can you write a two-line exchange for?
  - Which items would you spend most time on?
  - Which would you want to practise – and how?

Match the pictures to a word:

1 *scream*
2 *to fine*
3 *a raffle ticket*
4 *to snore*
5 *a scar*
6 *to arrest*
7 *angry*
8 *amazed*

Applying the principle

- Look at the coursebook you're using:
  - How often does it have exercises that focus on single words?
  - Is this the main type of vocabulary exercise?
- Choose a single-word exercise, and:
  - decide which items are most worth spending time on.
  - plan any questions you'd ask.
  - plan what you'd write on the board.
  - do it in class.
- If you have longer examples, you might just say these during the lesson and then, later, you can:
  - email them to the students, so they can study them at home.
  - provide them on a printed handout.
  - use them to make a revision task (see page 56 on 'whole-sentence exercises').

Collocation exercises

Developing both words and collocations

Principle

Many vocabulary materials and coursebooks now have exercises focusing on paired collocations. Some are similar to single-word exercises, and simply have single collocations instead of single words. This is still an improvement, as more words get recycled and because opposites and synonyms work better at the level of collocation.Other exercises have the students match words to one or more collocates, so you get answers like this:

watch TV / turn the ~ on / turn the ~ off
a tall man / a ~ building / He's over six feet ~
have an argument / cause an ~ / settle the ~

With exercises that result in single paired collocations, we can assume the students understand the basic meaning if they have the correct answer, and we can check by asking for further collocates.

- When doing this, you can ask about either word in the collocation. It depends what you think might be new or what is more relevant.
- As such, we could ask:
  What other things can you watch?
  What other things can you do to a TV?
  and / or draw on the board something like:

watch	TV	or	watch	TV
	?		?	
	?		?	

Where there are multiple collocates, you may have to check the students understand ones you think are new. So, above, we might ask: *Do you know what* ***settle an argument*** *means?* or *What happens when you* ***settle an argument****?* followed by an explanation, if necessary.

As we saw in Part A, different collocations of the same word can have quite different opposites, synonyms and co-text. It is therefore often better to ask concept checking questions and give examples based on the collocation rather than the single word:

What's the opposite of ***heavy rain****?*
What's the verb form of ***heavy rain****?*
What might you do if ***it's raining heavily****?*
What might happen if ***it's rained very heavily****?*

Practising the principle

- Look at the collocation exercise below. It's aimed at Intermediate/B1 students.

Match the words in 1–8 with the best endings in a–h.

1 *the light*	**a** *the TV on*
2 *the phone*	**b** *crashes*
3 *the screen*	**c** *a button*
4 *the computer*	**d** *rings*
5 *press*	**e** *freezes*
6 *switch*	**f** *flashes*
7 *plug*	**g** *the machine in*
8 *dial*	**h** *the number*

- What other collocates can you think for each word?
- Write a checking question for each collocation (like those on this page, and on pages 44–49)
- Choose the three items you would spend most time on.
- Write sentences or exchanges (see pages 41–43) for those collocations.

Applying the principle

Find the next exercise in your coursebook that is based on collocation – or find a collocation exercise from elsewhere. Do one of the following:

- As you go through each answer in class, ask for other collocates of one word in the collocation.
- Then write the students' ideas on the board in the style you saw depicted in *Principle*.

Alternatively,

- Before class, write two checking questions for each answer in the exercise.
- As you go through each answer in class, ask one of these questions.
- Write up some language you think is useful, or that will help the students during the practice phase.
- Give the other questions, either on a handout or written on the board, as a revision exercise in a future lesson.

Whole-sentence exercises

Making full use of examples

Principle

Many self-study vocabulary exercises and a few coursebook exercises feature whole sentences. Most commonly, you have to complete sentences by choosing from limited options or by finding words in a text (see the chapters on reading and listening).

Other tasks may have the keywords in bold in the sentences. Students then have to check the meaning and do things such as:

- put the sentences in the order they happen.
- agree or disagree with the statements.
- answer the questions.
- match questions to answers or statements and follow-up comments (see also page 57).

Whole-sentence exercises like this:
Can I come in late on Friday? I've got an <u>appointment</u> with the doctor.
are generally better than single-word (*appointment*) or single-collocation exercises (*have an appointment*) because there is usually more information about the keyword including collocation, but also co-text and grammar, and sometimes opposites, synonyms or related word-forms in context.

However, while we can assume that if the students get the correct answer to a gap-fill, they understand the basic meaning of the keyword, they often don't pay full attention to this surrounding context. We would suggest that students need to actively notice it if they want to produce this language accurately later.

When checking the item above, you could point out:

- what kind of people you have appointments with, and elicit other examples (*dentist/accountant*, etc).
- the pattern *I've got a … on Friday* – and ask/tell the students other nouns that could fill this slot.
- that *I've got* here refers to the future.
- that *come in* here means *come to work*, and give more examples of the verb or of other reasons to *come in late*.

We will look at other ways to exploit examples in the rest of this chapter.

Practising the principle

- Look at the exercise below on doctor-related vocabulary. It's aimed at Upper-intermediate/B2 students. The answers have been added and <u>underlined</u>.

1 That's a nasty <u>cough</u> you've got. You really ought to stop smoking.
2 I'm allergic to seafood. I get a <u>rash</u> on my arm after eating it.
3 I need to pop into the chemist's later to pick up that <u>prescription</u>.
4 Are you having any trouble <u>swallowing</u> at all?
5 I'll give you something to <u>relieve</u> the pain.
6 There's a really nasty <u>virus</u> going round at the moment.
7 I was jogging and I fell over and <u>sprained</u> my ankle.
8 I'm feeling so stiff today. I think I <u>overdid</u> it at the gym.

- What interesting features/patterns/chunks/collocations do you notice in each sentence?
- Plan what you'd say/ask about each item – and what you might write on the board for each item.
- If you were short of time, which items would you spend most time on? Why?

Applying the principle

- Look at the coursebook you're using, and find an exercise that features whole sentences.
- Check the answers, and see what interesting features/patterns/chunks/collocations you notice.
- Decide which items you'll spend most time on.
- Plan what you'll say/ask about those items, and what you will write on the board.

Sentence-matching exercises

Horizontal and vertical development

Principle

In the previous task on page 56, we noted that some whole-sentence exercises actually go beyond single sentences. In some vocabulary materials, you will find examples of matching exercises. The matched item is generally one of two choices:

- A follow-up comment by the same speaker:

1 *She's very bright.*	**a** *Everyone's going.*
1 *She's in a rush.*	**b** *She got straight As.*
1 *It'll be a great do.*	**c** *The train leaves at 10.*

- A response by another speaker:
  1 *She's very bright.*
  2 *She's in a rush.*
  3 *It'll be a great do.*

  a *I can drive her to the airport.*
  b *Is Selima going?*
  c *So why did she fail?*

These kinds of exercises fit with the idea of *horizontal* development – the way one person builds a longer turn or argument – and *vertical* development, which explores how two people build a conversation.

These kinds of exercises are good, because they:

- present co-text that the students need, but often don't see because they don't fit into typical lexical sets.
- help the students develop awareness of conversational and discoursal norms.
- treat coursebook sentences as plausible messages instead of simply discrete unconnected items.

As with other whole-sentence tasks, teachers will need to draw attention to features within the sentences. They can also elicit alternative ways each sentence could be developed horizontally or vertically.

This idea can also be applied to single-sentence examples that either appear in an exercise or that you give yourself. You will find that some sentences are more open to such development. This may well be connected to how natural the sentences are, and who you would say them to and why (see also page 43).

Practising the principle

- Look at the single-sentence vocabulary exercise below. It is connected to job applications and interviews. The gap-fill element focuses on prepositions. Answers are underlined.

1 I'm familiar with most kinds of design software.
2 I am quite knowledgeable about the history of art.
3 I'm serious about acting and drama.
4 I'm not keen on sitting behind a desk all day.
5 I'm well suited to research roles.
6 I specialised in employment law.
7 I'm very good with people.
8 I'm good at negotiating the best deals possible.

- For each sentence, try to think of a horizontal development – what the same speaker might say next – and a vertical development – the response by the interviewer and how the conversation might continue.
- Decide which sentences were easier to develop, and how.
- For the easier examples, try to think of one or two more possible follow-up sentences or responses.

Applying the principle

- Either find a matching exercise based on horizontal or vertical development that you are going to teach, and then:
  - think of alternative phrases to develop the initial sentence.
  - elicit alternative ideas for each item from your students, as you go through the answers
  - correct the language, and write up some of their ideas.

Alternatively,

- Look at the next single-sentence vocabulary exercise you want to teach, and:
  - decide for which sentences you can think of several ways they could develop horizontally or vertically.
  - for those sentences only, elicit alternatives from your students during feedback. You may need to prompt the students with one of your own ideas.

Memorisation tasks

Noticing and learning usage

Principle

Sentence or text-based vocabulary exercises are potentially better for students, because they feature more information about how words work. However, as we have already suggested, students may not actually notice the surrounding language or think about learning it because they are so focused on the 'gapped' word and the whole meaning of the sentence/text – rather than on the specific construction of the sentence, and how it might differ from their own L1.

Teachers can help to overcome this, by:
- asking questions about other items in the sentence (page 48).
- showing the chunks and giving more examples (page 56).
- drawing attention to grammar (page 59).
- eliciting alternative ways to develop a sentence horizontally and vertically (page 57).

However, we can also get the students to pay attention to language by asking them to spend a few minutes trying to memorise whole sentences, or even a whole exchange or text. Then, in pairs, either:
- one student tests the other, and corrects any errors.
- both students work together to write down what they remember, and then compare with the original.

Some students may initially complain that it is impossible to remember everything, but do persist because:
- there's no learning or speaking a foreign language without remembering.
- the aim in this first instance is to make the students notice, rather than produce fully correct answers.
- the exercise gives you another chance to see what the students don't fully know. So, for example, a student will not need to memorise 'depend *on*' if they already know that *depend* goes with *on*.
- you can (re-)teach points when the students finish.

* There is more information and a variety of activities on memorising language in Nick Bilbrough's excellent book *Memory Activities for Language Learning* (Cambridge University Press).

Practising the principle

- Look at the exercise below, connected to comparison and contrast. The answers have been added and underlined.

1 He bears very little <u>resemblance</u> to his brother.
2 I'm learning to appreciate the subtle <u>differences</u> between the various meats.
3 Any attempt to draw a <u>comparison</u> between the two situations is dangerous!
4 There's a growing <u>disparity</u> between rich and poor.
5 It can be hard to strike the right <u>balance</u> between technology and respect for human rights.
6 We ended up achieving the exact <u>opposite</u> of what we set out to achieve!

- Spend two or three minutes trying to memorise the sentences.
- Then cover the exercise, and write what you remember. Check your ideas, and:
  - note what you forgot and why.
  - consider what was easier to remember.
  - decide if you had enough time to memorise.
  - think of hints you could give your students, as prompts to remember or reduce the memory load.

Applying the principle

- The next time you use a vocabulary exercise that contains whole sentences or more, go through the answers and give the students time to memorise the language. Then tell them to close their books, and:
  - put them in pairs to write what they remember.
  - monitor and notice problems/give hints.
  - get them to compare with the original.
  - give feedback on any common errors.
- Alternatively, you could:
  - get weaker students (with their books open) to test stronger students.
  - set the memorisation as homework and test in the following lesson.
  - do it all as a revision task later in the course.

Grammar exercises

Opportunities to explore vocabulary

Principle

The vast majority of classroom materials maintain a strong division between vocabulary and grammar, and may reinforce this by ensuring that:

- vocabulary exercises avoid grammar, by focusing on single words or collocations.
- grammar exercises avoid 'new' words, and only focus on grammar rules or forms.

As lexical teachers, we want to break these divisions down by providing grammaticalised examples of words and, when they do appear, drawing attention to grammar and other features in sentence-based vocabulary exercises. We will look further at this in the chapter on 'Teaching grammar lexically'.

We also want to be alive to the possibilities of teaching more about words in grammar exercise:

- There may occasionally be words that are entirely new.
- More likely, there will be words that are partially known, and we might want to extend the students' knowledge of these – in the ways we have seen in this chapter.

For example, in the sentence *There* <u>*have been*</u> *many earthquakes in California over the years*, which tests the present perfect, the students may already know the meaning of the word *earthquake*. However, we can still ask questions such as:

What happens when there's an earthquake?
How does the government usually respond?
What other places often experience earthquakes?
What adjectives describe earthquakes?
What other 'natural disaster' words do you know?

In feedback to a grammar exercise, you will obviously first check the grammar, and then explore the vocabulary:

- as you go through the exercise item by item.
- as a separate focus on two or three words, after you have finished checking all the items.

Practising the principle

- Look at this grammar exercise below aimed at Intermediate/B1 students. It practises the use of the present perfect. The answers are in **bold**.

> **1** I **haven't mastered** Arabic yet, but I can communicate.
> **2** **Have** you **met** his parents yet?
> **3** I**'ve seen** that movie three times.
> **4** The army **has attacked** that city five times.
> **5** **Have** you ever **slept** in a cave?
> **6** She**'s talked** to several specialists, but nobody knows what's wrong.
> **7** You**'ve been** late for work too many times. You're fired!
> **8** We**'ve known** each other for fifteen years now.

- Decide which vocabulary you would explore.
- Decide if you think you'll need to explain the meaning of any of items – and how you'll do it.
- Decide what other examples you might give.
- Decide what questions you'd ask about the vocabulary, and what additional language it might generate.
- Decide what you would put on the board.
- Decide how you could practise that language.

Applying the principle

- Look at the next few grammar exercises that you plan to use:
  - Do they include any vocabulary that you could explore?
  - Remember that there may not be much.
- Decide which items you will cover and how.
- Focus on these words in your feedback to the exercises when you teach them.

Chapter Two

Teaching grammar lexically

When? Why? Who to?

Teaching the probable, not just the possible

Principle

As we saw in Part A, most coursebooks are still based on a 'grammar + words' view of language. When it comes to giving examples of how structures work, we believe this can cause problems because:

- the examples won't necessarily reflect the way the structures are actually used.
- little or no attention is paid to the language or patterns often used around the structure in question.
- the focus is generally on sentence-level communication, while real communication occurs mostly at discourse level.

Lexical teachers would hopefully:

- ensure that examples of particular structures can be used in everyday life.
- provide examples that reflect the way the words contained in them generally colligate or pattern.
- recognise that grammar structures are often restricted by lexis or by meaning.
- think about usage beyond sentence level.
- be aware of connected patterns and co-text.

One of the first steps towards teaching grammar from a more lexical perspective is to be critical of the examples given, and to try and improve them.It is useful to consider how many of the example sentences provided are likely to be *used*. To do this, we can ask:

- When would we say these sentences?
- Why – and who to?

If we are unable to easily answer one or more of these questions, we may well need to provide different examples. Once we have *better* examples, we can:

- add them as alternatives when checking answers.
- focus more on the sentences in exercises that *didn't* need to be improved on, and less on those that *did*.

Practising the principle

Below is a table of the kind often found in the back of coursebooks. It shows examples of many of the structures most commonly taught at lower levels. It includes active and passive sentences, as well as negatives and questions. Decide:

- which sentences – if any – seem *probable* to you.
- who you would say them to. When? Why?

Add to, or change in some way, the sentences that didn't seem probable to you. Ensure your new examples still illustrate the same grammatical structures, but are more likely to actually be used in day-to-day speech.

He *drives* cars.	He *drove* cars.
Cars *are driven*.	Cars *were driven*.
He *is driving* cars.	He was driving cars.
Cars are being driven.	Cars *were being driven*.
He *has driven* cars.	He *had driven* cars.
Cars *have been driven*.	Cars *had been driven*.
He *has been driving* cars.	Cars *had been being driven*.
I/You/We/They	*drive*.
I/You/We/They	*don't drive*.
Do I/you/we/they	*drive?*
He/She /It	*drives*.
He/She/It	*doesn't drive*.
Does he/she/it	*drive?*

Applying the principle

- Look at the grammar tables and examples in the reference section of the last coursebook you used.
- Think about how many of the examples are re-useable:
  - How many of them do you think your students might actually want to say, or might hear said by others?
  - Can you think of a context for them?
  - Who would *you* say them to? Why? When?
  - Can you think of any better examples?

Checking answers to grammar exercises 1

From explanations to concept checking

Principle

When going through the answers to a grammar exercise, it is obviously important to make sure we elicit – or give – the correct answers. However, we need to do more than this. If we don't, students who failed to get the answers right may be left not understanding why their efforts were wrong – and the class as a whole won't get the chance to have key concepts checked and clarified.

Given this, we need to ask questions in order to check whether the students know *why* an answer is right and whether they understand the underlying meanings of the structures. The questions we ask when checking:

- may sometimes require a simple *Yes/No* response.
- may also give options (*Is it x or y?*).

For example, if an answer is:
It said it might rain tomorrow.

We could ask:
'Is it *certain* to rain tomorrow?'
or
'Is rain a 100% chance, or more like a 60% chance?'

The correct responses would be something like:
'No. Only maybe.' 'A 60% chance.'

Many teachers learn this technique on initial training courses, but it's something that requires ongoing practice to get good at, and to be able to use with ease in the classroom.

One way to develop your ability to do this is to look at grammar explanations in a coursebook, and turn each one– or each part of each one– into questions.

Practising the principle

Look at the explanations below.

Write questions you could ask when going through the answers to any connected exercises. Your questions should check whether the students understand the basic concepts behind each piece of grammar:

- Use *Yes/No* questions or *Is it x or y?* questions.

Explanation 1
Use comparatives (*-er*/*more*) to compare two things:

- Add *-er* to one-syllable adjectives.
- Change *-y* to *-ier* with two-syllable adjectives that end in -y.
- Use *more* before other adjectives of two syllables or more.

Explanation 2
Use the present continuous to show that an action, feeling or event:

- is temporary and unfinished.

  or
- is arranged for the future.

Applying the principle

- Look at the next grammar exercise you are going to teach.
- Write concept-checking questions based on the explanations that accompany the exercise.
- Look at the answers to the practice exercise, and decide:
  - the concept-checking questions you will ask the students.
  - when you will ask them.
- Try to remember your questions.
- As you go through the exercise in class, elicit answers and write the correct answers on the board.
- Ask your concept question(s) as you are doing so.

Checking answers to grammar exercises 2

Drawing attention to co-text

Principle

In order to ensure that only one answer to a particular grammar question is possible, materials writers often (consciously or otherwise) include phrases that restrict the possible options.

For example, the only thing in the following sentence that forces the use of the present perfect simple – rather than, say, the present continuous – is the addition of the time adverbial *over recent months.*

Prices .... *dramatically over recent months.*(rise)

To take advantage of this, and to draw the students' attention to the co-text that often goes with particular grammar structures, a good follow-up question to ask, once you've asked the kind of basic concept-checking questions we looked at on page 62, is:

'Which words or phrases show ... (the concept/rule)?'

Look at the examples below. They are taken from an exercise aimed at Pre-Intermediate/A2-level students. The exercise contains ten examples of the present continuous. The students decide which refer to the time *around now* and which refer *to the future.*

1 *I'm working really hard at the moment.*
'So is this one temporary, or is it a future arrangement?'
(temporary)
'Good. OK. And which phrase shows *I'm working hard* is temporary here?'
(*at the moment*)

2 *Sorry I can't come tomorrow. I'm working.*
'And is this one temporary, or a future arrangement?'
(a future arrangement)
'Which phrase shows *I'm working* is in the future here?'
(*tomorrow*)

Practising the principle

- Match the questions (1-5) you might ask when checking answers with the words in **bold** in the completed sentences from various grammar exercises (a-e).
- Decide what probable answers to questions 1–5 you would expect the students to come up with.

1 What words show it's *a rule* or *obligation*?
2 What words show it's *an opinion*?
3 What phrase shows there's *a present result*?
4 What word shows it's *uncertain*?
5 What phrase shows that it was *before* getting home?

a I **might** go out later. It depends if I finish my essay.
b I don't think people **should** keep dogs here.
c You're out of breath. **Have you been running**?
d You **mustn't** bring dogs into the flats. You can be fined, if you do.
e I don't know the final score. The match **had finished** by the time I got home.

Applying the principle

- Look at your coursebook / classroom material, and choose two gap-fill or multiple-choice exercises focusing on tense or modal verbs that you will teach soon.
- Write concept-checking questions like those outlined on page 62.
- Identify any words or phrases in the exercises that reinforce the underlying grammatical concepts.
- Write follow-up questions, where appropriate:
  - Start each: *What words or phrases show ...?*
- Try to remember these questions and/or write them on your plan or in your coursebook.
- After eliciting a correct answer to a particular question, check the concept.
- Then ask *What words or phrases show ...?*
- You could then write the words/phrases on the board – or ask the students to repeat them.

Getting more from exercises 1

Same grammar, different co-text

Principle

Many grammar exercises use a fairly wide range of words to illustrate the form of a structure, and don't usually use each of those words more than once. While this may be good, in terms of showing how the form is constructed, it ignores the fact that some words are actually far more common with certain structures than others are.

For instance, an exercise on superlatives may have only one example of *best*, despite it being more commonly used with this structure than other adjectives.

This is problematic because, as we saw in Part A when discussing the work of Nick Ellis:

- basic patterns may well become established in the mind through repeated hearings of the most frequent combinations.
- once these patterns have been established, we are then able to both receptively understand new words we meet in the slots and add new items in them ourselves.

To tackle this issue, at the end of an exercise, once you've checked all the answers, you could take one or two sentences and look at how the co-text around them could be changed. Let's say an exercise includes the sentence below:

I've known Ben for 20 years. We were at school together.

Possible variations include the following:

- I've known Rebecca for 15 years. *We met when she started working here.*
- I've known Karim for twenty-five years. *We were in the same class at university.*
- My friend John has known his girlfriend for six months. *They met on the internet.*

Practising the principle

- Look at the exercise below. It's aimed at Intermediate/B1-level students, and focuses on '*should've* + past participle'. The answers are in *italics*.
- Decide which of the examples of the structure are the most common and might be exploited best.
- Think of some extra examples. Make sure your examples keep the same grammar, but add different co-text.

1 It rained. *We should've put up* a shelter over the barbecue.
2 You *should've seen* him. He looked ridiculous.
3 I *should've written* a shopping list. I'm sure there's something else we need.
4 You *should've told* me it was your birthday. I would've bought you a present.
5 They didn't do anything about him missing school. They *should've given* him a punishment.
6 It was really hot in there. They *should've opened* a window.
7 It's my own fault. I *should've listened* to you when you warned me about him.
8 I never learn! I *should've known* better after what happened last time!

Applying the principle

- Look at a grammar exercise you plan to teach soon.
- Choose two examples of the structure you think are more common and whose co-text could be varied:
  - If there are no good examples, you could change one or add your own.
- In class, write the example(s) on the board and:
  - give an example of a possible change, and show the students the pattern.
  - elicit other ideas/examples from the students.
  - set up a short pairwork practice where the students have to come up with more examples, or have conversations around the examples.

Getting more from exercises 2

Reformulating students' ideas

Principle

A lot of grammar exercises focus on single sentences or short responses, rather than longer stretches of discourse. One way we can overcome these limitations is to ask the students for their own ideas about how the discourse may develop. Doing this also helps language development by:

- giving the students the chance to integrate new grammar with what they already know.
- allowing the teacher to see how far the students have understood the grammar and its contexts of use.

Obviously, when you ask students for ideas, they may:

- struggle to express their ideas, and either use very broken English or fall back on L1.
- try to express ideas which you understand, but which need to be rephrased using structures that aren't necessarily being looked at at the present time – or that haven't yet been formally studied.
- suggest ideas which are either wrong or rather bizarre, and unlikely to be said about the given context.

This means that you may well need to:

- check you understand what the students are trying to say. Use L1 if possible, or ask questions in L2 and paraphrase*.
- say/write improved versions of the students' ideas.
- use some structures/lexis that the students have not yet formally studied, if they express the students' ideas.
- make judgments about naturalness or probability.
- reject some suggestions.

If your reformulation does lead to you introducing 'difficult' grammar or vocabulary, it's really not a problem because the students themselves have already provided the meanings, and can then learn the sentences/chunks you provide without having to analyse the underlying grammar structures (yet).

Practising the principle

Look at two examples that teachers have decided to explore. In each case, you can also see students' responses. For each response, decide:

- if you would accept it as it is, reformulate it, ask questions about it (if so, *which* questions?) or reject it.
- what – if anything – you would write on the board as part of your reformulation.

1

A: *Have you ever been to the UK?*
B: *No, I haven't.*

The teacher asks: 'What could you say here after *No, I haven't*? Any ideas?'

Student 1: *Have you been?*
Student 2: *It's great.*
Student 3: *How is it like?*
Student 4: *It's a place not my taste.*

2

I can't come on Thursday. I'm going to Liverpool.

The teacher asks: 'What else could you say here, apart from *I'm going to Liverpool*? Anyone?'

Student 1: *I'm having an exam.*
Student 2: *I make appointment my friend.*
Student 3: *I'm sleeping.*
Student 4: *I must to work lately.*

Applying the principle

- Look at a grammar exercise you plan to teach soon.
- Choose two sentences you think could be developed.
- In class, give an example of a possible development, and then ask the students what could be said instead.
- Listen to students' ideas and accept, reformulate or reject, as appropriate. Remember that you may sometimes need to seek clarification.

Getting more from exercises 3

From messages to mini-texts

Principle

As we have seen, grammar exercises often tend to focus on single-sentence 'messages'. On page 57, we looked at how we can encourage students to add comments after example sentences. However, we can also think about *broader* contexts for sentences.

In his book *Messaging: Beyond a Lexical Approach in ELT* (2013), George Woolard suggests a central role for an activity that he calls 'texting'. Woolard claims that the main goal for learners is to be able to create texts, which he defines as series of linked messages. He adds that 'we are more likely to remember a message as part of a larger text just as we are more likely to remember a word when it is contextualised in an appropriate example of use'.

To 'text' the messages that grammar exercises provide, take a sentence, and write what you think was said both immediately *before* and *after*. This may mean embedding the sentence within a longer turn by one speaker, or treating it as part of a dialogue between two people.

Note that you will find it difficult to do this with some sentences, as they may have been written solely to exemplify a grammar structure – with no thought being paid to whether or not they could potentially be used in everyday discourse.

If you find you're struggling to add *before* and *after* messages to sentences in an exercise:

- either choose the sentences which seem easiest to you.
- or, in class, put the students in pairs and encourage them to choose two or three sentences to text.

Go round and help the students:

- Let them use dictionaries.
- As they are writing, correct any errors and reformulate their ideas into better English.

Practising the principle

Look at the exercise on the use of articles below. Decide which sentences best lend themselves to being texted. In other words, for which ones can you most easily think what was said before and after?

For the sentences you do choose, write examples of what you think could be said before and after:

- To make your texts sound natural, you may find that you need to make small changes to the original sentences (such as replacing a word with a pronoun).
- This is something you can draw your students' attention to when they write their own texts.

1 My sister is married to a German. He's a doctor.
2 We go to the cinema about once a week.
3 Who's the guy by the door?
4 Did you remember to lock the door?
5 I usually leave work around 6.00 and get home at 7.30.
6 Women are normally less aggressive than men.
7 He has a beard and lovely blue eyes.
8 What a lovely day! We should go to the park.

Applying the principle

- Look at the next grammar exercise you plan to teach that is based on single sentences.
- Look at each sentence, and decide which could most easily be turned into a text by adding 'before' and 'after' sentences:
    - If you feel only *a few* are easy to use, then choose those for the students to do in class.
    - If *all* the sentences can be 'texted', let the *students* choose the two or three they'd most like to use.
- Put the students in pairs and get them to write their before/after sentences. Go round and help.
- When the students have finished, they can read out their texts to each other, or act them in pairs if they are dialogues.

Teaching grammar as lexis

Micro-presentation and practice

Principle

One core belief of lexical teaching is that, at lower levels in particular, students need to learn what Michael Lewis once called 'grammar as lexis'. Just as students in their first English class can learn the question *What's your name?* –without being told it's the present simple, and without any explanation of the underlying grammatical structure – so too can they acquire other useful examples of grammar in action.

If you listen to the ideas your students try to express, and help them to say these things better by reformulating them (see page 65), then you will sometimes give the students sentences that contain grammar they've not yet met. There are several advantages to doing this:

- The meaning of the sentence will already have been expressed by the students themselves.
- The sentence can be learned, revised and used as a whole. There's no need yet to fully study the structure.

When students do study the actual structures later on, they will already have some foundations in place.

If you want the students to briefly practise the sentences you introduce while reformulating, you need to provide different prompts that will encourage their production.

For example, an Elementary student may ask *How long you do it?* This might be reformulated as *How long've you been doing that?* You could then say the following as prompts to elicit this question from different students:

- I've got my Arabic class tonight.
- I go to yoga on Tuesdays.
- I'm learning to play the guitar.
- I paint quite a lot.

You can reply to each student with a different answer. The students could also work in pairs to write dialogues.

Practising the principle

Below are eight reformulations of things that Elementary and Pre-Intermediate/A1-A2 students said in class. For each one, try to think of four prompts that would elicit the sentence.

1. Sounds good.
2. I wouldn't do that if I were you.
3. You should've told me.
4. That must be hard.
5. It's supposed to be great.
6. I'd love to, but I can't.
7. How long did it take you?
8. I was going to, but I didn't.

Applying the principle

- The next time you hear students try to say something that they are not yet grammatically able to express, reformulate their output and write your new sentence on the board.
- Keep a record of all the reformulations you come up with over the next few lessons. Look back at them, and decide which are commonly used chunks/sentences.
- Think of prompts that could elicit each one.
- In your next class, present these sentences as revision. As you check the sentences, use your prompts, as outlined in *Principle*.
- Look out for opportunities to reuse these mini-presentations and practices in other classes you teach.

Grammar in vocabulary exercises 1

Asking about tense usage in example sentences

Principle

As we saw in Part A, one of the problems with a more traditional 'grammar + words + skills' approach to materials writing is the fact that when words are presented, there's often little attention paid to contexts of use or the typical co-text that occurs around the words. As a result, students are not always given the chance to see how words colligate: they fail to learn more about the typical grammar that often connects to words in texts.

Nevertheless, an increasing number of vocabulary exercises do feature whole sentences or even short dialogues for the students to complete with specific items. Where this is the case, teachers have the opportunity to ask questions about what tense particular sentences are in – and why:

- This helps to keep the basic underlying meanings of many of the core structures of the language fresh in the students' heads.
- It also ensures they're still studying grammar, even when the main focus is on vocabulary.

In some instances, there may only be one or two tenses featured in an exercise, but it's still worth asking about each of these at least once.

When going through the answers to exercises, you can just ask *What tense is this here? Why?* Alternatively, you could ask the kind of concept-checking questions we saw on page 62. This may work better with lower levels.

Practising the principle

- Look at the vocabulary exercise below. It's aimed at Upper-Intermediate/B2-level students, and focuses on adverbs and adverbial phrases. The answers have been added in **bold**. Decide which sentences would be best to ask the questions *Which tense is used here? Why?* about.
- Think about the answers you'd expect from your students – and any (brief) explanation you might give, to explain why particular tenses are used.

1 As he was coming round the corner, he was hit by a car. I **immediately** ran over to see if he was OK.

2 My friend Robert really loves Italian food and culture. **Surprisingly**, though, he has never been to Italy.

3 I looked into my bag and realised I'd left my wallet at home. **Fortunately**, I had my cash card with me.

4 Detectives searched the area for ages. **Eventually** they found the evidence they were looking for.

5 I found out today that I didn't get that job I applied for. **Obviously**, it was a big disappointment.

6 I was called into the boss's office and was told that I'd lost my job. **Weirdly enough**, I didn't feel that upset about it!

Applying the principle

- Look at a vocabulary exercise that you plan to use soon. Does it include any examples of different tenses that you could ask about? Remember that there may not be many.
- Decide which sentences you will ask about, and think about the answers/explanations you would expect.
- Try to remember your concept-checking questions and explanations. In class, ask why each particular tense is used, and then give your explanations if you feel further clarification is needed.

Grammar in vocabulary exercises 2

Drawing attention to syntax

Principle

In the 'Teaching vocabulary lexically' chapter,we suggested ways of asking questions that both checked meaning of vocabulary and generated connected language (see pages 44–49). You can also encourage students to notice more, and to pay more attention to, aspects of grammar around words by asking more closed and directed questions. For example:

- What preposition follows X?
- What verb form follows X? *-ing* or infinitive?
- Why do we use *much* – not *many* – here?
- Why do we use *were* here – not *was*?
- Is X a noun or a verb here? How do you know?

As you are asking questions like this, you might want to tell the students not to look at their books. You can also read out some sentences from an exercise, but leave out key grammatical words. These may be prepositions connected to particular adjectives or nouns, auxiliary verbs or modal verbs, or particular forms of certain words – noun forms, adjective forms, etc.

Instead of saying the words you're leaving out, simply say MMM – or say one MMM for each missing syllable.

For example, if two of the sentences are these:
We **go back** quite a long way.
They're **always there** for each other.

You can say:
We go back MMM a long way.
They're always there for MMM MMM-MMM.

See if the students can say the missing words.

You can also use one of the memorisation tasks that we looked at on page 58.

Practising the principle

- Look at the completed vocabulary exercise below. It's aimed at Upper-Intermediate/B2-level students, and explores the meanings and uses of some words that have the same form in different word classes. The answers have been added in **bold**.
- Decide which syntactical features you would ask about or replace with MMM – and what questions you'd ask about each one. Don't choose the words in **bold**!

1. I can't **bear** him! He never stops talking about football.
2. My daughter carries her teddy **bear** with her wherever she goes.
3. Ask her. I'm sure she won't **mind** if you leave a bit early.
4. You paid £300 for that? You must be out of your **mind**.
5. That shirt doesn't **fit** you very well. It's a bit too small for you.
6. She goes to the gym five times a week. She's really **fit**.
7. Of course I'll be there. I wouldn't **miss** it for the world.
8. I'd give it a **miss** if I were you. It's not very good.

Applying the principle

- Look at a vocabulary exercise you plan to use soon.
- Decide which syntactical features in which sentences you want to ask about or replace with MMM.
- Think about the questions you will ask about each one.
- As you're going through the answers to the exercise, focus on some of these other features.

Translation and grammar

Overcoming the objections

Principle

Some people object to the use of translation in EFL classes. They claim:

- students need to learn to 'think in English'.
- ideas can be translated in too many different ways.
- it encourages word-for-word translation, which doesn't work.
- it can't be done if the teacher doesn't speak the L1 of all the students in the class.

However, all of these objections can be countered:

- All learners refer to L1 in their heads, and it can be useful to make this process visible and to discuss it.
- A range of possible translations is often normal, and may simply reflect personal choices. Teachers can usually tell whether or not meaning has been grasped.
- Translating word for word from English can help the students appreciate how English sounds in their L1.
- Translation can make students more aware of the way grammar and words operate differently in L1 and L2.
- Even where you don't know students' L1, if you see them struggling or debating translations, it can alert you to the fact that further explanation/examples may be needed.
- Where the students have translated from L1 into English, the discussion is about how correct the English is, meaning knowledge of their L1 is not absolutely necessary.

Practising the principle

Think about why you you might do each of the following things:

1. Ask the students to translate a grammaticalised chunk (e.g. *How long've you been doing that?*) into their L1.
2. In a multi-lingual class, get the students who share an L1 to translate some sentences together. Ask them about any disagreements they may have.
3. Ask the students to translate sentences into L1 and to then translate back into English, possibly after a period of time. The students then compare their English sentences with the originals, and discuss the reason for any differences.
4. In multi-lingual classes, ask the students to translate sentences from a grammar exercise into L1 on a separate piece of paper. They should number the sentences. In pairs:
   - Student A then asks for a sentence from the exercise.
   - Student B tries to say the English, using their translation.
   - Student A corrects, where necessary.
5. Ask the students to translate sentences word for word into L1. Tell them these translations will sound strange and that, if there's no direct equivalent, they can simply use the English word.
6. In a monolingual group where you speak the students' L1, put students in pairs and tell them to decide on the best translations of certain sentences. Then check the ideas with the whole class.
7. Put the students with others who share their L1 and get them to do a speaking task in L1 first, and to then translate some of the things they were trying to say.

Applying the principle

- Either look at an exercise that you plan to use soon, or write a collection of between five and 10 sentences taken from exercises you have taught recently.
- Then use one of the techniques outlined above in your next class.

Chapter Three

Teaching speaking lexically

Before students speak

Understanding exercises by clarifying goals

Principle

In general, speaking tasks in classroom materials aim to get students to do at least one of the following:

- Break the ice at the start of a course, or warm up at the start of a lesson.
- Practise a specific grammar point.
- Practise specific vocabulary.
- Practise a specific interaction – usually functional – containing a mix of specific phrases and grammar.
- Generate interest in – and ideas about – the content of a reading or listening text.
- Share opinions/responses to texts.
- Simply practise speaking, and develop fluency.

To achieve these different aims, tasks vary a lot in terms of how much they allow the students to bring their own messages to the task and to use whatever language they want.

As lexical teachers, we feel *all* speaking has the additional purpose of providing teachers with feedback on what the students know/don't know, and gives us the opportunity to teach something new. So the more controlled a task is, the narrower the range of feedback we receive from the students.

We also believe speaking tasks should relate to the reasons the students learn English, as discussed in Part A: dealing with everyday life, exchanging ideas and feelings and understanding others' cultures.

It is good to look at all the speaking tasks, not just in one lesson but in a whole unit, and to understand their purpose, their content and how controlled they are. This can help you make decisions about how to model tasks, how to exploit feedback and whether to change anything. You may ask questions like these:

- Can I teach some language that will be useful later?
- If I teach some language now, will there be later opportunities to recycle and expand on it?
- Are there enough less-controlled tasks? How could I change a task, or where could I add freer tasks?
- Are there enough tasks that ask about the students themselves? If not, how could I change this?
- Where tasks are freer, what would *I* say here? What language might my students want to use?

Practising the principle

- Look at the speaking tasks from a unit on work aimed at Pre-intermediate/A2 students. For each task, decide:
    - what you think the purpose of the task is.
    - how controlled the tasks are – and what kind of feedback you might get from the students.
    - how far the tasks relate to the reasons for studying outlined in *Principle*.
- What is your overall opinion of the balance of the tasks? Would you want to change anything?

1. The students discuss what they think is the worst thing about a job they read about.
2. Students say sentences about a job using phrases just taught (*I work* in a hospital, *I have to* get up early, etc). Their partner tries to guess the job.
3. Using prompts to help them, the students ask *Do you have to ...?* questions about their lives. They then decide who has the easiest life.
4. The students listen to a recording, and discuss if the speakers used their time well or badly – and how good the students themselves are at managing their time.
5. In pairs, the students read different information about a job. They then ask each other present simple/continuous questions, based on prompts.
6. The students discuss some questions, such as *Have you ever had an interview?*, based on *have* collocations (*have ... an argument / a party / a qualification / lunch break*, etc).
7. At the start of the lesson, the students discuss three questions about when they work and study.
8. In pairs, the students read four scenarios where they need to apologise, give reasons or promises. They then act out the scenarios.

Applying the principle

- Look at the next unit in your coursebook.
- Find all the speaking activities, and do the same as in *Practising the principle*.
- Discuss your ideas with a colleague if you can.

Preparation

Ensuring the students speak

Principle

As we have seen, there are a number of reasons for students to speak in class – the primary one being to provide opportunities for new teaching and learning.

Sometimes, a traditional 'grammar + words + skills' approach fails to provide enough opportunities for interaction, as speaking is seen as separate to the teaching and the learning of language and is often just the final task in a lesson. In more traditional classrooms, teachers may lecture, and only allow speaking to take place through them – and often only via 'display' questions* that check the students have been listening.

A lexically taught lesson would aim for more frequent speaking opportunities, both between the students and in interactions with the teacher. Also, there would ideally be more chances for students to add their own ideas.

Providing more opportunities is one thing, but students still need to be able to take advantage of them. Some students from very traditional learning backgrounds may not see the point of a speaking task – especially when done in pairs or groups. They may want to move on to 'learning' tasks as quickly as possible. It is also possible that the occasional student may simply refuse to speak for personal reasons. However, far more often, the failure lies in the material and/or the preparation for speaking. For example:

- There are too few questions and/or:
  - they are all *yes/no* questions.
  - they are too obvious (eg *'Say what's in the picture'*).
  - The students don't have sufficient life or cultural knowledge to be able to answer the questions.
- The task is too open, and the students are unclear what they are supposed to say.
- The task requires too much language the students don't know, so they give up.
- The task requires too much imagination and/or knowledge to be done spontaneously.
- The students don't see the point of the task, because it doesn't relate to their lives and/or the language they are learning.

Practising the principle

- Look at the ways below that teachers may ensure speaking activities 'work' and that the students use the opportunity to produce language. Decide:
  - which you do regularly.
  - how they tackle the problems mentioned in *Principle*.
  - if you have any other ideas.

- The teacher models the task by giving their own answers to some or all of the questions.
- The teacher writes extra questions on the board.
- The teacher gets the students to do the roleplay in L1 first, and then helps with some translations before they do it again in English.
- The teacher explains the purpose of the task.
- Before starting the task, the students write notes and look up words they want to use in a dictionary.
- The teacher corrects some language or teaches something new, based on the students' speaking.
- The teacher does a quick tour of the class, to check the students are doing the task.
- Depending on the demands of the task, the teacher encourages the students to also talk about people they know – and not just about themselves.
- The teacher asks questions as they go through the answers to a vocabulary exercise. The questions generate related language (see pages 44–49).
- The students repeat the task with a new partner.

Applying the principle

- Over two or three lessons with the same group, record the learners and/or keep track of:
  - how many times they get the chance to speak with each other (in pairs or groups).
  - how long they speak before you stop them, before the first group stops, or before they go off-task.
  - what language is produced.
  - how open the interaction was, between you and the whole class.
- Decide if you would change anything next time. Would you use a different technique from *Practising the principle*?

Scaffolding speaking tasks 1

Predicting language

Principle

We saw on page 73 that speaking tasks can fail for various reasons. Failure is usually to do with:

- what the students are asked to do/discuss.
- the clarity of the instructions, in terms of what the teacher expects.
- the language the students need, to do the task.

We suggested that we could help prevent failure by, among other things:

- changing aspects of the task.
- modelling the task.
- allowing the students to plan what they want to say.
- doing the task in L1 first, and then offering help with translation.

Finally, we suggested that it's good to use speaking tasks to notice what students don't know, and to then teach them something new so they can improve.

In order to do these things effectively, the starting point should be thinking about exactly what you'd say when doing the task – and what you can imagine others (including your students) might want to say.

It is easy to assume that a task will produce lots of language, or that the language will be what students know or have just been taught, but then when you actually do the task yourself, you may find that you can't think of much to say, and thus realise you'll need to change it in some way.

Alternatively, you might find that potentially there's a lot to say, but the students will probably be unable to express very much in an accurate way. You might then be able to:

- elicit or highlight some useful new language, as you go through the answers of a language exercise or comprehension task.
- highlight some language, as part of a model.
- be ready to help the students when they prepare.
- be more attuned to what the students try and say, and the mistakes they make.

Practising the principle

- Look at the tasks below. Think what might be said about each. Remember: we want at least phrases, not just single words and a list of structures.
- Try one or two of these methods:
  - Write a list of sentences/phrases.
  - Write a dialogue of 'students' doing the task.
  - Do the task with a colleague.
  - Record yourself/colleagues doing the task.
- If you don't have much to say, how could you change the task? Check what you would say then.

Discuss these questions:

1 Where did you *grow up*?
2 How do you *get on* with the rest of your family?
3 Has anyone ever *fallen out* in your family? Why?
4 How often do you *eat out*? Where do you go?
5 What are you *looking forward to* doing at the moment? Why?

In pairs, tell stories about bad journeys you've had.

Explain what jobs are needed to get the tea from the fields to your home, where it can be drunk

Applying the principle

- Find two tasks you plan to do that should generate a good amount of speaking.
- Think of language that might be used to do the tasks. Use a method from *Practising the principle*.
- Notice any language that might be useful, but:
  - hasn't been taught in the lesson.
  - the students probably won't know.
- Introduce some of this language during the lesson, through one or more of the methods in *Principle* (see also page 73).

Scaffolding speaking tasks 2

Modelling tasks

Principle

We have suggested that one way we can support students with speaking tasks is by modelling. It is easiest to model a task that involves answering questions, commenting on statements, telling a story or producing some other longer stretch of speech, but you may also be able to model a conversation with one of the stronger students in your class.

Modelling a task can help in a number of ways:

- It shows the students how you expect them to answer – for example, that you want them to go beyond simple *yes/no* responses.
- It can reinforce the purpose of the task – for example, by emphasising the fact that you are using language that has just been taught.
- It can allow you to feed in some new language or remind the students of useful language, by:
  - writing key phrases on the board.
  - saying key phrases with additional emphasis (slower and/or slightly louder).
- It gives the students some time to start thinking about their own responses.
- It shows you are willing to share ideas and personal experiences, which may make the students feel more comfortable about doing the same.

You might support your students further by asking one or two of them for their ideas in front of the whole class, and then helping them with any new language they need. You can write some of this up on the board, too.

See also 'Teaching low-level classes' in Part C on page 137.

Practising the principle

What follows is based on a task called 'Scars' in *Vocabulary* (Morgan and Rinvolucri, 1986). The task is best done with students, but could also be done with colleagues. It helps develop the skills of modelling, as well as responding to students (see page 78):

- Think of a story about a scar you have, or an accident you once had.
- Write down the story, and underline words/phrases that you think would be useful for others telling similar stories.
- Tell the story in class. As you do, emphasise the key language orally and/or write the language on the board (or on a piece of paper, if working with colleagues).
- Get one or two students to tell their own stories, and write on the board useful words they say – or language they could have used, but didn't. If you're working with colleagues, write this language on your piece of paper.
- If you're doing this as a class activity, put the students in pairs and ask them to tell their own stories.

Applying the principle

- Find the next two speaking tasks that you plan to do in class.
- Write down or record the models you will give. If the task is a series of questions, choose two or three.
- Think about the language you will highlight, and how.
- In class, model the task and, if appropriate, ask one or two students for their ideas, as in 'Scars' above.

Feedback on speaking 1

Cheating!

Principle

A central purpose of speaking activities (apart from practising speaking for speaking's sake) is the opportunity it affords teachers to teach new language or new aspects of language that the students half know.

Ideally, this teaching will come in response to specific things that your students try to say. However, the reality is that when students are talking in class, it can be hard to hear much of what is being said. Even when you are able to hear things that the students are saying, as we suggested in Part A (page 15), noticing gaps in their knowledge and turning this into new input can be very difficult. Sometimes, correcting on the spot is tricky even when listening to just one student, and being able to note gaps in student output and then write the language on the board in a way that will potentially involve the whole class is a further difficulty.

For these reasons, you might want to cheat! Rather than using your students' output, you can use some of the language you predicted the students *might* use (see page 74) as the basis for the feedback you give.

We would suggest that this is justifiable – and better than giving no feedback at all on speaking tasks – for the following reasons:

- It allows you to revisit and check aspects of grammar and lexis more frequently (see page 31).
- It allows you to focus on new aspects of words you have taught before.
- It may allow you to reflect on more complex language.
- It can still provide some 'negative evidence', which some say helps the learners acquire correct usage.
- The language chosen may have actually been an issue for some students, and thus is a response!
- It reinforces the value of doing speaking tasks and so, over time, perhaps encourages participation.
- It allows you to practise writing on the board and involving the students in feedback.
- It may help you relax and be more able to hear the students, if you know you already have something to give as feedback.

Practising the principle

- Look again at the task below (aimed at Intermediate/B1 students) and at a possible list of things people may want to say. Decide:
  - which sentences would be best for these students.
  - which aspects you would focus on, and how (think about frequency and wider use).
  - any other language you would prefer to use.

Explain what jobs are needed to get the tea in the fields to your home, where it can be drunk.

It could be almost any job.

Everybody connects to someone else in some way.

If you didn't have doctors to keep everyone healthy, there'd be no-one to work.

What about people who are directly involved?

Obviously, you need people to pick the tea.

What do you call the thing that you put the tea in?

Isn't it all done automatically?

Don't they have machines to do that?

You need factory workers to process the tea.

Who does that? Is it a tea company like Lipton's, or do you think there is another stage/a middle man?

You'd need someone to design the packaging.

You need a marketing manager to promote the product and sales people to sell it.

You'd need truck drivers and people to transport it.

Applying the principle

- Before your next lesson, write down some language that you plan to introduce as feedback on the speaking tasks.
- In class, write some of this language on the board, for feedback. Spread this out by writing one or two items:
  - immediately after checking the students are on task.
  - between listening to the students.
  - just before you start feedback.
  - after finishing feedback on the language you had written up so far.
- You can introduce this language by saying '*I heard someone trying to say …*'.

Feedback on speaking 2

Engaging the students

Principle

While we may sometimes partially 'cheat' by preparing language that we are going to look at during feedback on a speaking task, if we want that language to be taken in we still want to check that the students:

- have understood the meaning.
- have noticed aspects of form and structure.
- try and relate it to their existing knowledge.

We might initially do this by:

- gapping words in sentences we write up.
- writing incorrect sentences for the students to correct.

With these techniques, you can focus on different aspects of language:

- You can focus on grammar:
  He must __________ had something to do with it.
  I haven't seen him _________ ages.
  X The economy booms. You see cranes everywhere.

In these cases, you can simply ask your students to say the missing word or correct the mistake– and give them the answers if they can't. You may also explain words that some students may not know (eg *crane*).

- You can focus on aspects of vocabulary:
  The economy is really b__________. You see cranes everywhere.
  You see a lot of people smoking marijuana, but the police turn a _____ _____ to it.
  X We're going to make a party on Sunday.

With vocabulary, if you think the word/phrase may be new, you will need to prompt the students by giving the translation or some other kind of explanation. For example: *'The economy is doing very well, it's …'* or *'The police ignore it, they turn a …'*. (See pages 37 and 38.)

Practising the principle

- Look at the sentences below that were prepared as feedback on speaking done by Intermediate students who roleplay conversations sharing good and bad news.
- Decide how you will present them on the board – turn at least one into an error to correct.
- Think of the explanations (if any) you would use as a prompt, to elicit words and corrections.

Are you OK? You look a bit upset.
My brother has got to have an operation.
I'm pregnant.
Congratulations! When's it due?
Did I tell you I'm going to Mexico in the summer?
Did I tell you X and Y are splitting up?
Did I tell you I've got an interview for that job I applied for?
My girlfriend's dumped me.
I failed my exams.
I've got a scholarship to study at X.
Wow! That's great!

Applying the principle

- Before your lesson, write down some language you plan to introduce as feedback to the speaking tasks you'll set.
- Decide what aspect of the language you want to focus on:
  - and how you will gap it, or what mistake to include.
  - what explanation (if any) you will give.
- In class, write some of this language on the board.(Make sure to add an X to indicate mistakes.)
- Introduce this language by saying: *'I heard someone trying to say …'*, and explain the part of the task it relates to.
- Elicit corrections and language as you see fit:
  - by asking the class and letting students shout out ideas.
  - by nominating specific students.

  (Make sure you give the students enough time to answer before you decide to provide the answers/explanations.)

Feedback on speaking 3

Correcting students' mistakes

Principle

Anticipating things the students may want to say, and mistakes they might make during a task, can help you to extend their knowledge of words, to revisit and to encourage noticing of grammar, and to maybe present new forms and meanings. However, as we discussed in Part A, there is evidence that some of the most effective teaching and learning takes place *during* communication – and in particular when communication becomes difficult or breaks down altogether (see page 13).

Firstly, this principle may mean that you ought to reconsider the kinds of errors you focus on. Primarily, try to notice when communication becomes difficult. You can see this happening when a student:

- reaches for a dictionary.
- asks you/a classmate *How do you say ...?*.
- makes use of L1 to do the task (not for chit-chat).
- hesitates, and says something in a different way.
- looks confused, or asks *What do you mean?*
- says something you don't understand, or you think a non-EFL teacher wouldn't understand.

You may also notice other aspects of student language that are 'incorrect' – particularly in terms of what you have taught – but if it doesn't cause problems, then the above should take priority. This should be the case, even if the grammar required has not been taught yet.

Secondly, this principle implies a different response to error than in a 'skills-based' fluency task. Rather than letting the students get on with it and perhaps only listening 'from the outside' to note errors, you should listen *to intervene* when communication becomes difficult, because that's the best moment to teach the language to help your students say what they want.

You can still make a note of errors to write on the board and then deal with them, as you would do with prepared sentences (see page 76). You might also refer to the student who asked for the language or who made the errors – *they* may even explain the correction or give the missing language to the other students.

Practising the principle

- Look at these things students said in different speaking tasks. Decide:
  - which you would intervene in when listening.
  - what you would change the language to.
  - what you would write on the board.
  - how you would engage the students.

Sorry. Underground problem. Horrible. Horrible.

A: *How long is it taking you to get here?*
B: *About 25 minutes. I come by bike.*
A: *Oh, I think you are very healthy.*

A: *Does 'montar'... is making IKEA furniture DIY?*
B: *Yeah, I think so.*
A: *I make the IKEA furniture. It's awful, because the instructions – sometimes they're really difficult follow.*
B: *Yes ... I bought a bike – those fixed bikes for exercise and I couldn't ... How do you say 'montar'?*

A: *Have you been to America?*
B: *No, I haven't. ... er ... Have you been to America?*
A: *Yes I have. I ... it was good. Have you been ... have you been to ... somewhere not Europe?*

I did some volunteer work – I was younger – a long time ago. It was with prisoners and they were going to ... um ... quit prison. They were going to become ... There was a forest and they were sent there to help deal with the forest fires. So they needed to be very fit and we were there to make them to be fitter.

Applying the principle

- For the next lesson you plan to teach, look at how many freer speaking tasks there are.
- In class, as you listen to the students talk, notice any signs of difficulty.
- Engage with one or two students, and correct them at the moment they have difficulty.
- Include this language in your post-task feedback.
- In the different speaking tasks in your lesson, try to engage with *different* students.

Beyond correction

Putting emergent language to use

Principle

If you intervene in a student's communication and provide the language they need, you are addressing several of the steps involved in learning mentioned in Part A. It can be assumed that the learner you help:

- understands the meaning of the language,because they generated that meaning.
- hears or sees 'correct' language when you give it.
- will probably use it as they continue speaking. (If, of course, they don't just say *'Yeah – that!'*.)
- will pronounce it accurately enough if they do use it.

However, when we highlight that language for *other* students during feedback, only the first two steps may take place, and none of the students will have:

- repeated these steps over time by encountering/using the item again in other contexts.

If we think about this 'emergent' language in the same way as the prepared language we teach through materials, we should want to do the same things that we do with vocabulary and grammar exercises. We have already suggested using gap-fills and error correction with sentences on the board, but you could also:

- give additional examples.
- draw attention to chunks or patterns.
- ask questions about vocabulary/grammar (see pages 44 and 62).
- elicit additional comments or responses (page 57).

You also want the students to (re)-use the language. If you know it will re-appear in a text or language exercise in your book, you might leave it till then. Otherwise, you could:

- get the students to repeat the task they just did with a new partner or in a shorter time.
- set a new task.

Expanding on the language and inventing a task may be too difficult to do on the spot. However, you can plan to do it at the start of your *next* lesson. If a similar language point comes up with a different set of students after this, you may also be prepared to deal with it on the spot then.

Practising the principle

- Look at the language below that was corrected during feedback on the language in the previous task (page 78). Decide:
  - what questions you might ask about vocabulary here.
  - if there are any patterns you would highlight with additional examples.
  - if there are any responses/additional comments you could elicit.
- Think of ways that the students could practise some of this language (see pages 52 and 67).

Sorry I'm late. There was a problem on the underground...

... The train was stuck in the tunnel for 30 minutes. It was really crowded and I could hardly breathe. I thought I was going to die. (This came from further discussion with a student – and reformulation.)

A: *I usually cycle to work.*
B: ~~*I think you are*~~ *You must be very fit.*

(montar)
put together IKEA furniture

I did volunteer work once.
quit prison be released from prison
They were going to become fire fighters.
They were going to be sent to fight forest fires.

Have you been to America?
➧ *No. I've never really wanted to.*
Have you been anywhere outside America?

Applying the principle

- In your next lesson, record all the language that you put on the board during feedback. Take a photo of your boardwork if you can.
- Prepare the sentences that you wrote on the board as a handout or on an IWB. You might want to gap different parts.
- Prepare ways in which you will expand on the language and practise it – as outlined in *Practising the principle*.

Chat

Further opportunities to develop speaking

Principle

As lexical teachers, we would argue that *all* speaking is an opportunity to get feedback from students and to teach something new. We would argue that this includes speaking that goes on in and around a class, but which is not explicitly 'a speaking task'. For instance:

- Chatting as the lesson starts or ends – and in breaks.
- Students asking you questions or asking permission to do things.
- Jokes, banter and side-tracks in Ll.

However, teachers can sometimes be reluctant to correct errors or engage with language during such speaking, as it is often a one-to-one exchange and:

- they feel they may be ignoring other students.
- they feel it is a distraction from their lesson aims.
- they feel it might be rude or discouraging to turn a personal comment into a learning opportunity.

On this last point, teachers might have been put off by stories of crude exchanges like this:

Ss: *Sorry I didn't come to class last week. My mum breaked her leg and I must help her.*
T: *Breaked? It's broke. My mum broke her leg.*

Obviously, the best thing is to respond as you would to a friend outside of class:
Oh no! Is she OK? and/or *How did she do that?*

Of course, most chat isn't sensitive in this way, but, even here, the student would normally just answer and, at this point, the teacher may need to supply language to help. In our experience, when you do this, *the students themselves* often ask for items to be written on the board. You can do this and still continue to chat. So, to exploit these moments, you need to:

- be prepared to see them as teaching opportunities.
- respond first as an interested person.
- continue the conversation beyond basic responses.
- reformulate/help the students when communication breaks down, rather than 'correct' the grammar.
- write new language on the board (if appropriate).
- perhaps get *all* the students to practise similar conversations (depending on the language and scenario).

Practising the principle

- Look below at the common ways we may start a chat in class:
  - Decide which you've had or taught in your classes.
  - Did you teach any language during them?
  - Did you get any other students to practise it?
- For any situation you haven't taught language for:
  - Think of two or three ways the conversations might develop over four turns (A-B-A-B).
  - Decide what language could come up.

Chat starters

- *What did you do last weekend?*
- *Are you going away in the holiday?*
- *Sorry I'm late.*
- *Oh dear. What have you done to your leg?*
- *Are you OK? You look tired.*
- *I can't come to the class next week.*
- *Teacher, can you open the window?*
- *Did you see the game last night?*
- *I'm afraid* (teacher's name) *isn't here today.*
- *You've had your hair cut!*
- *You're back! I was starting to wonder what had happened to you!*

Applying the principle

- Next time you chat with a student, see if you can teach something!
- Either within the same lesson, or in a follow-up class:
  - expand on the language point.
  - get all the students to practise.

From speaking to materials

Backward design

Principle

Most of the tasks in this chapter relate to the different kinds of speaking tasks that you'll find in coursebooks – and how to deal with them.

However, there are serious questions about the degree to which speaking tasks in coursebooks reflect real life and, as a consequence, whether the things the students end up saying will be of use to them outside of class. For example, the classic task of describing a picture for someone else to draw could produce this:

A: *There's a man in a chair. He's wearing a red jumper.*
B: *What's he wearing … on his legs?*
A: *Jeans – and he has brown shoes and green socks. He's reading a paper. Opposite the man, there's a woman sitting in an armchair,* etc.

It's hard to imagine this conversation happening outside class. It's even hard to imagine some of the individual sentences being said in other contexts.

So one thing you might consider is setting tasks and conversations that reflect the kinds of conversations your students might have:

- Think about common conversations you have.
- Ask the students for ideas.
- Look in books such as *Teaching Unplugged* (Thornbury and Meddings, 2009).

In the first instance, you might set up a scenario and see what students come up with, perhaps allowing them to have the conversation in L1 first (see page 73). You will probably also want to brainstorm some language that you might say and feed this in during and after the task (see pages 76–78). You can then re-do the task.

You can later turn this language into formal exercises that you can use to present language in future classes. You may use these exercises in ways we discussed in Chapters 1 and 2, and then end with the original conversation.

Another interesting take on conversation and materials is George Woolard's *Messaging* (2013). He suggests providing translated dialogues – which the students then think about how to vary, with their teacher's help.

Practising the principle

Look at the six speaking scenarios below. Choose one, and work backwards:

- Write the language you'd use in it (see page 73).
- Write a vocabulary exercise. Bear in mind ways the vocabulary could vary within each conversation.
- Think of a speaking task to focus on the vocab.
- See if there is any grammar or structure worth teaching?
- Write a task in keeping with the final conversation.
- Add a messaging type of task (see page 66).
- See if there are any other opportunities for speaking?

Scenarios

- You and one other person are waiting for a lift. Have a conversation till you arrive at where you want to get to.
- Take a taxi ride from the airport to your home/hotel. Have the conversation from start to finish.
- Someone knocks over a drink in your home/a café/the classroom. Have the conversation.
- You are reading a lifestyle magazine/a newspaper/a book. Have a conversation around it.
- You have a problem with your landlord. Try to resolve it.
- You're going to have a staff meeting at a student's place of work. They should allocate a role and explain what each person does. Write the agenda. Have the meeting.

Applying the principle

- Use your material in a lesson.
- Get some feedback from the students about the task – and any other material you used.
- Change aspects of the task/material that didn't work, or add more language and exercises based on feedback.
- Try it out on another class and see if it works better.
- Revise it again – or write material for a different task!

Chapter Four

Teaching reading lexically

Reading lessons

Stages and procedures

Principle

In many 'traditional' classrooms, reading lessons involved students taking turns to read a text aloud, the teacher then asking a few comprehension questions or explaining unknown words, and finally some grammar exercises or translation.

With communicative language teaching, the focus shifted to skills. Tasks now reflected the different ways we read real texts (eg skimming and scanning) and how schema theory explained comprehension (eg prediction tasks).

As we saw in Part A, the 'top-down'* approach of schema theory has been largely discredited as the primary way that readers process texts. Most recent research reasserts 'bottom-up' processing* – essentially moving from letters to words to chunks – and the importance of automaticity* in how readers:

- hear language in their head.
- recall meaning.
- retain this language and meaning in the memory.

William Grabe's *Reading in a Second Language: Moving from Theory to Practice* (2008) gives a very thorough review of current thinking. As well as emphasising language knowledge, Grabe also stresses the value of:

- extensive reading beyond the class.
- repeated readings of texts (he suggests up to ten!).
- encouraging faster reading.
- developing motivation for reading.

Teaching reading lexically does not necessarily mean changing the stages or tasks in coursebooks that are based on 'skills' teaching. Rather, as lexical teachers, we also want to ensure these stages and tasks help:

- us to pre-teach words and phrases.
- us to get feedback from students about what they know/don't know, thus enabling further teaching.
- our students to notice other aspects of words they already know the meaning of (increase 'primings').
- our students to recognise chunks more automatically.
- us to teach language to talk about texts.
- our students to be motivated to read and reread.

Practising the principle

- Look at the tasks below, and use the criteria presented in *Principle* to decide:
  - how each one might help develop reading.
  - what a teacher could do, beyond simply getting the students to do the task.
  - how many tasks you might do in a reading lesson.
- Think of other tasks that fit the criteria in *Principle*.

1. Set a vocabulary exercise to begin a reading lesson.
2. Get the students to discuss the general topic of the text before they read.
3. Predict the content of the text, based on a photo.
4. Give a glossary of some words in the text.
5. Get the students to read the text a second time and answer *true/false* questions.
6. Ask the students to match some words in the text to their meanings.
7. Get the students to share their opinions about the text and/or discuss how it relates to their experience.
8. Get the students to find words in the text to complete some sentences.
9. Ask the students if they have any other questions about the text, after tasks about a reading.
10. Ask the students to find out more about the issues raised in the text for homework, and to report back.

Applying the principle

- When you next do a reading lesson, record yourself and the language that you teach.
- After the lesson, consider:
  - how many of the activities (or similar ones) in *Practising the Principle* you did.
  - what language you highlighted and how.
  - how much of that language was in the text.
  - how many times the students looked at the text – or at parts of the text.
  - if you would change anything about the lesson.

Preparing for a reading lesson

What language is there?

Principle

We have suggested that, for lexical teachers, reading lessons should be primarily language-focused. The starting point for planning should, therefore, be to read the text and notice the language it contains.

Analysing the text on page 97 using a 'grammar + words' focus might result in us saying the text contains:

- many examples of the present perfect.
- contrasts between different present tenses.
- new words: *elite*, *notorious*, *undergo*, *wounds*, etc.
- a lexical set around economics and politics.

A lexical view of language would lead to the analysis you see on page 97. You can start from single words that your students may not yet fully know (shown in **bold**), but then look beyond the single words to the whole chunks that include these words and that have been **highlighted**. Finally, notice how words that should be familiar to students at this level combine (highlighted only – no bold items).

We would suggest this highlighting of chunks offers a better analysis for a reading lesson because:

- it reflects the way fluent readers process texts.
- it will enable you to highlight some of these chunks at different stages in the lesson.
- it may highlight grammar and syntax common in reading texts, but not often taught.
- it often highlights frequent words that do not fall into lexical sets, and are thus not often taught.

Word frequency in corpora like the British National Corpus is generally more biased towards written language. It is reasonable to assume that the more frequent a word is in such corpora, the more likely it is that it will help students with their future reading.

While coursebook materials may fail to focus fully on this language, we do *not* suggest teaching *all* of it. How much time we focus on individual items depends on:

- which words your students 'know', what they know about them, and how many there are.
- the frequency of words (see page 36).
- how far chunks can be varied (page 64).
- if your students need them for speaking and writing.

Practising the principle

- Look at the text on page 98. It is aimed at Intermediate/B1-B2 level. Divide it into chunks, as demonstrated in *Principle*:
  - Circle what you think might be new or only partially-known words.
  - Highlight the whole chunks they are part of.
  - Next, look between these chunks and highlight phrases containing words you think students at this level will know well.
  - If you have a very long single chunk, think about how it could be split into two pieces.
- Check how frequent the keywords you circled are.
- Look at the 'known' chunks:
  - Are you sure the students will know these combinations?
  - If not, are they frequent?
  - Can any of the chunks be varied easily?
  - Would they help your students get better at speaking/writing?
- Choose the ten words/chunks you would spend most time on:
  - At what stages of the lesson do you think you could draw attention to these different chunks, and how?
- Compare your analysis with a colleague, if possible.

Applying the principle

- Look at the next two or three reading texts you plan to use in class.
- Chunk the texts in the way you have practiced:
  - If there is a high proportion of unknown words, you may want to consider replacing the text or doing more intensive language work.
  - If there are exercises that go with the text, consider how many of your chunks are focused on in them.
- Decide what chunks you might spend extra time on (if any).

Before the text 1

Vocabulary exercises and feedback

Principle

One of the impacts of a focus on skills can be a reluctance to pre-teach language in the text. The argument goes that we are preparing students to be able to deal with texts outside of the class, where they will not have someone to pick out words they do not know before they read, and, therefore, the students supposedly need to learn how to:

- get the gist by predicting – based on what they know about the text (where it is found, titles, photos, etc).
- get the gist by making use of words they *do* know.
- ignore or guess the meaning of unknown words.

This goes counter to the view that improving reading depends on 'the massive over-learning of words and much recognition practice in transferable and interesting contexts' (Alderson, 2000). Some of this practice can come *before* the texts we read in class.

In the case of coursebook materials, you may find grammar or vocabulary exercises earlier in the lesson – or earlier in the unit – that include language that reappears in the text. This is a good thing.

If we have analysed texts well, we can ask questions as we go through the answers to these exercises that enable us to show *more* language that we know will appear in the text later. In other words, we can provide extra recognition practice. For example, imagine these items came up in pre-text exercises:
The economy <u>has grown</u> by 5% over the last year.
undergo changes / a transformation

For the text on Rwanda on page 97, we might ask questions and guide the students to the language in brackets:

What's a noun phrase for 'the economy has grown'? (economic growth)
How might you get economic growth? (encourage/attract/bring in foreign investment, boost tourism)

How can you describe changes a country undergoes? (social/political/significant/remarkable)
Why might a country need to undergo a transformation? (There's a lot of corruption, it's politically unstable, it's been hit by floods, there are inter-ethnic tensions, etc).

Practising the principle

- Look at this language exercise that comes before the text on pets on page 98.

Say if the animals in the box are normally:
a) pets b) farm animals c) wildlife

dog	donkey	snake	goat
eagle	hamster	rabbit	mouse
bear	horse	fox	cattle

Which animal(s) are being talked about?

1 Can you take it for a walk?
2 We went for a ride.
3 It killed some of our chickens.
4 I keep them in a cage in my room.
5 You can see them flying in the sky near here.
6 It's not poisonous.

- Identify any language from this exercise that already appears in the text.
- Notice any connected language in the text:
  - What questions could you ask to generate some of this associated language when checking answers?
- Try out your questions with a colleague. See how easily you can reformulate or guide their responses to language you want.

Applying the principle

- Look at the next reading text you plan to use in class and analyse the language, as on page 97.
- Look at language exercises that come before the text in the unit. Notice the language in the exercise(s) that will be in the text, and think of questions to ask, as above.
- Ask the questions in class. Remember that when you guide students you may need to help by:
  - giving the first letter of the word you want.
  - reformulating (*'Yes – we also/usually say …'*)
- If you are using your own text, decide the language in it that could be pre-taught in a vocabulary exercise.

Before the text 2

Speaking tasks and feedback

Principle

Most reading texts in published materials will have a speaking before the text. This is a product of the view that we rarely read a text without motivation or some prior knowledge. The speaking, therefore, is to:

- generate interest.
- activate schemata.

The task will typically involve such things as:

- generalised questions around the 'topic' of the text.
- getting the students to say what they know about a topic.
- a prediction task (see page 87).

We feel that these kinds of tasks can motivate students to read. However, remember that they are also speaking tasks in their own right, providing opportunities to teach new aspects of language (see page 76).

To some degree, as with other speaking tasks, you will want to respond to what the students say, and that can vary wildly. However, as the focus is on developing reading, we would suggest you should aim to introduce at least some of the 'new' language that the students will see in the text. As with other speaking tasks, you can do this by:

- preparing sentences beforehand (see page 76).
- reformulating what the students say (page 78).

Below are examples of pre-reading tasks and some things from the text that we might be able to highlight:

- Do you know any economies that are doing well? Why?
  the economy is booming, good leadership, etc
- Why might people go to these places on holiday and why might some not want to? Which would you visit?

the Greek islands	Egypt	Rwanda
Iceland	Nepal	Peru

  gorillas / protected / unstable / reputation for ... / notorious (+ lexis describing the history of Rwanda)
- In groups, list everything you know about Rwanda.
  tiny state / east Africa / a wave of killings / Tutsi / ethnic minority / have a growing reputation, etc

Practising the principle

- Analyse the language in Text 2 on page 98, if you have not done so already (see also page 85).
- Do the pre-reading speaking task below in your head or with a colleague, and:
  - write a list of things the students may want to say.
  - note opportunities to teach language in the text.

How far do you agree with the statements below?

1 Owning a pet is like being a parent.

2 Pets take a lot more than they give in return.

3 The only easy relationship is man and dog.

- Think of two more pre-reading speaking tasks that you could do to generate language found in the text.
- Make sure you do the task (ideally with a colleague) to check it produces a good range of language.

Applying the principle

- Take a text you plan to teach, and analyse the language in it.
- If it is part of published material:
  - Check what language has been taught earlier in the lesson and the unit.
  - Look at the pre-reading speaking task and see what language from the text could be generated.
  - Replace it with a new task if you want.
- If it is your own text or from an 'authentic' source:
  - Think of a pre-reading task, and check what language it produces.
- In class, introduce some of the language in the text during feedback to the speaking (see pages 76–78 in the 'Teaching speaking lexically' chapter).

Before the text 3

Prediction and using language from the text

Principle

Asking students to predict from photos and so on what they will read has been criticised using evidence from exams, where discussing pre-reading prediction tasks had no positive effects on reading comprehension (see Alderson, 2000). Given this, you might wonder what the value of doing prediction tasks is.

As with the tasks on page 86, we feel they provide a strong motivation to read in class, and can have a positive effect on readers and class dynamics. However, more importantly from a lexical teacher's point of view, they offer a more focused way to pre-teach language and to help the students develop the automaticity of recognising words/chunks that helps reading.

As well as predicting based on photos and headlines, tasks often give single words from the text that the students then use to guess the story or how they may be connected to the photo, etc. For example, for Text 1 – on Rwanda:

killings	*booming*	*leadership*	*gorillas*
minority	*tourism*	*equality*	*start-ups*

As lexical teachers, we could also ask questions about the words, as we do in vocabulary exercises. In addition, we may get the students to generate other language they expect to see, which we can then reformulate.

If we are choosing the words ourselves, we might start off with collocations rather than single words, to help the students process texts in chunks:

wave of killings	*economy is booming*
ethnic minority	*tourism brings in cash*

You might even use whole sentences (perhaps edited):
Most people will probably associate Rwanda with the terrible wave of killings that swept the country.
A significant factor in development has been leadership.

In all cases, feedback should focus on understanding of the vocabulary rather than correct predictions. You may also get the students to re-use the words you selected when re-telling the text at a later point (see page 91).

Practising the principle

- Find a colleague or colleagues to do this task with.
- You should each find a text. It does not need to be graded or from an ELT source. Analyse the language. Alternatively, use Text 2 on page 96. Compare the words you chose.
- Choose the words or collocations that you would use for a prediction task.
- Give your colleague/s your list of words, and get them to make predictions. You may give additional photos, headlines, a general introduction about the text – or nothing!
- Ask two or three supplementary language-generating questions about your list of words.
- As your colleague/s make predictions, write some down – especially those containing language which is in the text or which can be reformulated to match what is in the text.
- Swap roles. Then read each other's texts.
- Discuss how easy/difficult the prediction task was to do, and help each other with suggestions.

Applying the principle

- Look at the coursebook you use – or one you have used. See how it gets the students to predict content. Find out:
  - how many tasks explicitly pre-teach language.
  - how many are based on single words, and how many on larger chunks.
- When you next use a text in class, set a prediction task based on language in the text. Remember:
  - Give yourself sufficient space on the board to write student language/your reformulations.
  - The focus is not the correctness of the predictions – accept all ideas that use language well.
- Your first reading task should then be telling the students to read and see if they were right / if their language was used.

Reading aloud

The pros and cons

Principle

Reading aloud in class has been strongly criticised, and it has been almost totally abandoned in many ELT settings. There are some good reasons for this, principally that:

- most reading is silent.
- reading aloud may discourage reading fluency because it is often a slower, word-by-word process.
- some students find it embarrassing.
- many students find it boring and/or may switch off when they are not reading themselves.

However, hearing students read aloud does shed light on such student internal processes as:

- pronunciation difficulties they may have.
- omissions or replacements of words.
- a lack of chunking or mis-chunking of the text.

Catherine Walter (2008) has argued that issues with pronunciation are still important, even when reading silently. Poor pronunciation can hinder a student's ability to retain short amounts of text in the short-term memory. This leads to the student having to reread sections or making mistakes when decoding* the text.

Walter suggests that spending time on 'increasing exposure to the spoken language, and improving receptive and productive phonology' might be better than trying to improve reading skills that students already possess in their own language, but cannot fully employ because of problems with phonology.

So there is clearly a place for reading aloud, if the students are also getting plenty of practice in reading silently at speed. Furthermore, we would suggest any reading aloud:

- needs a pronunciation focus.
- does not have to focus on the whole text.
- does not have to involve the whole class.
- does not have to only happen in 'reading' lessons.

A number of activities in the chapter on 'Teaching listening lexically' will also make use of reading aloud.

Practising the principle

- Look at the reading aloud activities below. Consider the following:
  - How many do you do already?
  - How might they prevent some of the problems associated with reading aloud in *Principle*?
- Can you think of any other reading aloud tasks?

1. Only do reading aloud for the first paragraph of a text. Use the paragraph for a prediction task (see page 87).
2. Set a reading task. Read out the text – or play a recording of it – as the students read.
3. The students mark a dialogue they have listened to for some feature of phonology (eg word stress) and they then read it out in pairs.
4. Make the students read out whole sentences when eliciting answers to a vocabulary exercise.
5. Give half the students a text with underlined words. They read the text to a partner, but stop before each underlined word and see if their partner can say what it is.
6. At the end of a reading lesson, the students work in pairs. They read the text out, taking turns to say a sentence at a time.

Applying the principle

- If you normally ask your students to read texts aloud:
  - Do a few reading lessons with no reading aloud.
  - Then consider how you and the students felt about this change.
- Next, try doing a few of the activities above and see how you and your students feel about them.
- If you would not normally do any reading aloud, try to include some of the activities above in your next few lessons. Then think about these questions:
  - Did you have any of the problems discussed in *Principle*?
  - How did you and your students feel about the classes?
  - What aspects of phonology did you look at?

Comprehension tasks

Feedback focusing on language

Principle

Many coursebooks and exams feature a variety of question types that aim to facilitate different ways of reading, such as skimming and scanning, making inferences, etc. While we have raised questions as to how far different skills can be separated and developed, it is also clear that only using the type of open comprehension questions of old (*Why? Who? Where?* and so on) might get boring and demotivating.

Also, a *variety* of different question and task types can motivate students to reread texts several times, which can be highly beneficial (see page 83).

However, also interesting from a lexical teacher's point of view is how often comprehension tasks essentially draw attention to words, phrases and aspects of word knowledge. In many cases, when going through answers, the teacher can treat feedback as a 'reading aloud' task and vocabulary exercise.

For example, for the text on Rwanda on page 97, students might answer *true/false* questions like this: *Only one region was affected by the problems in 1994.*

Rather than simply eliciting the correct answer (*false*), we might ask a student to read out the relevant part:

T: *Why? Read the bit that shows it's false.*
S: *The wave of killings swept the country.*
T: *OK. Exactly … so all over the country, not just in one part – and listen how we say it: 'swep(t) the country'. You don't really hear the 't'.*

We can then also explore this language further:

T: *Often stories in the media talk about things sweeping the nation. Maybe a craze for something has swept the country, or a storm has swept the country or a wave of protests. OK. Number 2 anyone?*

You may feel that this distracts from the reading lesson, but, in doing the task, the students practise their reading 'skills'. We suggest that the best way to improve reading is to work on the language.

You might also write questions about this language for the students to discuss later in the lesson (see page 52): *What things have swept the country? When? Why?*

Practising the principle

- Look at Text 2 on page 98, and do the comprehension exercise in the box below. Note that, unlike normal coursebook exercises, we have used a variety of question types to show how the principle can apply to different exercises.

1 Which person:
a was persuaded to get a dog?
b is worried about the effect of dogs on the environment?
c doesn't like the character of dogs?

2 Are these statements true or false?
a Piper doesn't think pet rabbits know who you are.
b Justin's kids never help to look after their pets.
c Having a pet can be bad for wildlife.

3 Answer the questions:
a What does Piper like about Dizzy?
b What arguments does Justin give for not getting a pet?
c Why does Asher mention driving?

- Decide what language you would focus on when the students (finally) give the correct answer. Think of one or more of the following:
  - A further example you'd give.
  - How the chunk might be varied.
  - Questions you might ask to generate related language.
  - Questions you might write to practise this language later in the lesson.

Applying the principle

- Look at the next text you are going to use.
- If it is a text in a coursebook, plan your feedback for the comprehension questions as in *Practising the principle*.
- If you are using your own material, write some questions that will allow you to focus on some useful language, and prepare feedback as above.

Talking about reading texts

Encouraging and scaffolding natural responses

Principle

As outlined in Part A, we believe that the reading texts we use in class should be treated as real messages. This means that part of our planning should involve thinking about the kinds of things the students might want to say in response to what they read.

Ideally, the kinds of speaking activities about reading texts that are set should provide your students with opportunities to:

- explain their thoughts and/or describe their feelings about what they've read.
- discuss and debate any cross-cultural issues that the text may have raised.
- think more critically about what they've read – and analyse and explore factual claims made in the text.

It may sometimes be the case that the best way to encourage this is to have the students discuss in pairs/groups questions related to the general topic they've read about. For example, we might give the questions below after the text on Rwanda on page 97:

- What surprised/shocked you the most in the article?
- What do you think has been the most important factor in Rwanda's development? Why?
- Would you now consider a holiday there?
- Can you think of any other countries/places that have changed dramatically over recent years?

Alternatively, you could ask the students to complete as many sentence starters* as they can. For example:

- What surprised/shocked me most about this was ...
- I'd like to know a bit more about how/why/what ...
- I didn't understand the bit about ...
- What I found most incredible was the fact that ...

The advantage of this approach is that it provides models of how texts are often discussed outside of class. At very low levels, you may want to provide whole responses, and simply ask the students to say whether or not they agree with them. For example: *It's great when lots of women are in parliament.*

Practising the principle

- Look at Text 2 on pets on page 98. Write five questions about the general theme of the text that the students could discuss in pairs/groups. Use the ideas outlined in *Principle.*
- Compare your questions with a colleague:
  - Try to answer each one together.
  - Decide which questions work best.
- Now write four or five sentence starters (or whole sentences) the students could complete to express their ideas, opinions and questions about the text. To help you, think about how you would complete each one.
- Decide which approach – questions or sentence starters – you think works best with the text, given its content and level.

Applying the principle

- Look at a reading text you plan to use in class soon. If it has a speaking task following it, decide:
  - if the task allows for the genuine exchange of thoughts and feelings – or if it is more of an extended check of comprehension.
  - if you're happy with the focus. Could it be adapted to encourage more meaningful speaking?
- If there is no speaking task, create your own – using one of the three formats we have looked at:
  - Try answering them yourself – or answer them with a colleague – to check they work, and note what language comes out of your answers.
- When the students are engaged in your post-text speaking task, listen and try to teach some new language during your round-up. Ideally, some of this new language might be taken from the text itself

Retelling texts

Getting more from a limited language focus

Principle

Many coursebooks have post-reading language-focused exercises that require students to guess the meaning of words from a text, or to match the words to meanings. You may well want to go beyond this. One way you can do this is by encouraging retelling of parts of the text, using items in the exercises.

Alternatively, you may want to choose items from a text yourself and get the students to retell parts of what they read, using them. When choosing items, the priority is to choose language that is central to the story/argument, even though some of this language will already be at least partially familiar to the majority of the students in the class. It's also usually easier for students to tell the story of what they've read if we give collocations or larger chunks instead of single words.

For the text on Rwanda page 97, for example, we might take chunks like these:
elite ethnic minority groups
become more notorious
attracted international attention
the main source of income

The students can be given these key chunks and asked to say as much as they can about how the items were used. This involves considerable retelling and reconstruction. They can then reread the text to check their ideas before we explore 'new' language around these items when eliciting ideas from the class, highlighting overlooked features or uses.

The dialogue scaffolds and extends what the students can produce. It may work something like this:

T: *OK, so* ***elite ethnic minority group****?*
Ss: *The Tutsis.*
T: *Yeah, and what happened to them?*
Ss: *They were killed.*
T: *Yeah, and what's the adjective to describe the murder of LOTS of people?*
Ss: *Mass.*
T: *Right. And* ***the mass murder*** *of huge numbers of the* ***elite ethnic minority group****, the Tutsi, did what?*

Practising the principle

- Look at Text 2 on page 98, and choose three items from each section – Piper's, Justin's and Asher's. Remember that retelling works best if the items are:
  - a central part of the message in the text.
  - more than just single words.
- Decide which approach to retelling would work best with these items:
  - Asking the students to say as much as they can about how each item was used.
  - Asking them to decide which person used each item – and why.
- If you can, get a colleague who has read the text to retell key parts of the text using your items and task. Alternatively, return to the task yourself after a few days. See how much you can recall, and then check your ideas by looking at the text again. Think about:
  - what you forgot– and why you forgot it.
  - how you could ask questions and elicit from a class, to get at the language you forgot.

Applying the principle

- Look at the next reading text you're going to use in class. If there is a 'guessing words' or 'matching words to meaning' exercise after it, decide:
  - if the items in the exercise are all central to the text and will work well in a retelling task.
  - if there are any items you want to take out, or replace with other items from the text.
- If there isn't a language-focused exercise, choose between 6–10 items as prompts for retelling, as you did in *Practising the principle*.
- After the students have done the 'matching/guessing meaning' exercise in the book – or after you have given the students your words:
  - put them in pairs to retell the text.
  - monitor and help with any problems.
  - ask them to reread the text quickly. Set a time limit.
  - go through the answers with the whole class (with books closed), eliciting as in *Principle*.

Mining texts for language

Setting and checking noticing tasks

Principle

We have already noted that the best readers know the most language – and automatically recognize and process it in different contexts. Given this, we need to view texts not only as genuine messages, but also as a rich source of both new lexis and extra information about items already studied.

However, there are a number of reasons why students often fail to pay much attention to the lexis in texts:

- They are focused solely on processing meaning and being able to show comprehension.
- They're so keen to discuss the content of the text, they fail to notice much about the language.
- They're too busy dealing with single words – often less frequent ones that they've not met before.
- None of the post-text tasks encourage them to.

As such, you may need to make exercises that check how much the students notice about language in texts they read. Here are some of the many types of exercises you can use to do this, based on the text on page 97:

- Complete these sentences from the text by adding the missing words/prepositions.
  (eg *Coffee is one of the main sources of ….*)
- Match verbs with the nouns they went with in the text.
  (eg (1) *hold* (2) *heal* // (a) *wounds* (b) *a seat*)
- Look at these adjectives from the text. Can you remember what they described?
  (eg (1) *elite* (2) *adventurous* (3) *average*)
- Complete the sentences with words/phrases from the text. The definitions in brackets will help you.
  (eg *The economy is …… . (growing quickly)*)
- Correct the words in italics in the sentences below, using words from the text.
  (eg Rwanda has *sustained* a major transformation).

There are three main aims to these tasks:

- To make students more aware of the fact that understanding meaning is not the same as noticing and being able to re-use language;
- To get them to reread the text with this in mind;
- To highlight and to then further explore the more frequent/useful new language in the text.

Practising the principle

- Look again at the list of ten words/chunks that you picked out of the text on page 98.
- Decide which of the exercise types outlined in *Principle* you think best checks how much readers noticed about the language on your list. You may:
  - decide the exercise type would work better if you discarded some items from the list, and added some others from the text.
  - feel a completely different exercise type is required.
- Write the exercise. Ideally, it should focus on 6–10 items.
- If you can, ask a colleague to try it and see how well they get on. Alternatively, return to it in a few days' time and – without looking back at the text on page 98 – see how well you can do it.
  - You will almost certainly find it impossible to remember everything, and will need to reread. The students will probably remember even less than you do. Raising awareness of this fact is one of the points of the exercise.

Applying the principle

- Look at a reading text that you plan to use in class soon. If there is a post-text exercise that focuses on language, decide:
  - if it focuses on the most useful/frequent language in the text.
  - what aspect/s of word knowledge the exercise explores.
  - the questions you could ask and extra examples you could give, as part of your feedback.
- If there's no post-text exercise that focuses on language – or if you want to replace what's there already – then you'll need to write one yourself. Select the language you want to focus on, and decide which exercise type best allows exploration of this language.

Exploiting and expanding on lexis

Deepening connections with key items

Principle

As we've previously said, one of the main values of texts in the classroom is that they can potentially serve as excellent ways of bringing new high-frequency lexis, or items that may well be relevant to a particular topic area, to students. We may just decide to focus the students' attention on the way language was actually used in the text they've just read (see page 92).

However, we may also want to take some of the most useful language from the text and further develop the students' knowledge of how these items are used. There are several ways we can do this, offering varying degrees of expansion. Here are three examples, based on the text on page 97:

- Write pairs of sentences/phrases, and ask the students to complete the second phrase with the correct form of the word in **bold**. It's easier if the missing words are from the text.
  1 ***invest** in property* *encourage .....*
  2 *a **corrupt** system* *deal with .....*
- Select 6–8 key nouns, verbs or adjectives. Most should be words the students are already familiar with. Get the students to match them to groups of possible collocates. You may want to make some of the collocates match those used in the text. To make the exercise harder, you could *not* give the items selected but, instead, ask the students to find words in the text that go with each group of collocates.
  1 *a lack of social ~ / enforce workplace ~ / gender ~*
  2 *deal with ~ / expose ~ / face ~ charges / is rife*
- Highlight or pull out 6–8 collocations/chunks from the text. Then write sentences featuring a slightly different use of one word from each chunk. Ask the students to complete each sentence with one word from each collocation/chunk.
  1 *He stayed in hospital overnight and is now in a ..... condition.*
  2 *Orders came ..... in from all over the country.*

When going through exercises like these, make sure you don't just check the answers. Also explore, explain and exemplify any new collocations, chunks or uses.

Practising the principle

- Analyse the language in the text on page 98, if you have not done so already (see also page 85).
- Choose 8–10 items that you want to focus on.
- Choose which of the ways outlined in *Principle* you want to use, in order to expand on them. Note that you may then need to discard some items and add others, depending on the exercise type you decide to go for.
- Write your exercise. Remember that you can increase the level of difficulty, by:
  - not including the items you're focusing on, but, instead, highlighting them in the text.
  - not even highlighting them in the text, but telling the students to find the missing items.
  - not including any collocations/co-text from the reading text in the exercise at all.

Applying the principle

- Find a text you plan to use sometime soon that doesn't have a post-reading focus on language.
- Choose 8–10 words, collocations or chunks that you want to explore in more depth.
- Write a relevant exercise. Decide what aspect of knowledge about your items to explore, and how difficult you want the exercise to be.
- When checking the answers to the exercise, be sure to explore, explain and exemplify new collocations, chunks or uses.

Other kinds of speaking around texts

Exploiting new lexis, roleplays – and more

Principle

If we have mined a text for lexis (see page 92) or taken lexis from a text and explored broader uses and other meanings (page 93), we may also want to provide further opportunities for students to speak. As with language that students meet in vocabulary exercises, language that emerges from texts needs to be practised and students need to have the chance to connect it to their lives – and to the language they already know – in some way.

There are several ways this can be done. For example, the students can:

- discuss questions that use some of the new lexis. These questions may be personal, they may involve some broader world knowledge, and they may not always be directly connected to the original theme of the text. A mix usually works best.
  (eg *What're the biggest* ***ethnic minority*** *groups in your country? Can you think of any films* ***set in*** *your home town/city?*)
- discuss how far they agree with statements that contain some of the new language – and explain why.
  (eg *The world would be a better place if more women* ***held seats in parliament.***)
- choose three or four of the new items that they feel they will use most, and explain in pairs when and how they think they'll use them.

Other kinds of speaking are also possible. You could get students to:

- roleplay scenarios mentioned in/suggested by the text.
  (eg *Student A – you're a Rwandan government official. Explain to Student B –a foreign business person – why they should invest in your country.*)
- predict what happens next. This works particularly well with more narrative-driven/literary texts, where the students can read to find out real answers.
- watch a film version of what they've read (or a film that's connected in some way) and then compare and contrast similarities and differences.

Practising the principle

- Look back at the list of language from the text on page 98 that you have previously decided would be worth focusing on. Also, look at any connected post-reading vocabulary exercises you have written.
- Write 6–8 questions/statements that use some of the lexis you've selected. Try to ensure:
  - they encourage discussion of personal experiences, opinions, world knowledge and topic areas not directly connected to the theme of pets.
  - They are generally quite open, rather than being closed *yes/no* questions.
  - that at least some of them encourage the students to try and produce further language connected to the language being practised.
- Next, look again at the text on page 98. See if you can think of any other speaking tasks connected to it that could be done, once the students have finished reading. These might be:
  - roleplays involving one or more of the characters in the text.
  - prediction tasks of some kind.
  - debates based around issues raised in the text.
- Finally, decide which of the possible speaking activities you've thought of would work best, in terms of encouraging speaking and generating language.

Applying the principle

- Look at a text you plan to use in class sometime soon. Analyse the language in the text, and in any exercises based on the text. Then:
  - Decide which items work best in questions/statements for discussion.
  - Write a short exercise using these items. Within it, highlight the lexis you're focusing on.
- Decide if any other possible connected speaking activities, such as roleplays, might work better – or could even be used as additional tasks.
- Set your speaking activity in class, and use your feedback on the speaking as an opportunity to teach some language and recycle some you have previously taught.

Encouraging further responses

Allowing space for open questions

Principle

Once students have read a text, tackled a gist task, discussed what they've read and explored in more detail some of the lexis that's been pulled out, they may have had enough and be ready to move on. However, it may also be the case there are still things they're curious to learn more about. These could be related to:

- new lexis. They may have underlined individual words, collocations or larger chunks.
- grammar. There may be particular uses of structures/patterns the students are curious about.
- content. They may have questions about things they read about, aspects of the text that still puzzle or bemuse them.
- aspects of discourse. The students may not grasp what a reference word such as this relates to.

Near the end of a lesson based around a reading text, giving the students a few minutes to look back one last time and decide whether they have anything they'd like to ask about usually ensures at least a few interesting questions from the class as a whole. For instance, students who've read the text on Rwanda on page 97 may come up with questions such as these:

- What does *advance* mean here, at the end of the fifth paragraph?
- Can I say *make a transformation* here, instead of *undergo*?
- Why is it an *-ing* form here –*With so many more people passing through it*?
- How were these killings allowed to happen?
- How long has Paul Kagame been in power?

When dealing with such questions, you may want to:

- make it clear they're asking about single words, when the issue is a larger chunk (eg it's not *advance*– it's *book* trips up to a year *in advance*).
- give/elicit answers, and add extra examples.
- simply say it's a good question and that you're not sure of the answer, but will find out.
- give your own opinions about content-related questions. Then ask the rest of the class for theirs.
- encourage the students to research some content-related questions on their own at home.

Practising the principle

- Look at the questions below that students have asked about the text on page 98. Decide:
  - if the focus of the question is OK or if it'd be better to broaden the focus to larger chunks of language.
  - if you could answer the question on the spot. If so, how? Would you give any extra examples? Would you write anything on the board? Would you involve the class in the answer in any way? How?
  - which you'd admit to not being able to answer on the spot, but would find answers to at home.
  - which are best answered via a whole-class chat.
  - which would be best dealt with by telling the students to read around the topic more at home.

1 What does *company* mean here, where Piper uses it?
2 Why is it *mice coming here* – not *mice to come*?
3 Justin says *we'd say no*. Is this *we had* or *we did*?
4 When do British kids start getting pocket money?
5 Is *the wild* the same as *the countryside*?
6 How can a dog produce so much greenhouse gas?

Applying the principle

- Look at the next text you plan to use in class. Bearing in mind how you'll already be exploiting it, can you think of any *other* questions the students may try to ask about it? How would you answer them?

- In class, try to leave time at the end of the lesson. Tell the students to look at the text one last time and see whether they have any final questions they'd like to ask – about the language or the content.

- If you don't have time for this, ask the students to reread the text at home and think of at least one question they'd like to ask about it. You could then begin the next lesson with their questions:
  - Encourage the students to ask their questions. You may want to give them a few minutes to discuss in groups first, and then ask each group for one question.
  - Try to answer the questions as best you can.

The benefits of extensive reading

In-class ways of encouraging out-of-class reading

Principle

Extensive reading involves students reading primarily for their own enjoyment. It can be done in class time, but more usually it's something that teachers encourage students to do at home. There's a growing body of research that outlines the many benefits of extensive reading, and there seems to be at least some evidence to suggest it can, among other things:

- consolidate and extend knowledge of vocabulary, and develop primings.
- enhance general language competence.
- help reading fluency, and develop automaticity.
- result in improved writing capabilities.
- encourage students to take more responsibility for their own learning.
- help develop general world knowledge.
- foster a love of and enthusiasm for reading.

Given all of this, it is perhaps surprising that there isn't more of a drive to encourage extensive reading outside the classroom. It's worth considering some of the factors that may explain the relatively low uptake:

- The students may not see how reading outside of class connects to their in-class learning.
- They may struggle to find texts that interest them.
- They may struggle to understand much of the texts they do choose, and this may reduce motivation.
- They may not have much time to read outside of class.
- Teachers may not encourage it, as they see no way of testing or assessing its value.
- Teachers may not be happy accepting the more hands-off role that extensive reading usually requires of them.

However, even if all of these obstacles can be overcome, it remains a fact that the purpose of extensive reading is not *explicit* learning of new words. As lexical teachers, if we want to ensure that students not only read for enjoyment, but also consciously use reading texts as an aid for vocabulary development, we may well need to provide advice and guidance on how this can be done.

Practising the principle

- Look at the ways below that teachers can support and encourage extensive reading. In each case, decide:
  - if you've ever tried anything similar.
  - what particular problems are being addressed.
  - how much time is needed to create and implement it.
  - what issues might arise in class.
  - how easy it would be to set up in your own context.
- Think of any other things that could be done to encourage extensive reading.

1. Set up a class blog, and encourage the students to write short reviews of everything they read there – and to comment on other reviews as well.
2. List websites that contain excellent graded reading practice, and that can be accessed remotely (eg *http://www.bbc.co.uk/learningenglish/english*).
3. Set aside time at the start/end of class for the students to discuss what they've been reading.
4. Encourage the students to use Twitter or WhatsApp to send examples of English they particularly enjoy – or items of lexis they have enjoyed learning.
5. Begin a lesson by getting the students to work in groups and explain three or four new bits of vocabulary they've learned from their reading texts.
6. Ask the students to bring an interesting text to class. Give them time to read the first couple of paragraphs, and then ask them to explain in groups whether the article is worth finishing.
7. Persuade your school to invest in a range of graded readers. Make sure these include a range of non-fiction works, as well as fiction.

Applying the principle

- If your students already read extensively outside of class, choose one of the above that's new for you – and see how it works with *your* students.
- If you don't yet encourage extensive reading, think about what's stopping you from doing so, and how you could maybe overcome those hurdles.

Appendix

Chapter Four

Text 1

From hell on earth to holiday resort

If they've heard of Rwanda at all, then most people will probably **associate** this **tiny state** in central east Africa with the terrible **wave** of killings that **swept** the country in 1994, leaving between five hundred thousand and a million people – almost 20% of the population as a whole – dead. The **mass** murder of huge numbers of the **elite ethnic minority** group, the Tutsi, shocked the world and the country became even more **notorious** with the **release** of films such as *Shooting Dogs* and *Hotel Rwanda* that were **set** during that terrible time.

However, in the two decades since those dark days, Rwanda has **undergone** a **remarkable** transformation and today the country is politically **stable** and **united** – and the economy is **booming**. While China has **attracted** international **attention** for its growth over recent years, the fact that the Rwandan economy has grown by around 9% per year since 2000 is far less recognised. The main **source** of income for the country is the coffee and tea that is grown locally and then exported, but **tourism** is also starting to **bring in** huge amounts of foreign cash. How has this been possible? And what does the country have to offer the **adventurous** tourist?

Back from the brink

Perhaps the most **significant** factor in Rwanda's development has been good **leadership**. The recent period of growth has happened during the time that President Paul Kagame, who is a Tutsi, has been in power. Kagame has worked hard to help the country **heal** its **wounds**: he's **encouraged investment** and has used the **aid** that's **poured in wisely**, dealing with ***corruption*** in the **process**; he's fought hard for greater **equality** between the main ethnic groups, the Tutsi and the Hutu, and he has also fought for **gender equality**, with Rwanda today having the highest percentage of women **holding seats** in parliament – a **massive** 68%.

Some of the worst killers of the 1990s have been sent to jail. However, by learning to **live with** the **horrors** of the past, the Rwandan people have achieved incredible things, and it is this, along with recent **social** changes, that has enabled the country to move forward to a **brighter** future for all. Rwanda is also a young country: the average age is just 18, so many of the adults of today were not even alive during the terrible times. The large number of educated young people may also help to explain the country's **growing reputation** as a centre for new technology.

Gorillas and five-star hotels

As a result of this economic growth and social **stability**, tourists have started **flooding** in to the country, which is sometimes referred to as the land of a thousand hills. The main attraction is the mountain **gorillas** and a lot of work has been done to make sure the animals are protected from **hunters**. In addition, only a limited number of visitors are allowed each day, so some people book their trips up to a year **in advance**.

With so many more people **passing through** it, the capital Kigali is growing fast and is now home to a number of luxury hotels. It's also very well connected to the Web, with great Wi-Fi and many new **start-ups**, all part of the country's dream of moving from an economy **dependent on** farming to a **knowledge-based** one. So if you feel like exploring somewhere different this year, maybe it's time to give Rwanda a try.

Appendix

Chapter Four

Text 2

Good pet, bad pet

Our readers talk about their views on pets.

Piper

When it comes to pets, I'm very much a cat person. They're just easier to look after than dogs, and they're also more interesting than something like fish or rabbits. I mean, they recognize you and you can have a relationship with them, but they're not as needy as dogs. Dogs demand that either you take them out for a walk and give them attention or they'll make a lot of noise. They're like little kids who scream and shout when they don't get what they want. I've had my cat Dizzy since I was five years old. She's lovely. She sleeps on my bed and keeps me company, but she's also useful because she stops mice coming into our house.

Justin

We bought all kinds of pets for our kids when they were growing up. It always followed the same pattern. One of them would ask us if they could have this or that kind of pet and we'd say no, but then they'd keep asking and I'd say, 'we can't afford it' or 'who's going to take care of it?' and they'd say, 'Well, I can pay for some of it from my pocket money. You won't have to do anything. I'll feed it and keep it clean'. I'd then say, 'you said that last time', which was followed by denials or promises to do better. Eventually, I gave in and we got a hamster or rabbit or dog or whatever. There was always some initial excitement and enthusiasm when they kept their promises, but six months later unless there was a huge argument, it was always us cleaning the cage or taking the dog for a walk.

Asher

I love wildlife. I often go out in the countryside and go bird watching or see if I can take photos of animals in the natural habitat. I don't want to have a pet, though. Pets are actually bad for nature and the environment. For example, cats kill thousands of birds each year and just think of the damage and mess dogs cause! Then there's all the meat they eat, which takes up a lot of space we could use to grow food for people and it also creates a lot of greenhouse gases: a dog creates twice as much as driving a large family vehicle does! And there are eleven million dogs in the UK. That's one for every six people!

Chapter Five

Teaching listening lexically

Similarities and differences with reading

Starting points for planning

Principle

In part A, we discussed listening and reading in the same section. This is, in part, because in most coursebooks, both reading and listening lessons tend to follow a very similar pattern. There are usually:

- pre-text tasks, including prediction.
- comprehension tasks, to be done while tackling the text.
- responses to the text, or some other speaking task.
- language development exercises related to the text.

As we also made clear in Part A, as lexical teachers, much of our approach to reading and listening texts is the same, because we believe that students' abilities in both areas are primarily based on 'bottom-up' processing. With listening, this involves:

- knowing more language (especially words and chunks).
- automaticity of hearing words and recalling meaning.

Implicit in that last statement, of course, is a fundamental way in which listening does differ from reading: when listening, students need to be able to *hear* the language before they can recall its meaning. Helping students *hear* language, and the different approach to analysis, tasks and feedback that this requires, will be the major focus of this chapter.

However, as *a starting point* for planning a listening lesson, we suggest doing something similar to what you would do with a reading lesson:

- Analyse language in the listening in the same way.
- Use pre-listening tasks to pre-teach language.
- Use feedback to comprehension tasks to focus on language.
- Ensure the students get repeated opportunities to hear the text.
- Use other speaking around the listening as a chance to notice gaps in your students' knowledge. You may then correct or teach new connected language.

It is probably best to make sure you have read the chapter on 'Teaching reading lexically' before starting this chapter.

Practising the principle

- Look at listening Script 1 on page 111. It is a conversation in a language school between the director of studies and some teachers at a staff meeting. It is aimed at Upper-Intermediate/B2 students.
- Analyse the language, as you did with the reading text (page 84):
  - Underline words or phrases that students at this level may not know.
  - Highlight the full chunks.
  - Highlight other chunks of familiar words.
- Think about a pre-listening task, and how it could generate both interest and language from the text.
- Think of a comprehension task and what language it might allow you to focus on.
- Think about questions that will encourage the students to respond to the text. (See pages 94–95.)

Applying the principle

- Look at the coursebook you are using and at the listening lessons it contains. Ask yourself:
  - if they follow the same stages as the reading lessons.
  - if there are any additional stages or tasks – for example, a focus on hearing language or phonology.
  - if the scripts are conversational, or if they are more of a monologue.
  - if the language in them sounds natural.
  - how much of the language contained in the scripts is explicitly focused on during the different stages of the lesson.
  - if the focus is on single words or chunks.
  - if there is a focus on frequent words.

If you normally create your own lessons using other kinds of listening materials or videos, review your recent lessons and ask yourself the same questions as above.

Analysing language

Soundshapes in the greenhouse, the garden and the jungle

Principle

Richard Cauldwell, in his superb book *Phonology for Listening* (2013), talks about the varied 'soundshapes' of words as they occur 'in the greenhouse, the garden and the jungle'.

In what he calls the *greenhouse*, soundshapes follow the phonetic transcriptions you see in a dictionary.

The *garden* represents controlled connected speech, where there are features such as:

- weak forms: when 'grammar' words (*to*, *for*, *me*) are unstressed, they include a weak sound – /ə/ or /ɪ/.
- elision: sounds disappear across word boundaries in formal contractions (*I'm*), double consonants (*big guns*) or, for example, when a /t/ falls between consonants (*last night*).
- linking: where final consonants 'move' to the start of a word beginning with a vowel, or a consonant (/r/, /w/ or /j/) is inserted between a final vowel and a beginning vowel (*to (w) Andrew*).
- assimilation: a sound changes due to surrounding sounds, so *handbag* sounds like *'hambag'*.

The *jungle* is normal everyday speech, where strings of words are in fact one continuous stream of speech. Here, the neat rules of connected speech above combine and are stretched further, depending on speed of speech, how phrases are chunked and how words are stressed at the moment of speaking.

So the words in 'Guy's just speaking to a student' could have these soundshapes:

- greenhouse gaɪ ɪz dʒʌst spiːkɪŋ tʊː aɪ stjʊːdənt
- garden gaɪz dʒʌspiːkɪŋ tʊːwə stjtʊːdənt
- jungle gaɪdʒəspɪkəntwəstjʊːdənt

As fluent speakers, we become deaf to these changes because we have learnt to understand that /dʒə/, /dʒʌs/ and /dʒʌst/ are all sound representations of 'just', so a key step towards helping our students is to re-sensitise ourselves to how words really sound in natural speech.

Practising the principle

- Try one or more of the following, to become more aware of varied soundshapes.

- Watch Richard Cauldwell's videos on Cool Speech: *http://www.speechinaction.org/cool-speechhot-listening-fluent-pronunciation/videos/*
- Read Richard's blog posts on the stream of speech that start at: *http://www.speechinaction.org/2015/02/*

- Find an authentic piece of listening material. A good source is the BBC/British Library Listening project: *http://www.bbc.co.uk/programmes/articles/MrHK9VQvVkc6Jc8m2CzL7k/find-a-conversation*
- Within the piece you chose, find a section you think is very fast, but you can write down the words for.
- Record the section, using an audio editor such as Audacity (available free at *http://audacityteam.org/*).
- Play around with the short recording, isolating individual words and their soundshapes.

- Choose 4–6 chunks that you identified in the audio scripts on pages 111 and 112.
- Record yourself, or a non-teaching fluent speaker, saying them fast and then more carefully.
- Can you identify any features of connected speech from 'the garden', or any crushed soundshapes from 'the jungle', that are discussed in *Principle*?

Applying the principle

- Listen to several examples of listening material you have used in recent weeks:
  - How varied is the speed of speech?
  - Do you notice any examples of faster speech with elements of the garden or the jungle?
  - Does the material focus on these, or help the students deal with them in any way?
  - Did you focus on this or help the students with it? How?

Highlighting the stream of speech

Using the board and drilling

Principle

In the previous task, we saw how students often struggle with decoding what they hear because of the variation in the soundshapes of words. Many teachers and writers ignore the reality of the stream of speech and the extreme variations of soundshapes that Richard Cauldwell highlights (see page 101).

Course materials will often focus on weak forms of grammar words, such as /wɒz/ and /wəz/ for *was*, but won't mention /wə/ as a possibility. This avoidance is partly because we are unaware of the sounds we make when speaking naturally, but may also be due to a view that reduced forms are a sign of laziness or of slang, and may be used 'inappropriately' by students. This can be seen in the often disgusted reaction to teaching 'gonna'.

There has also been some resistance to presenting reduced forms because of the idea that, in the context of English as a Lingua Franca, native-speaker norms are no longer the best models for students.

While teachers may not want to use 'jungle' soundshapes as productive models, Cauldwell suggests that getting students to try to reproduce these sounds is an important way to develop their ability to decode.

Before students get to that stage, however, there are other ways we can show aspects of the stream of speech 'in the garden' and 'in the jungle' (see page 101). We can:

- give several models of chunks and sentences we teach (greenhouse, garden and jungle versions).
- focus on fast speech in listening texts.
- say fast speech slowly while retaining the same soundshapes.
- mark features of connected speech on the chunks we write on the board. For example:
  - Cross out elided sounds.
  - Draw lines between words that link, and add in extra sounds.
  - Circle prominent sounds.
  - Mark /ə/ or /ɪ/ to indicate weak forms.
- write versions of what the students hear in phonetic script or Latin script.

Practising the principle

- Choose 6–8 of the chunks that you identified in the audio scripts on pages 111 and 112.
- Mark each chunk with the features of connected speech ('the garden') that you might expect to hear. Remember that there may be knock-on effects. For example, in 'just speaking' we first elide the 't', as it comes between two consonants, but then we also elide an 's', because we don't pronounce double consonants. Thus, we get 'juspeaking'.
- Record yourself saying each chunk, as in:
  - the greenhouse (carefully).
  - the garden (fairly slowly, but using your marked-up version above).
  - the jungle (as fast as you can).
- Is the 'jungle' version different to your 'garden' one?
- Try to write a phonetic or Latin script version of the jungle form.
- Practise saying the fastest form slowly, while still retaining the soundshapes. Record it and listen.
- Practise backchaining* – where you drill the chunk section by section from the end, to help the students say it better. Try it with the garden and jungle versions. For example:

  now
  doinow
  chadoinow
  wotchadoinow?

Applying the principle

Do one or more of the following:

- Photograph your boardwork over a series of lessons:
  - Are you highlighting aspects of phonology?
  - Were there opportunities to highlight features of connected speech that you missed?
  - Can you try to use more phonology in each lesson?
- Write down common chunks or examples of traditional grammar you plan to teach:
  - Think about phonological features to highlight.
  - In class, highlight on the board and/or drill the language fast and slowly.

Generating appropriate language

Pre-listening tasks for conversational texts

Principle

One key way in which conversational listening texts differ from most reading texts is that, in conversations, language is often used to do things in the here and now, while reading texts more often describe what was – or will be – done.

Also, in conversations, we rarely describe everything that took place or will take place in much detail. This difference is important when it comes to pre-text tasks in listening lessons, because, as lexical teachers, we then aim to pre-teach language as it will be heard.

Many pre-text tasks that we saw in the chapter on 'Teaching reading lexically' encourage students to come up with descriptions, opinions and stories, whereas, in listening lessons, we want the students to generate some of the actual language they will hear. Take, for example, these two pre-listening tasks for Script 1 on page 111:

1 Do you ever go to meetings? When? What for? What do you think makes a good/bad meeting?
2 Can you think of eight things that might be discussed at a teachers' staff meeting?

When doing these tasks, the students may well:

1 talk about starting on time or people arriving late, but probably won't come up with language used to start the meeting on time, such as: *Are we all ready? Can we start? We've got quite a lot to pack in in quite a short time, so maybe we should just get started and they can catch up.*
2 try to say words like *assessment* and *parents' meeting* that appear in the text, but not the kinds of things said about these words in a conversation.

We can try to take account of these gaps between description and language used in conversation, by:

- giving pre-listening tasks that encourage output more like conversations the students will hear.
- asking the students to predict what will be said, and how the conversation will develop – rather than just asking for predictions about content.
- showing exchanges, rather than just sentences, when reformulating students' ideas and suggestions.

Practising the principle

- First, look at Script 2 on page 112.
- Below are short examples of different tasks that could be used before playing this recording in class. Do them in your head or with a colleague, and note:
  - what language each task generates.
  - how much of the language generated appears in – or could be reformulated into language from – the audioscript.

1 Work in pairs. Discuss these questions:
- How often do you eat out?
- Where do you usually go? Why?
- What's your favourite foreign food? Why?

2 In pairs, roleplay a conversation starting:
A: *Are you hungry?*
B: *Yeah, a bit. And you?*

3 The questions below come from the listening:
(a) Put them in the order you expect to hear them.
(b) Decide two possible ways each might be answered.
1 *Have you got anywhere in mind?*
2 *Are you hungry?*
3 *Shall we walk, or do you want to get a cab?*
4 *Do you want to get something to eat, then?*

4 Look at the keywords from the first four lines of the listening. Predict what you think will be said:
A: *hungry?*
B: *bit / you?*
A: *am / want / get / eat?*
B: *OK / anywhere / mind?*

Applying the principle

- Look at the next listening you plan to do in class and the task/s that precede it. Decide:
  - if the language it generates appears in the listening.
  - if anything potentially generated could be reformulated into language in the audioscript.
  - if there are any other tasks you could do instead, which might generate more featured language.

Withholding the correct answer

Checking hearing in comprehension tasks

Principle

Unless they have particular literacy problems or are unfamiliar with Latin script, the difficulty most students have when reading is not strictly one of decoding. Instead what makes reading hard comes down to the meaning of the words they see. They may:

- not know the meaning of the words.
- choose the wrong meaning for the context.
- take too long to recall or work out the meaning.

As such, in reading lessons, it is reasonable to move straight from comprehension tasks to work on vocabulary meaning and usage (see page 89).

In addition to these problems, with listenings, the students will have problems because they cannot decode what they hear. This includes words they actually know the meaning of. As a result, when checking answers to comprehension questions, we need to know whether the mistakes that the students have made are due to not having heard the correct word or are, rather, the result of not having got the meaning, as outlined above for reading.

If the problem is decoding, we can help students by:

- letting them hear key parts several times.
- providing a choice of words to listen for as a guide.
- highlighting pronunciation features in difficult sections.
- drilling the language as it sounds, or giving examples of fast and slow versions (see page 102).

The temptation can be to accept the first correct answer we hear, or to give the correct answer when a student gets things wrong. Neither action provides us with information on what the students heard. Instead, it may be better to withhold the correct answer, and ask the students to say what they heard. Even if this is correct, we might then ask other students if they agree. If there are disagreements, we need to find out what *those* students heard, and to then replay the recording to check who is right.

Once everyone has the right answer, we may then focus on other examples or on asking about aspects of word knowledge, as suggested for reading comprehension.

Practising the principle

The task below is adapted from John Field's excellent book *Listening in the Language Classroom* (2009). We suggest it as a way of developing the skill of withholding correct answers and guiding comprehension in a 'bottom-up' way. You can do it as a comprehension task with any listening text. However, it will be more effective if you choose a challenging listening for some/most of your students.

- Briefly introduce the text students will hear. For example: *You are going to hear ...*
  - *a school staff meeting.*
  - *two people deciding where to have dinner.*
- Divide the board in half:
  Completely sure **Not completely sure**
- Play the recording. Tell the students to note down what they hear.
- Ask the students to compare their ideas in pairs. Monitor, to find out what they all seem to agree on.
- Ask different students to say what they heard, and whether they are completely sure or not.
- If there are disagreements, both ideas should go on the 'Not completely sure' side, perhaps with a '/'.
- Play the recording again, Ask the students to:
  - add more details.
  - move anything from *not sure* to *completely sure*.
- After comparing again, check ideas on the board. Some of the new information may need to go under 'Not sure', and some previously *not sure* information will be moved to 'Completely sure'.
- Repeat these last two stages once or twice more. You may stop the recording and repeat a short extract, to resolve disputes

Applying the principle

- The next time you do a listening in class that has a comprehension task such as *true/false* statements, try to withhold the correct answers.
- Before confirming the answers, use disagreements as a lead-in to replaying the listening and as a way of establishing what the students heard. Then move on to focus more on meaning and word knowledge.

Gapping texts

Focusing on chunks and pronunciation

Principle

In the chapter on 'Teaching reading', we noted that students may sometimes get the gist of what they have read without paying close attention to the language, and thus soon forget it. This is equally true of listening, but, rather than asking the students to reread a written text to check what they remembered, it is better to replay the recording. It is good to gap two-to-four word chunks in the audioscript to help the students to notice language. This encourages students to process language in chunks, but also gives practice in hearing how words sound together (see page 101).

Apart from fast connected speech, your gaps may also focus on things such as these (see the audio script on page 111):

- **Traditional grammar**
  Present continuous: *Guy's just speaking*
  Reported speech: *said he might be …*
- **New words/keywords**
  a lot to pack in *they can catch up*
- **Chunks**
  on her way *up to date with*
- **Other features and patterns of spoken language**
  Uses of *just*: *we should just get started*; *you'll just have to miss*
  Persuading: *But if I could sort it out?*; *What if I made sure …*
  Talking to a group: *Any other issues with anyone?*

You may be able to have a single focus, but more likely it will be a mixture. Because of the practicalities of listening and writing answers, you will need to:

- limit the size of the chunk (eg two to four words).
- limit the number of chunks.
- spread the chunks evenly over the whole text.

As well as drawing attention to phonology, when checking the answers to the gapfill, we can:

- check grammatical concepts.
- ask questions about the vocabulary.
- exemplify and vary chunks and patterns.

Practising the principle

- Look at the two audio scripts on pages 111 and 112. For each, select a number of 'gaps'. Either number and underline each gap, or write the gapped words on a fresh piece of paper. As you choose them, consider:
  - the number of gaps you have (Are there too many? Are they too close together?).
  - the features of phonology you could emphasise, and how you will highlight them (see page 102).
  - what other ways you could exploit the phrases you gapped as you go through the answers.
- If you can, work with a colleague. Swap your 'gapped' texts and roleplay being teacher and student:
  - Elicit each 'gapped' phrase.
  - When your partner says each gap, drill the group of words and draw attention to features of phonology, as appropriate.
  - Ask a further question about the language or give further examples, as suggested in *Principle.*
- When you have both tried this, discuss your choices and the way you did the feedback.

Applying the principle

- Copy the audioscript for the next listening you plan to do, and gap any language you want to focus on.
- Hand out the gapped audioscript after you have played the recording at least once and done at least one comprehension task.
- Give the students a few minutes to read the script and to discuss in pairs what they think is missing. Don't expect them to remember much!
- Play the recording all the way through again. Ask the students to try to complete the script and compare ideas.
- Play the recording again to just after the first gap, and elicit the answer.
- If the students don't have the answers or disagree, replay the gapped section (repeatedly if necessary).
- Elicit the answer. Drill it and highlight connected speech, and/or ask your question(s) about the language.
- Play the recording up to the next gap. Repeat the steps above.

Using scripts

Purposes and feedback

Principle

We have already looked at using audio scripts by gapping words. We can use scripts in other ways to:

- practise pronunciation.
- encourage students to memorise and recall language.
- adapt conversations in creative ways.

It is worth reiterating at this point that we are referring to two kinds of pronunciation here – productive and receptive – and that this will impact on the kinds of feedback we give during and after tasks using scripts.

With *productive* pronunciation, we are talking about the ability to produce individual sounds and words in a broadly intelligible way, rather than be 'native-like'. This ability is also important for the 'internal voice' that can impact on reading (see page 88). Acting out scripts in pairs offers the teacher opportunities to notice problems in these areas and work on them.

Tasks on connected speech, however, should be seen as essentially *receptive*. While there are 'rules' for connected speech, we do not make use of them when we speak. The tasks, therefore, aim to raise students' awareness of changing soundshapes (useful for listening), but any active correction of pronunciation would still best focus on individual sounds and words.

An exception to this may be very common chunks and collocations, where practising what Richard Cauldwell (2013) calls 'garden' or 'jungle' versions for productive use is good because:

- they are typically said faster than non-formulaic language (see Alison Wray, 2008) so the students need to develop automaticity in decoding.
- they are actually easier for students to say than the 'greenhouse' version (*las night* / *gonna*).

We may memorise and adapt scripts for the same reasons we outlined previously (page 91). However, to make it worthwhile, the script should contain lots of re-usable chunks. In feedback, focus on:

- re-noticing grammar students misremembered.
- (in)effective changes to the audio script.
- pronunciation, as above.

Practising the principle

- Look at the listening script on page 112. Do each of the tasks in the box below yourself or with a partner.
- Notice the process involved in each one, and decide:
  - what the purpose of the task is.
  - any problems there may be.
  - how the task could be made either simpler or more challenging.
  - what feedback you might give.
- Can you think of any other ways to use the script?
- Would all the tasks work with the script on page 111?

1. Listen and mark the script with stressed sounds.
2. Underline any chunk in the text you could often re-use. Practise saying the chunks as fast as you can. Then read out the dialogue in pairs.
3. Read out the dialogue in pairs, but only speak when you are looking up at each other.
4. In pairs, each memorise one role. Write one word in each line as a reminder. Then act out the script.
5. In pairs, mark words in the script that link together.
6. Read out the script in pairs, but refer to real places you know.
7. Play the recording or read it out while the students whisper along.
8. Tell the students to number the lines. Then ask them to practise reading out the text, but, when they reach a particular line (eg line 6), they must say something different to the script and continue the conversation, based on this new line.

Applying the principle

- Look through the audio script in your coursebook, and identify a dialogue that the students could read out.
- Alternatively, find a suitable conversation from another source, or write your own and record it.
- Do one or more of the tasks above when you do the listening in class.
- Consider what pronunciation issues came up and the feedback you gave and how to improve it.

Beyond the listening lesson 1

Focusing on individual sounds

Principle

Students often struggle with sounds in English that they do not have in their mother tongue. This is not just a productive problem, as students are also often unable to hear these sounds correctly, which can affect their ability to comprehend texts.

Perhaps the most common solution to this problem is to get students to repeat the individual sounds, sometimes as part of a 'minimal pair'* – a pair of words with only one different sound (eg *very–berry, ship–sheep*).

However, in order to improve, students need to actually see and understand how the sounds they find hard are produced. Robin Walker's excellent book *Teaching the Pronunciation of English as a Lingua Franca* (2010) provides advice on how to tackle this in class.

While working on individual sounds is important, it is worth remembering that the students are less likely to confuse words if they learn, hear and process them as part of collocations, rather than as single items. For a Japanese student, say, the individual words lock and rock may sound the same, but they share few collocations or colligations:

lock the door	*rock from side to side*
fit a new lock	*listen to rock music*

Students in multilingual classes struggle with different sounds, so a focus on collocations means some students will find some sounds easy to produce/hear, but others won't. Such a focus is more relevant to everyone, and avoids any explicit focus on discrete minimal pairs.

Coursebooks often have word lists, but rarely include common collocations. You can choose words from the lists that include problematic sounds for your learners. Think of collocates that go with these words. These can be given as a dictation (see page 109). It is good if problem sounds appear in different positions in words.

When checking answers, you can also help with the productive side of pronunciation, working with either individuals or with the class as a whole.

Practising the principle

- Make a list of phonemes* that you think the students you teach struggle with:
  - If you teach monolingual students and share your students' first language, you probably already know which English sounds are tricky for your learners.
  - If you teach monolingual students but don't speak their L1, you may still have noticed problems with particular sounds. You could also use a reference source such as the Robin Walker book mentioned earlier, or *Learner English* (2001).
  - If you have multilingual classes, choose different sounds that are hard for two or three of the main language groups you teach.
- Look at the audio script on page 112. Find as many words as you can that include the phonemes you have chosen. From this, make a smaller list of 6–10 items. To help you choose, try to find:
  - words that may well be new – for learners at Pre-Intermediate /A2-B1 level.
  - words that feature problem sounds in different places (as initial, middle, final sounds, etc).
  - words for which you can easily think of frequent, natural-sounding collocates.
- Write a list of collocations using the words you selected. Choose more than one collocation per item.
- If you don't know already, find out exactly how the problem phonemes you have selected are made.

Applying the principle

- Either look at an audio script for a listening you have recently done, or at the word list for a unit you have recently finished teaching.
- Make a list of 8–12 words from the audio script/list that contain tricky phonemes for your students.
- Write collocations based on these words, and dictate them in your next lesson.
- Let the students compare ideas in pairs. Then elicit answers from the whole class. Write the answers on the board and drill the collocations. Help the students with tricky sounds, by showing them how they are made.

Beyond the listening lesson 2

Focusing on sound–spelling

Principle

The relationship between spelling and pronunciation in English is very inconsistent. Sound–spelling problems mostly involve vowel sounds, but also occur with certain combinations of letters, such as *-ough*. Students often only see words written down, and so may be unable to hear them when listening.

Given this, practising pronunciation through spelling is necessary. It also provides opportunities to revise language, especially if followed by pronunciation exercises with new questions about the language being practised (see pages 44–49). When revising, you should be able to ask questions without any extra explanation or examples.

Many coursebooks have word lists you can use to focus on sound–spelling. For example, with the list below, you might explore ways the letter 'a' is pronounced in the words that include it:

access	*original*	*original*	*search*
advantage	*essay*	*pretend*	*save*
affect	*finance*	*promise*	*straight*
appear	*harm*	*quote*	
assume	*law*	*recognise*	
create	*mix*	*retake*	

- In class, give some keywords containing 'a' as examples of the different ways the letter is said:

  cat *walk* *make* *part* *around* *mountain* *said*

- The students can then match the ways 'a' is pronounced in the words in the list to these keywords.
- When checking answers, you may sometimes need to correct the students' pronunciation. You might also give examples of usage (thus ensuring the students hear the sounds in context) and ask extra questions.
- Note that the main key to ensuring vowel sounds are comprehensible is maintaining the difference between long and short vowel sounds such as /iː/ and /I/ and between 'monophthongs'* (single vowel sounds like /e/ or /u/) and 'diphthongs'* (compounds of two sounds such as /ei/).

Practising the principle

- Look at the word list below based on a B2-C1/Upper-Intermediate lesson. Decide what to focus on:
  - Choose a vowel and a consonant sound that are pronounced in a range of different ways within the selected words.

boiling	*discovery*	*mosquito*	*soldier*
bomb	*effect*	*occasion*	*storm*
boost	*evidence*	*pet*	*sense*
cancer	*environment*	*protect*	*smell*
cage	*fund*	*rare*	*terrorist*
conduct	*investigate*	*rocket*	*term*
detect	*insect*	*snow*	

- Think of other words that students at this level should already know, to show the sounds you want them to find/practise (see *Principle*).
- Finally, decide:
  - what questions you would ask about the words above that you focus on.
  - what examples might result from these questions.

Applying the principle

- Look at the word list from a unit you have recently completed in your coursebook.
  - If you don't have a word list, make your own.
- Choose one or two key sounds/spellings that you want to focus on.
- Choose some lower-level parallel words that illustrate the different sounds connected to your particular letters or combinations of letters.
- Write them on the board.
- Ask the students to go through their word list and match words with the same sound to your list of simpler words on the board.
- Elicit answers from the whole class.
  - Make sure that the students say the words, and correct pronunciation when necessary.
- At this point, you may also ask questions about the words and give extra examples.

Beyond the listening lesson 3

Dictation, dictogloss and grammaring

Principle

Dictation was once popular in language teaching, but fell out of favour during the Communicative Language Teaching era. It came to be seen as a relic of the Grammar Translation, and was condemned for not being in line with the way fluent users utilise language.

However, it has since been reappraised and today there is increased awareness of its many advantages, namely:

- It practises 'bottom-up' processing. When students listen and try to write down what they hear, they need to process individual sounds and sound combinations, and then also use lexical, syntactical, discoursal and contextual knowledge.
- It provides listening practice, but also involves writing, reading and speaking (when the students check/compare texts).
- It can raise awareness of words the students are not hearing/noticing when listening – and of any sound–spelling issues.
- It gives students a chance to notice such features of spoken English as weak forms, linking, elision, etc.
- It can be used at any level.
- The focus can be shifted more towards lexis, grammar or texts.

At this stage, it's worth noting the difference between a dictation, which usually focuses on phrases/sentences that can be held in the short-term working memory, and a dictogloss*, which focuses on longer stretches of text and involves more of what Diane Larsen-Freeman (2003) called grammaring* – adding knowledge of grammar to the key verbs and nouns that are heard.

In class, it's good to:

- first read out your phrases/sentences/text at a relatively fast natural speed, with weak forms, etc.
- give the students time to complete their notes on their own, and to then compare ideas with a partner.
- hear the phrases/sentences/text again, this time perhaps said slightly more slowly.
- elicit ideas from the whole class. Write up the correct version/s on the board, highlighting – and drilling – relevant features of connected speech or problematic sound–spelling issues.

Practising the principle

- Look at the classroom activities in the box below. Think about:
  - when each one might be done – and why.
  - what aspect/s of phonology each one might test.
  - if any other lexical, syntactical, discoursal or contextual knowledge may be required.
  - what problems the students may have in each case.

1. Dictate the first two lines of a conversation that the students are going to listen to later.
2. Dictate a range of sentences based around a particular structural pattern (eg *How long have you been doing that? How long have you been waiting?*)
3. Give the students eight keywords and then dictate eight sentences, each of which features one of the words.
4. Dictate eight minimal pairs (eg *vest–best*).
5. Dictate a short text of between 50–60 words based on a topic that has been – or will be – studied.
6. Give the students eight key nouns or verbs. Dictate a range of collocations/chunks containing each one. These should be things you have previously covered. The students then write whole sentences for each item.
7. Dictate pairs of sentences that feature different meanings of words (eg *The roots go a long way down / We need to get to the root of the problem*).
8. Dictate 8–10 sentences previously covered in class, but, before each one, say how many words the sentence contains. The students then compare in pairs.

Applying the principle

- Choose one of the activities above that you have not done. Include it in your next lesson. Think about:
  - the lexical or grammatical areas you want to focus on.
  - the phonological aspect/s of the language you want to dictate that will cause most problems.
- Before class, practise saying the phrases/sentences/text that you are going to dictate, first fast and then more slowly. Try to keep the features of connected speech.

Beyond the listening lesson 4

Receptive and productive drills

Principle

In the past, drilling was often used as a way of encouraging students to produce grammatical structures. However, it is now widely recognised that being able to hear and reproduce particular examples of a structure over a short period of time is in no way guaranteed to result in an ability to use the structure in any broader sense. There has also been criticism of the fact that many of the examples of structures that were drilled lacked any real meaning for the learners.

However, as lexical teachers, we believe that drilling collocations, chunks and whole sentences can have value, as it:

- provides intensive exposure to features of connected speech – and encourages practice of these.
- gives the students a chance to get their tongues round potentially tricky bits of language.
- may help develop both receptive and productive automaticity, with regard to particular chunks.
- can be used in a meaningful way.
- can be energising, motivating and fun!

In class, you might:

- drill new language both chorally – with the whole class – and individually, listening for problems and then remodelling or slowing down accordingly.
- break down longer sentences like *You'll just have to wait and see* down by backchaining them – starting from the end and working back, so the students repeat *see, wait and see, have to wait and see*, etc.
- start by drilling slowly, and then speed up.
- ask several individual students the same question, so they hear it repeated and have a chance to get used to the way it sounds. However, instead of repetition, encourage natural/true answers. (eg *How long've you been learning English, Andreas? / For six months. / And Mika, how long've you been learning English? / Too long!*)
- use sentences as prompts, to elicit recently taught responses (eg *I work in a bank / That must be tough // I work in a bank / That must be well-paid //* I *work in a shop / You must work long hours*).

Practising the principle

- Look at the language in the box below. Decide:
  - which phonological aspects of each sentence the students might find hard to hear/reproduce – and how this will change, depending on whether the students hear a 'greenhouse, garden or jungle' version (see page 101).
  - at which level you might drill each sentence.
  - which might need to be backchained – and where you'd break those ones for drilling.
  - which could be varied.
  - which could be used receptively to prompt natural/true answers or responses from the students.

1. Unfortunately – *Unfortunately I couldn't.*
2. Toothpaste – *Have you got any toothpaste?*
3. *So how often do you go running, then?*
4. *Why did you decide to study here?*
5. *It's a waste of time.*
6. *There's no pleasing some people.*
7. *I wouldn't eat that if you paid me.*
8. *I haven't made up my mind yet.*
9. *What have you been doing since the last time we met?*
10. *I'd been thinking about doing it for ages, and in the end I just decided to give it a try.*

Applying the principle

- Look at the language in the next unit you of your coursebook – or in the next lesson you plan to give. Choose 6–8 collocations, chunks or whole sentences that you think would be good to drill. Think about the issues outlined above in *Practising the principle*.
- Decide at what exact point in your lesson you are going to drill each item – and how you are going to do it.
- Try to implement your plan in class.
- Afterwards, think about what went well and what – if anything – you might do differently in the future.

Appendix

Chapter Five

Script 1

Ana: OK. OK. Are we all ready? Can we start?

Ben: Maya's on her way. She'll be here in a second.

Cal: Guy's just speaking to a student. He said he might be five or ten minutes.

Ana: OK, well, we've got quite a lot to pack in in quite a short time, so maybe we should just get started and they can catch up. Anyone else not here? No? … No? Good. OK then well, we're getting to the end of term so we need to make sure we're all up to date with tutorials and paperwork. And make sure … er … you need to have completed all the assessments in time to write the reports. Remember, the parents' evening is on the 9th.

Dan: The 9th! I thought it was the 16th?

Ana: Er … no. I think it was fairly clear.

Dan: It's a Tuesday, isn't it?

Ana: Yeah. I did send an email about it a while ago – and it's on the staff noticeboard. Did anyone else have it down wrongly?

Cal: No. No. I have it down as the 9th.

Dan: OK. Sorry. It's my fault.

Ana: Is it going to be a problem?

Dan: Well, someone offered me a ticket for the Champions League game.

Ana: Right. What time does it start?

Dan: I need to be there by half seven really.

Ana: Well, there's not much we can do. You'll just have to miss the start of the game.

Dan: What if I made sure all my appointments finished by, say, 7.15?

Ana: I'm not sure you'll be able to fit them all in and some parents might not be able to make it before then.

Dan: But if I could sort it out …

Ana: Listen, I'm not saying no, but I think we need to discuss it.

Dan: OK.

Ana: I can't promise anything – it's not me who's double-booked, but catch me after the meeting.

Dan: OK.

Maya: Hi. Sorry I'm late. Have I missed anything?

Ben: Not really. End of term, paperwork, parents' evening and all that.

Maya: OK.

Ana: Any other issues with anyone about the run up to the end of term?

Cal: Well, kind of yeah, I mean I know I've mentioned it before … and er I don't know if I'm speaking for everyone, but I do find – especially this term with the parents' evening and also the bank holidays interrupting things and the extra assessment, that it's just, well, it's all a bit too much coming at the same time and, you know, well, I was wondering whether it was possible to, you know, either cut out some things or spread things out a bit more.

Dan: Yeah, it IS difficult getting everything done.

Ana: OK – what does everyone else think?

Guy: Hi, sorry. I was just dealing with a student.

Ana: Yeah, Cal said – no problem, I er I was just. Well, Cal was just saying she finds the end of this term a bit much, with all the assessments and everything and was asking if we could change things and I was just wondering how everyone else felt.

Guy: Right, yeah. Yeah. I mean, personally, yes I find it is a lot to do, 'cos, for example with the bank holiday, I was supposed to do an assessment that day and because we were off I had to put it off to this week and now I'll be struggling to get it all marked and the reports done.

Maya: Yeah, the same thing's happened to me.

Ben: The reports are a bit of a pain, to be honest. I mean, they take ages to do and I'm not sure how useful they are – especially when we're going to meet the parents anyway.

Ana: … er right. Well … *[fade out]*

Appendix

Chapter Five

Script 2

A: Are you hungry?

B: Yeah, a bit. And you?

A: Yeah, I am – quite. Do you want to get something to eat, then?

B: Yeah, OK. Have you got anywhere in mind?

A: Well, there's a good Turkish place just round the corner.

B: Ah, to be honest, I don't really feel like Turkish. I had a big kebab on my way home last night, so ...

A: Oh, right. OK.

B: So if it's alright with you, I'd rather have something different. Do you know anywhere else good round here?

A: Well, there's an Indonesian place up in Hendon.

B: Is it very spicy? I can't take it if it's too hot

A: It's not too bad, no, and anyway, there are loads of dishes to choose from, so you're bound to find something you'll like.

B: Well, if you're sure.

A: And the food was great last time I was there.

B: OK. Go on, then. You've talked me into it.

A: Cool. So shall we walk or do you want to get a cab?

B: Let's just walk. It's such a lovely evening. It won't take long, will it?

A: No, half an hour at most.

Chapter Six

Teaching writing lexically

Issues around writing

Finding the right focus for your students

Principle

It could be argued that the dominant model of language in ELT is a written one, as grammar is often presented via written texts, and practice frequently involves students writing whole sentences. As previously discussed, such sentences can often seem quite unnatural in conversational contexts.

Furthermore, if you start by thinking about whole conversations and examples, you may also find that students need quite different language to what you expected or have taught. We believe it is mainly this language gap that causes difficulties when speaking – rather than any lack of skills.

In reality, though, some of these same issues apply to writing, particularly when students tackle specific genres (kinds of texts). They may not know:

- the specific language common to texts within the genre (see page 115).
- the way texts are normally structured (page 116).
- how parts are linked and made cohesive (page 117).

You can, therefore, help students by starting with a generic text, then drawing attention to the aspects above and providing focused practice to help the students use these aspects in their own texts. Indeed, this may be easier to do for writing than for speaking, because students will usually want to write a restricted set of texts in English.

Many cousebooks do have specific writing lessons based around a model, but you may still consider if the models:

- reflect any writing that the students need to do.
- are a decent representation of what they need to write.
- are analysed and exploited for language, structure and linking as above.

If the students have no need for the writing, does the lesson offer any benefit – or could you do something different?

Practising the principle

- Make a list of the different kinds of texts that your students may need to write in English in their lives outside of class. Work with a colleague if possible.
- From your list, choose two types of text – and, ideally, find one or more models of each text. Alternatively, imagine their typical features. Then discuss:
  - any specific language connected to each text.
  - the way each text is normally structured.
  - how the parts are linked.
  - how you might focus on these things in class.
- If you think your students do not need to learn how to write any specific genres of writing, discuss:
  - whether you think writing might have any other value for the students.
  - what writing you might ask them to do.
  - what it might be better for them to do instead of writing – particularly for homework.

Applying the principle

- Interview your students or give them a short questionnaire, to find out:
  - what they write in English outside the class (not including set homeworks).
  - if they intend to do an exam in English in the next couple of years and, if so, which one.
- Look through the coursebook you are using, or the writing lessons you have previously given, and decide:
  - if any of the models reflect the needs of your students.
  - if the models are fully exploited and, if not, how you might improve on this.
- Finally, consider how you might cope if the students have very differing needs:
  - Would you help all the students with all the text types needed?
  - Could the students somehow work on different texts?

Analysing written texts

Genre and a lexical view of language

Principle

Genres are types of writing marked by consistent features of organisation, lexis and patterns across texts within the genre. For example, the following two extracts express similar meanings in different genres:

Situated in the heart of the city, just a two-minute walk from the Sagrada Familia, the four-star Neptune Hotel is an ideal base for exploring Barcelona.

This is the link for the hotel we stayed in. It's a bit pricey, but it's worth it just to be so central. The Sagrada Familia is literally just round the corner.

A 'grammar + words' view of the 'guide' genre could well lead to teaching and practice of such areas as:

- formality (eg no contractions in more formal texts).
- long noun phrases (eg *a two-minute walk from the Sagrada Familia*).
- participle clauses (eg *Situated in …, …*).
- positive adjectives (eg *ideal*, etc).

However, as lexical teachers, we would argue that writers do not write generic texts from rules in this way. We prefer to focus first on the specific chunks and then on limited variations – if the chunks can be varied at all:

Situated in the heart of …, [the place] is …
a two-minute walk from / a ten-minute bus ride from …

This is the link for … the hotel we stayed in
the gallery I mentioned

You can also draw attention to grammar, by asking concept questions such as 'Why is it *two-minute* and not *two minutes*?' (see also page 62). Where you do expand on grammar, practice is best restricted to examples the students might use in their own writing within the same genre.

Practising the principle

- Look at the extracts below. Decide:
  - what each genre is.
  - what chunks or patterns could be highlighted and exploited.
  - whether you would concept check any grammar.
  - what vocabulary you would use if you were going to practise that grammar further.

1 I am writing to enquire about the possibility of doing an internship with your company.

2 *Man on Wire* is a gripping documentary recounting Philippe Petit's 1977 high-wire act between the World Trade Center's twin towers.

3 In terms of transport links, more could be done to coordinate the different services.

4 Just a quick one to let you know there'll be six of us coming later.

5 Recent theory suggests that accuracy in face recognition is influenced by motivation, with people being particularly motivated to remember in-group faces, as opposed to those 'out of group'. The study sought to examine whether multicultural experience moderated this effect.

6 A two-bedroom, first-floor flat situated on St. John's Way in the sought-after area of Lower Highgate. Consisting of 16' 8 reception room with bay windows, separate kitchen, two bedrooms and bathroom.

7 Gone to shops. Back 10-ish.

8 The snow had been falling all night and it lay thick on the ground.

Applying the principle

- Look at a model of a text you plan to teach, and underline any chunks or patterns.
- Decide how you will exploit these in class.

Helping students organise written work

Macro-structures and micro-structures

Principle

We have already seen how a 'grammar + words' view of language can lead to the study of specific examples of 'written' grammar, not all of which will necessarily be useful when practising a given genre. In addition to this, ELT materials often emphasise the importance of paragraphs and topic sentences* – the opening sentences of paragraphs that summarise the content to come. The advice given is often quite general. The students may be told, for example, that 'an essay consists of an introduction, a discussion and a conclusion', or that it's best to 'start a new paragraph for each big new idea within your essay'.

This is a start, but it overlooks the fact that many genres of writing not only have relatively fixed macro-structures*, but also contain fairly predictable micro-structures: parts of the whole will often pattern in similar ways. This is why certain chunks often perform particular functions within genres.

Take, for instance, the kind of short 'for and against' essays featured in the IELTS exam. The macro-structure of such pieces is often:

1 Introduction.
2 Explore a 'weak' point of view you disagree with.
3 Explain why you disagree, and present 'stronger' views.
4 Conclusion.

However, within this, there are other micro-structures that students benefit from seeing. For example, as can be seen in Text 1 in the Appendix on page 124, we often begin such introductions by describing current trends or problems connected to the title. This shows we grasp the importance of the issue. To do this, we tend to use the present perfect or present continuous. We may well then use *As such* to introduce a question connected to the essay title, before making it clear what our own opinion about the issue in the title is.

Practising the principle

- Look at the writing tasks in the box below. Decide how you would expect each of the different kinds of texts to be structured. Think about:
  - the number of paragraphs – and what the function of each paragraph typically is.
  - whether any particular paragraphs pattern in relatively predictable ways. If so, how?
  - any chunks that might be commonly used to perform particular functions at particular points within the texts.

1 You are on holiday. Write a postcard to a good friend.

2 You recently had a bad experience with an airline company. Decide what problems you had. Then write a short letter of complaint.

3 Write a short email making a request to a hotel or company.

4 You are applying for a summer job as a youth camp leader. Write a covering letter to accompany your CV.

5 Write a story beginning with the sentence: *I felt angry as I got off the bus.*

6 Write a review of a book, film or exhibition you have enjoyed recently.

7 Write a report of between 250 and 300 words on the topic of public transport where you live.

8 Write a short essay on the problems of global obesity. Suggest some ways of tackling the problem.

Applying the principle

- Look at the writing lessons in the coursebook you are using, or at writing lessons you have given. Decide:
  - how much information is given about the general structure of each text type the students have to write.
  - if any information is given on micro-structures.
  - if any structural aspects of the texts have been overlooked, and how they could be focused on.

Linking words and phrases

Moving beyond function

Principle

Given that they are among the few pieces of language that generally recur across a range of different genres, it is no surprise that linking words* and phrases often feature in writing lessons. They are frequently presented in groups that have shared functions, such as contrasting (*Although*, *Despite*, *In spite of*, etc) or addition (*In addition*, *Furthermore*, *Not only ... but also*, etc).

While such items are obviously worth spending time on, looking at them in groups or as synonyms can be problematic. There are several reasons for this:

- No two items ever function as exact synonyms, and linking words are no exception. Each item tends to be used with particular grammatical patterns, and may well also frequently occur with specific chunks.
- Items may also either link ideas within sentences or across them – and appear in particular parts of texts.
- One linking word or phrase may occur more commonly in a certain genre than another with a similar function.

Even when students learn a range of linking words and phrases, they still need sufficient language within which to embed them. For example, in many ways, knowing the words *Firstly*, *Secondly*, etc, is the easy part. Filling the gaps between these words is more challenging.

All of the above suggests that when we tackle linking words in class, we need to pay attention to more than just their meanings and functions. We also need to focus on:

- grammatical patterns that often go with particular linkers – and their locations in sentences/texts.
- whether some linkers are more common in certain genres.
- any chunks that frequently co-occur with the linkers.
- additional language that will help the students integrate the linking words and phrases into specific texts.

Practising the principle

- Look at the groups of linking words/phrases in the box below. Use your own knowledge, a learners' dictionary or sites that allow access to corpora – such as *www.phrasesinenglish.org* – to find out whether:
  - the grammatical patterns connected to the words/phrases, in each group differ at all.
  - the words/phrases more commonly link ideas *within* sentences or *across* them.
  - certain words/phrases are commonly used in particular kinds of texts.
  - any items recur with particular chunks.

1 *despite, whilst, that notwithstanding, on the other hand* (contrast)

2 *otherwise, unless, as long as, in case* (conditions)

3 *subsequently, during, the second, afterwards* (time/order)

4 *so as to, so that, consequently, thus* (purpose/result)

5 *thanks to, on account of, due to, a result of* (cause)

- Next, try to write one example for each linking word/phrase in order to illustrate how it might be used in a short 'for and against' IELTS-style essay of the kind shown in Text 1 on page 124. When you have finished, decide:
  - if some linking words/phrases within each group were easier to think of examples for. If so, why?
  - if there were any items you found it very hard to think of examples for. If so, why?

Applying the principle

- Find a writing lesson you have done or want to do that includes a focus on linking words/phrases. Decide:
  - to what degree the lesson looks at the areas mentioned in *Principle*.
  - how it could be improved.
  - which items are most relevant to the genre being looked at – and why.

Exploiting model texts

Tasks focusing on aspects of text construction

Principle

If you have a model text illustrating the kind of writing that you want your students to try and produce, you can initially use it in similar ways to a reading text. You may have some kind of pre-reading discussion and then set a gist task (see pages 86–87). However, it is unlikely that you will want to have more detailed comprehension questions or to use the text for practice of such 'skills' as skimming and scanning. Instead, greater attention ought to be paid to the features of text construction that we have already looked at. Certain kinds of tasks are particularly well suited to focusing on certain aspects.

To focus on chunks relevant to the genre, you can:

- remove them from the model and present them in a box. The students then fill the gaps.
- highlight in some way key verbs or nouns, and ask the students to find collocates in the text.
- highlight chunks. Ask the students to cover the text after reading and do a vocabulary exercise based on them.

When checking answers, repeat some of the techniques from the 'Teaching vocabulary lexically' chapter.

To focus on macro- and micro-structure*, you can:

- ask the students to discuss the function of individual paragraphs or of specific parts within paragraphs.
- present the text as one long paragraph, and ask the students to split it up. They then discuss their ideas.

To focus on linking words and phrases, you can:

- include pairs of similar linkers in the text, and let the students choose the correct one by focusing on surrounding patterns, etc.
- remove the linkers and either give them to students in a box and ask them to gap-fill the text, or else simply let them decide what they think the missing items are.

Practising the principle

- Look at the model Text 1 on page 124, and write an exercise or task focusing on each of the areas below. You may want to use some of the task types given in *Principle*, or you may have other ideas:
  - The macro-structure of the piece.
  - Any micro-structures you can see within individual paragraphs.
  - 6–10 collocations/chunks typical of this kind of writing.
  - Linking words or phrases.
  - Grammatical features or patterns that you think are typical of the genre.
- Finally, think what kind of feedback you would give on each task – and if there are any additional examples you would give, or questions you might ask.

Applying the principle

- Find a writing lesson you have done or want to do that includes a model text. Look at the exercises directly connected to the text and decide:
  - which features of text construction (chunks, structure, grammar, linking words/phrases) are looked at.
  - if you think the exercises that are there already exploit these areas to a sufficient degree. If they don't, what's missing? How could they be improved?
  - on one extra exercise or task that could be added to focus more on an area currently overlooked.
- Add the extra exercise or task to the material. Think about where in the lesson it would make most sense to include it – and how you will set it up and then give feedback on it in class.
- When you (next) teach the lesson, include the improvements and additions that you came up with.

Process writing

Brainstorming and planning to focus on language

Principle

As discussed in Part A, many teachers advocate what is often described as a process approach to writing, which emphasises developing the skills of being a good writer:

- Brainstorming ideas and doing research.
- Planning and ordering ideas.
- Drafting and rewriting (and sometimes starting again!)
- Final editing.

As professional writers ourselves, we agree that these are important skills. However, we also know that when we do the things above, we do so with our prior knowledge of language and genre. As we have seen, some of this knowledge can be presented to students via model texts. However, 'skills' tasks can also have a language focus.

For example, if the students brainstorm ideas about what to include in a hotel advert, they may say 'centre' or 'near the airport'. A skills view may see this as sufficient, but lexical teachers would also feed in examples like *it's in the heart of the city*, *it's a ten-minute drive from the airport*, etc. Brainstorming can also be more language focused: eg the students can try to come up with synonyms or collocates of words that are key to the genre.

When the students do research to write a text, you can ask them to find key quotes to support their arguments, but you can then also encourage them to look at ways of paraphrasing these quotes or introducing them within a text (*As Smith notes/states in his article …*, etc).

When the students plan, they could suggest phrases for starting emails, for example, or write initial topic sentences for each paragraph. These can be corrected and discussed before they write a complete first draft.

Later in the chapter, we will look at editing and redrafting.

Practising the principle

- Look at the model Text 1 on page 124, and underline any collocations or phrases that you think are more common in written English than spoken English.
- Look in the box below at different brainstorming and planning ideas for the essay *'Some sports stars earn far too much money'. How far do you agree?*
  - Make a list of the responses you think might be generated. If you can, check your ideas by doing some or all of the tasks with your own students.
  - Reformulate the responses you or your students came up with as they might be written.

1 Discuss in pairs your own opinions on the question.

2 Think of six reasons to support the statement and six reasons to oppose it.

3 Discuss which you think are the most persuasive arguments for and against the statement. What evidence could you give to support these arguments?

5 Think of reasons why sports stars' pay might be an issue. What examples of high earnings can you think of?

4 Underline the keywords in the essay question. What other words/phrases are connected with those keywords?

6 Imagine you agree with this statement. Discuss how you might start each paragraph in your essay.

Applying the principle

- For the next writing task you plan to do, decide:
  - what brainstorming or planning tasks you will do.
  - the written language you hope to generate.
- In class, provide some of this language as you monitor, and do feedback to the task(s).
- Use some of the techniques discussed in the chapter on 'Teaching speaking lexically'.

Completing the process

Encouraging drafting and redrafting

Principle

Hopefully, students will write their texts after studying an appropriate model and some relevant language. Ideally, they should also have brainstormed ideas and planned what to write. Typically, the writing is then done at home, the teacher grades the texts and then hands them back. In many cases, that is the end of the process.

From a process writing point of view, this is bad because the students are not learning to develop such good writing strategies as making corrections and writing multiple drafts of a text. It should be noted, though, that students may already be 'good writers' and may have corrected and rewritten parts or all of the text before submitting it as their 'best' version.

This may not always be clear, as the text may be hand-written. Nevertheless, it is still clear that good writers rewrite in response to feedback as well, and this probably should be encouraged.

From our point of view, there is the additional issue that the students may be missing out on an opportunity to learn language from the errors they make. As we saw in Part A, for learning to take place, students need to:

- pay attention to items and notice their features.
- do something with the items – use them in some way.

Evidence suggests that students don't pay close attention to corrections if they don't have to rewrite texts. This is especially true when texts are graded: the grade becomes all that counts. A simple way to encourage students to pay more attention is to get them to rewrite their texts, taking account of suggestions and corrections you make.

Learning can then be further stimulated by encouraging the students to revisit previous mistakes and language fed in during the redrafting stages when they attempt future writing tasks. This may be particularly effective if the students are writing within the same genre.

Practising the principle

- Mark Text 2 in the Appendix on page 124 as you would if it had been written by a student of yours at B1 level.
- Compare your marking with a colleague and discuss:
  - if you normally get students to rewrite their texts.
  - how far the way you mark may help them rewrite.
- Discuss how the strategies below might encourage:
  - self-correction before handing in the 'first' draft.
  - redrafting in response to your feedback.
- Can you think of any other strategies?

1. Ask the students to word process their essays.
2. Show them how to use a spell checker.
3. Ask them to use the track changes feature when writing in Word or a web-based processor such as Google Docs.
4. Withhold grades until the students do a second draft.
5. Ask the students to read their text aloud to themselves or to each other before handing it in.
6. Tell them to read for one particular error, then read for a second kind of error, etc.
7. Limit the number of comments you give, focusing first on structure and then on language.
8. Ask the students to grade their own and each other's texts.

Applying the principle

- The next time you do a writing with your students, make sure they redraft their texts before handing them in, and again in response to your feedback.
- Try strategies from *Practising the principle*.
- Reflect on how you feel about the process.
- Ask your students how they felt about it.

Using criteria for feedback

Linking teaching, evaluation and learning

Principle

Grades for writing may be necessary, and students may be desperate to see how they have done; but grades can also be fairly meaningless and have little to do with improving performance. This is because students often have no real idea about what is being graded, and while teachers may have a general idea of what they want, they may also vary grades based on other factors – such as mood, attitude to the students, or comparisons with other texts. Grades also offer little or no information about how texts can be improved. As such, they just end up reinforcing the students' existing beliefs about their abilities.

Professional testing bodies try to overcome this by using criteria against which texts are evaluated. Markers compare marks to develop consistency. While 'double marking' may be impractical in your context, using criteria should make grading more consistent and provide a framework that shows:

- what you are expecting before the students write.
- how they might improve their writing in their redraft.

You could just use an exam board's criteria for an exam at your students' level. These are generally freely available on the web. However, the feedback derived from these criteria are quite general. If we write criteria based on a genre, it can make teaching and learning more 'visible' (see Hattie, 2011) by highlighting:

- structure and features, such as titles and subheadings.
- specific examples of grammar/patterns in the genre.
- specific examples of the kind of vocabulary used in the genre.
- an error you are working on.

The criteria should still reflect the level of the students, so a top grade at B1, for example, would not be faultless and may still contain pointers as to how the student may develop.

Practising the principle

- Look at the criteria below for the writing in Text 2 on page 124. Consider:
  - how they reinforce genre.
  - what the criteria for a lower grade would be.
  - how you would grade the writing and what feedback you could give using the criteria.

8–10
The story is of interest and includes a clear ending with a comment on the whole story. We learn the background to the story and the main events are clearly described using two or three past tenses – mainly correctly – and sentences are linked with words such as *while*, *as* and *just then*. Other errors don't confuse the reader. The writer uses a variety of vocabulary, including some examples of expressive words such as *rush*, *crunch*, *terrifying* or *fortunately*. There are no errors with verb–person agreement.

6–7
The writer clearly describes the events story, but there is no comment on the whole story. The writer uses one or two past tenses, with some errors, and only basic linkers such as *and*, *then*, *after*. Other errors only cause slight confusion. The vocabulary is generally simple, such as *go*, *run*, *make a noise*, *scared*, etc, with one or two exceptions. There are errors with verb–person agreement.

Applying the principle

- Before you set your next writing task, write criteria.
- Explain the criteria to the students before they write.
- Write feedback on the students' first draft, based on the criteria and showing how they can improve the text.
- Get the students to rewrite, and then look at the text again and give a final grade (no comments or corrections).

Providing language-focused feedback

Correction codes, reformulation and explanations

Principle

As previously stated, the first thing to do when looking at a piece of student writing is read it all the way through, to see how well it conforms to our expectations about genre and structure. If the text fails to meet these expectations, then the accuracy of the language is basically irrelevant. Providing feedback on such work (and redrafting it) is made easier if we have written and shared the criteria by which the work is judged.

However, as lexical teachers, when we deal with student writing that broadly meets expectations, we also want to use feedback to tackle error and to teach new things.

One common way of tackling language errors is to use a code, where, for example, GR signifies a grammar error, and SP a wrong spelling. Codes can highlight errors that students then correct. These will basically be signs of a failure to correctly use items already studied. However:

- codes work less well with most errors, which occur simply because students do not know any better ways of expressing particular ideas.
- they are also problematic as they stem from a 'grammar + words' view of language, and thus fail to recognise how grammar and vocabulary impact on each other.

Consider this sentence: *The area has been deserted after a huge flooding three years ago.* The issue here is both lexical and grammatical, and if we assume this is the best version a student could produce, then a code approach won't result in much improvement. Given this, we need to reformulate and provide further explanations/examples. We may also need to ask questions and give options. For example:

Do you mean the area was evacuated during the terrible floods three years ago? Or that it has been uninhabitable since then? Or something else?

Note, by the way, that we use the past simple with 'three years ago' and the present perfect with 'since then'.

Practising the principle

- Look at Text 2 in the Appendix on page 124 again. First, choose *one* type of mistake (ideally a recurring one) that you think B1-level students would be able to correct on their own if you told them to look for it, underlined it or marked it with a code in some way.
- Next, find all the other things in the text that you think are wrong in some way. (Remember that many of these errors will be down to the fact the writer did not know a better/more accurate way of expressing their ideas.) Choose three to focus on.
- Reformulate these three errors and add explanations, where relevant. You may want to:
  - clarify why the use of particular words or structures was wrong.
  - give examples of more correct uses of items that were used wrongly.
  - explain and give examples of how to use any new items/structures from your reformulation.
- If you can, compare your reformulations and explanations/examples with a colleague. Discuss:
  - the similarities and differences in the way you approached the text.
  - whose feedback you think is better – and why.

Applying the principle

- Next time you look at a piece of student writing that meets your expectations in terms of genre and structure, highlight one (recurring) error that the students should be able to correct themselves.
- Then choose 3–5 parts of the text to reformulate. You may also want to explain why the students' efforts were wrong, and add extra information/examples.
- After you have returned the writing, ask the students how they feel about this kind of feedback, and discuss your rationale for trying it.

Other reasons for writing

The value of non-genre-based practice

Principle

So far, we have discussed teaching writing in terms of the production of texts within genres – for reasons made clear at the start of this chapter (see page 114). As we suggested there, many students have little need to write in English and are more concerned with developing their general language and speaking abilities. However, while we believe that improving speaking requires plenty of practice, writing – especially as a homework activity – may still have a role to play, even with these students.

Writing may help language development, because when students write, they:

- have more time to use a dictionary to find words.
- have more time to pay attention to various aspects of any 'new' language they may be practising.
- are doing something with the new language, and trying to integrate it with what they already know.

Writing may also allow teachers more time to:

- consider student errors and gaps in their knowledge.
- get to know more about the students as individuals, and build better relationships with them.

If you take the goals of general learning rather than genre practice into consideration, your feedback on writing may also change. You may just choose to respond as an individual, and ask questions or comment as you might in conversation. Where we do give feedback on language, as lexical teachers, we will want to maintain a focus on collocation and other chunks – not just surface grammar.

As this kind of writing is a purely formative exercise, with no 'ideal' answer, grading seems unnecessary. If you were to grade such tasks, however, the students would still need clear criteria, perhaps based on a measurement of effort.

Practising the principle

- Look at the non-genre tasks below. Consider:
  - what the main goal of each one is.
  - what feedback – if any – you might give.
  - what you like/do not like about each one.
  - what the criteria would be for a top grade, if you were to grade each one.
- Discuss with a colleague which of these kinds of writing task you have done – and explain any other tasks that you think would be good for this purpose.

1. Keep a personal diary.
2. Write a summary of a speaking task you did in class.
3. Write a conversation based on a topic you have studied.
4. Write sentences showing how to use ten new collocations.
5. Write a story including 8–10 words you learnt this week.
6. Write your thoughts about a text you studied this term. Include any extra information you have found out about it since.
7. Write about something you read this week (in English or L1), why you read it and what you thought of it.
8. Write all the new vocabulary you learnt this week in a vocabulary notebook or on cards. Add examples.

Applying the principle

- Present the writing tasks above to your students, along with any others that you came up with.
- Talk about why these tasks may be useful to do.
- Get the students to choose one task (individually or as a group) to do for homework.
- Explain what feedback you will give (if any) – and the criteria for grades, if relevant.

Appendix

Chapter Six

Text 1

Sample piece of generic writing:
An IELTS 'for and against' essay.

'Some sports stars earn far too much money.'
How far do you agree with this statement?

The amount of money that top footballers and other sports stars earn has increased dramatically over recent years. The stars of today earn more in a week than most fans can dream of earning in a year. As such, it is worth asking if they are paid too much and whether action now needs to be taken. Personally, I think there are good reason why wages should remain high.

There are several arguments against maintaining the current high level of pay. Firstly, such wages seem disproportionate when compared to the far smaller amounts earned by public sector workers such as nurses or fire fighters. Secondly, many claim that having access to so much money at such a young age inevitably corrupts and encourages poor behaviour in people who are role models around the world.

However, despite this, the current situation still seems the best option to me. The fact is that sport generates huge amounts of revenue and it is only fair that a decent proportion of this goes to the stars themselves. In addition, top athletes can change the course of sporting events, and this, in turn, can bring in large sums to the teams they represent.

In conclusion, while it may seem unjust that top sports stars earn the amounts they do, it is wrong to claim that they are overpaid. Their high wages merely reflect their market value.

Text 2

Sample piece of student writing:
The following piece of writing was written by a student at B1 level in response to this task:

Write a short story that starts with the line:
It was three in the morning and the phone rang.

It was three in the morning when the phone rang. It was my best friend Lorena, and she told me she needs help because her car was broken. Inmediately, I dress up and I get my car quickly, and I went to see her. When I arrived there she was crying, she had an accident and smashed the windscreen She was really worried because the was her father's car. we didn't know what to do, so we decided to call a friend. Ten minutes later the police appears and we called my friend's parent and we explained to them all. We though that her father would be really furious, but he was really calmed, and he understand everything. They stay there, and I went home at 5 o'clock.

Chapter Seven

Recycling and revising

Recycling

Teacher-centred ways of ensuring repeated exposure

Principle

Recycling involves ensuring informal re-encounters with 'taught' language, as opposed to formal revision exercises that test it and encourage reproduction of it.

A lexical view of language stresses that knowing an item is complex, and learners cannot learn everything about a word or a grammatical structure in their first encounter. As such, learners will only ever have a provisional knowledge of language they have 'learnt', which will then be consolidated or altered as they learn more language or experience the restrictions that grammar and vocabulary place on each other.

This means that, for language to become useable, we need to repeat the process of learning over time in new contexts. If we only focus, say, on meaning in repeat encounters, students do not deepen their knowledge. By definition, recycling places language in new contexts.

Ideally, class material will recycle language in texts and other exercises. However, the teacher can also recycle language when:

- modelling speaking tasks – models can include previously taught items, and you can use stress and volume to draw attention to them (see page 75).
- giving explanations and examples of new language, such as an 'old' collocate with a new word.
- reformulating student output – particularly grammar words and forms that you write up and gap on the board (see page 77).
- writing your own exercises, or adapting published ones, to include items you have already explored.

Recycling is often quite passive, so, to be most effective, we may need to actively draw attention to new features.

Practising the principle

- Think about how often you consciously include grammar or vocabulary items you know you have previously taught when you are:
  - modelling speaking tasks.
  - reformulating student output.
  - explaining or exemplifying new language.
  - writing on the board examples of how new items are used.
  - writing your own worksheets/lessons.
- Try to think of five examples of particular items you have recycled recently. Then consider whether:
  - the inclusion of the items was planned or spontaneous.
  - you did anything to draw attention to the recycled items or to check understanding.
  - you drew attention to any new features, such as a new collocation or aspect of grammar.
- Finally, examine the coursebook or materials you are using in class in order to see if you can find examples of items being recycled within a unit, across the whole book – or even across the series.

Applying the principle

- Write a list of 20–30 items that you have taught in recent classes.
- Look at the material you are planning to use in your next two or three classes, and decide:
  - what opportunities there might be to recycle some of the items on your list.
  - how you will include particular items in your teacher talk and/or boardwork.
- In class, try to recycle the items as planned. Also, be aware of opportunities to include items on your list when reformulating student output – either orally or on the board.

Revising

Student-centred ways of ensuring active remembering

Principle

On the previous page, we stressed the need to see language in multiple contexts in order to deepen knowledge of the item. However, multiple encounters are also necessary to retain language in our long-term memory. There is plenty of evidence that consciously trying to recall language (not just passively seeing it) can speed up this process. Perhaps this is why actively revising words with flashcards enables the quicker learning of words than passive recycling within extensive reading.

In the rest of this chapter, we will look at ten revision tasks that we frequently use in class ourselves. For a far more comprehensive discussion on memory, and extra examples of activities, see Nick Bilbrough's book *Memory Activities for Language Learning* (CUP).

Of course, the first stage of revision is choosing the language to revise. Coursebook review units:

- often focus more on grammar than lexis.
- may only focus on single words and meaning.
- rarely revise language from reading/listening texts.

As teachers, we may do the same, perhaps adding in some language that came up in class and that we wrote on the board. This language may include relatively infrequent items that were a response to a particular student's need in a particular conversation. While that may have been good to do, you may not want to revise this with the whole class, and might instead choose something more frequent or generally useful.

While revision tasks may start from looking at language as the students first encountered it, you can still explore other aspects of word knowledge during feedback. Indeed, the more easily words are recalled, the more we should try to go beyond students' current knowledge.

Practising the principle

- Do you keep a record of language you have covered in class? If not, why not?
- If you do keep a record, does your list include:
  - language you have taught spontaneously and given examples of on the board?
  - language from vocabulary exercises in any classroom material you have used?
  - language from any listening/reading texts that you have explained or given examples of?
  - grammar? Just the name of the structures looked at, or actual example sentences?
- How do you decide which language – from your list or from the classroom materials you use – to revise?
- How often do you do revision in class?
- How long do you spend on revision in any given lesson – and at what point in a lesson do you do it?
- What feedback do you give? How far do you explore other aspects of word knowledge or new examples of grammar?
- Look at the activities on the next pages, and decide:
  - which you do already.
  - what aspect of the language is tested.
  - if there are any problems with the task.

Applying the principle

- Decide what language you want to revise in your next lesson.
- Decide if you want to test the same aspect of word knowledge you taught before, or a new one.
- Choose one of the revision activities on the following pages that you think fits best.
- Consider the feedback you will give, to expand on the items.
- Do the task.

Revision activity 1

Gapped sentences and dialogues

- Choose 10–15 items you have previously taught. Look at the contexts in which the students met them and either use the same sentences or write new sentences where the items retain the same meaning.
- Gap one or two words in each sentence. Once you have decided on your gaps, look again to check that the only possible answers are those you expect. For instance, for an Elementary/A2-level class that has recently looked at how to talk about experience, you might include something like this:
  Have you ever .... to Japan?
  > No, never. .... you?
  Yeah. I .... there on holiday a few years ....
- In class, give out your handout and let the students see what they can remember on their own. When some have finished, put the students in pairs to check their ideas and help each other. Then elicit the answers from the whole class.
- Write the correct answers on the board, so that all the students can see them. You may also want to:
  - elicit the pronunciation of certain items, and mark the stress and the number of syllables.
  - drill certain items – both as individual words and as part of the wider chunk they appear in (eg *ago – a few years ago – I went there on holiday a few years ago*).
  - concept check any grammar that comes up in the exercise (eg *What tense do we use here? Why? Yes, right – because of 'a few years ago'*).
  - elicit – or give – extra examples/variations of particular items (eg *last year, a couple of years ago, years and years ago*, etc).
- There are two ways you can vary the task to make it easier for the students:
  - You could provide the first letter of each missing word.
  - You could also give the missing words in a box at the top of the page, and simply ask the students to use them to fill in the gaps.

Revision activity 2

Language-generating questions

- Choose 10–15 items you have taught in class that you asked extra questions about – or that you now see you *could* have asked extra questions about. Most typically, these will be questions exploring:
  - collocation.
  - co-text.
  - contextual opposites (antonyms).
- Write questions about each item for the students to discuss in class. These should not be personal questions. Rather, they should be questions that allow further exploration of different aspects of usage. They may be questions you already asked the class in a previous lesson, or questions exploring slightly different aspects of usage (see page 45). Here are several sentence starters you can use:
  - *What does X-ing involve?*
  - *Where might/would you X?*
  - *Is X-ing good or bad? Why?*
  - *What's the opposite of X in this situation?*
  - *What kind of things can you X?*
  - *Say three different ways you could X.*
  - *What happens when you X?*
  - *What might you need to do if something X-es?*
  - *Say three things you could describe as being X.*
  - *Say two possible ways you could respond if someone said X.*
- In class, put the students in pairs, hand out the questions, and allow time for discussion. You may want to ask one question to the whole group and elicit answers in order to model the task.
- As the students talk, monitor and help with any questions they particularly struggle with.
- Round up by eliciting answers from the group. Reject any plainly incorrect ideas.
- Try to add some boardwork that expands on what comes up:
  - For instance, if one question is *What do you need to do if your car breaks down?* and a student replies '*garage*', you might write *My car broke down and I had to call a garage. They sent a mechanic out to repair it.*

Revision activity 3

Personal questions

- Choose 10–15 items you have taught in class that you think the students might be able to connect to their own lives/experiences of the world.
- Write questions for the students to discuss, using each item. You might want to highlight each item you are revising by marking it in bold. It is important to make sure the questions are open rather than closed.
- Here are some starters you can use:
  - *Have you ever X-ed? When? What was it like?*
  - *Have you ever been/felt X? When? What happened?*
  - *Have you got an X?*
  - *Have you ever used an X?*
  - *Have you ever been to an X?*
  - *Would you like to X? Why? Why not?*
  - *Can you think of an example of X? When did it happen? How much do you know about it?*
- With questions that could be seen as personal, it's better to ask, for example, *Do you know anyone who has …?* or *Have you heard of anyone who has …?* – rather than *Have you ever …* This allows for a broader range of responses, and yet still allows the students to talk about themselves, if they want to.
- In class, put the students in small groups, hand out your questions and allow 10–15 minutes for discussion. You may want to answer one question yourself – before the students start talking – in order to model what you expect. You could choose the question yourself or let the students pick one to ask you.
- As the students talk, monitor and help by sorting out any communication breakdowns and providing any new language the students require to express their ideas. During this time, you should also be looking to get some of this language onto the board.
- Round up by looking at some of the things the students tried to say. Ideally, while the students were talking, you found time to write whole sentences/short dialogues on the board and to choose which words to gap. Elicit/give the missing words.

Revision activity 4

Using translations

- Choose 10–15 items you have recently covered in class and enter them into a grid like the one shown below.
  - Note that, as lexical teachers, we use collocations or whole expressions with this particular activity, rather than just single words.

English	Your language
I had to take out a loan.	
Someone hacked into my account.	
Inflation rocketed.	

- Once you have completed your grid, with monolingual classes you can:
  - add translations yourself if you share the same first language as your students.
  - give the grid out and ask the students to work in pairs and agree on the best translations for each item. If you share the students' L1, elicit ideas to check. If you don't, ask for translations and if the students seem to agree, accept them.
- With multilingual classes, you can:
  - still get any students who share an L1 to help each other with translations.
  - get the students to translate on their own, asking for clarification of any items they are unsure of.
- The students can later use the grid to revise. They can work in pairs and take turns to cover the grid. One student says – or points to – the L1 expressions, the other tries to remember the exact words in English.
- With monolingual groups, the teacher (or a student) could read the L1 sentences and elicit the English from the whole group.
- Online sites can be used to make bilingual flashcards for students to revise from at home. See:
  www.quizlet.com
  www.memrise.com

Revision activity 5

Student-to-student elicitation

- Choose 12–16 items from recent classes. These might be single words, collocations or short phrases. For example, with an Upper-Intermediate class who recently studied language connected to the economy, items might include the following:

  in recession *cut bureaucracy*
  go bankrupt *boost the economy*

- Type the items out and then divide them into two equal lists of 6–8. Print the lists, and cut out enough copies so everyone can eventually get both lists.
- In class, divide the students into two equal groups. Give one group one set of cards, the other group the second set. Give the students time to check with other members of their group that they remember the words. They may need to ask you, check in dictionaries or ask other students for translations.
- Explain that each student will talk to a member of the other group, who has different words. They should not show their words or say them – even in their own language. Instead, they should take turns to explain their words and see if their partner can remember them. They should only say the words after they have tried and failed to elicit them. You may well want to do one example (not from the list) with the whole class to model the task.
- In lower-level classes, the students can act or draw the words rather than explain them.
- Pair the students with partners from the other group. As they explain their words, help out where necessary, monitor and write up some gapped examples, exploring other ways in which some of the better known items are used.
- Stop the activity. Send the students back to their seats and give out the lists of words their partners from the other group had. Give the students a few more minutes to check they understand all the items.
- Round up by looking at the boardwork. Elicit/give the missing words.

Revision activity 6

Choose three expressions

- Either compile a list of 20–30 items you have covered in class in recent lessons, or else simply ask the students to look through their own vocabulary records. Tell the students to choose three items, using one of the following criteria:
  - You like them and think they'll be useful.
  - You have used them recently– or have heard them being used.
  - You have forgotten what they mean and/or how to use them.
  - They remind you of a time or experience or person in your life.
  - You think they are good words for three other people in the class.
  - You don't like them – for whatever reason!
  - You could use them all in one short story.
- To model the task give one or two examples yourself, before the students choose.
- The students work in small groups or mingle and share their choices with their partners, explaining as much about each item as they can.
- While the students are talking, monitor and help out where necessary. Note problem words you may need to re-explain and write gapped examples on the board, to explore other aspects of word knowledge once students have finished.
- A more thorough alternative to this exercise involves encouraging the students to look at the whole list and to forge new connections with *all* the items. To do this, you could:
  - give out your list, ask the students to tick any items they can't remember and to then mingle in order to find someone who can explain them.
  - ask the students to organise all the items on the list into groups. Either provide the groups yourself (eg rooms in a house, countries, people in the class) or let the students decide on their own groups.

Revision activity 7

Text reconstruction

- Reading and listening texts are great sources of language that perhaps we don't revisit frequently enough, so, at the end of a class in which the students have read or listened to a text, tell them to try to remember as much of it as they can at home and make it clear you will come back to the text again. In the next lesson, you can:
  - read out the text (or selected parts of it), stopping in the middle of particular sentences, collocations or phrases. The students then shout out or write down what follows.
  - print a selection of gapped sentences/phrases from the text and ask the students to complete them with the missing words they saw/heard used.
  - select 6–10 verbs or adjectives from the text and print them along with the nouns they were used with, with the order mixed up. The students then match them and try to re-tell as much of the text as they can remember, using these items.
  - get the students to discuss in pairs what they remember about the text. Then elicit ideas from the whole group reformulating where necessary to ensure recycling of the language that was actually used in the text. For instance, if in one lesson you played a listening about an accident, the conversation next lesson with the whole group might include the following:

    Ss: *They went round a corner.*

    T: *Yeah, OK. So the accident happened when they were going round a … not a corner, but a …?*

    Ss: *bend.*

    T: *A bend, yeah, and if it's the kind of bend you can't see round, it's very MMMMM …*

    Ss: *tight?*

    T: *A tight bend, yes.*

Note: This kind of retelling forces the students to meet language a step up from what they currently produce, and pushes them to start taking on some of this new language.

Revision activity 8

Repeat (and extend) activities

- Choose an exercise from a previous class that you want to revisit. It should include a clear speaking task and (ideally) some language linked to and practised in this speaking. It could be from any class earlier in the course, recent or not.
- In class, tell the students they are going to repeat a speaking activity that they have done before, but this time they are going to do it better! Allow the students time to look at the language connected to the speaking task, marking anything they had forgotten.
- Put the students into groups to help each other with any language that has been forgotten. Monitor and give feedback.
- (If relevant) tell the students to close their books and to then repeat the speaking task. You might:
  - write up basic errors involving language from recent classes. Then encourage self-correction.
  - write gapped sentences featuring new items the students need, and then elicit the missing words.
  - add a further practice/extension where students personalise the task/language more.

Note: There is often a fear of repetition in language teaching, a sense that students will be bored if asked to revisit language or activities. Nevertheless, it remains true that repetition is central to the development of automaticity. It is also true that, for many students, repeating activities is reassuring, as it allows for the consolidation (and development) of language already studied – and avoids the extra level of challenge that occurs when a task requires practice of new language.

Asking the students to revisit exercises studied in previous lessons, to check how much of the language they remember and to repeat any connected speaking activity gives them the chance to perform better second time around – and can also give the teacher the chance to address any issues that may arise and to add in any new language that may be needed, thus also ensuring a level of challenge for the stronger students in the class.

Revision activity 9

Test and remember

- This activity usually works best if done at least twice – once just after students have finished an exercise, and once in a following lesson. It requires exercises that focus on matching:
    - questions with answers.
    - statements with possible follow-up responses.
    - the beginnings of sentences with their endings.
    - verbs, nouns or adjectives with collocates.
    - descriptions or definitions of things with the actual names of the things described.
- In class, go through the answers to the exercise, work on any language that has caused problems, asking questions about it, providing extra examples and maybe writing up some extra boardwork.
- Next, give the students a minute or two to try and remember the language from the exercise.
- Put the students into pairs (A and B) and tell the Bs to close their books. The As read out their sentences, the Bs try to say the correct responses, with the As correcting them if necessary. After a few minutes, stop the students and change the pairs round, so that, this time, B is testing and A is trying to remember.
- It is often a good idea to make the stronger student of each pair a B. This means the weaker student – A – gets more time and more opportunities to see and hear the language before they are tested and required to reproduce the language.
- The students can be encouraged to repeat the exercise at home as a way of revising, and you can then repeat it in a subsequent class – either by putting the students in pairs or simply by playing the role of Student A, with the whole class then shouting out the responses that B said the lesson before.

Note: Encouraging memorisation of the language in exercises and repeating the testing task is a covert way of reminding the students that it is not enough to simply do exercises, practise them in class and then move on. Instead, they need to notice and try to remember the language in exercises, and extend this process over time (see also page 58).

Revision activity 10

Team games

- Either make a list of at least 25 items you want to revise or in class ask the students to tear out a piece of paper, rip into two or three pieces and, on each, write an item from their notebooks or the coursebook. If you choose the latter option, collect each piece of paper as the students write, rejecting duplicates and checking that the words are legible!
- Once you have your items, divide the class into two equal teams. Put one team on one side of the room, the other team on the other, and place two chairs at the front of the room, each facing one of the teams.
- One person from each team comes and sits at the front of the class with their back to the board.
- Write an item from the list on the board.
- Each team should then explain the item to their team member at the front of the class. Tell the class not to say any part of the item or to use L1.
- The first person to guess gets a point for their team. Record the scores on the board and bring another pair of students to the front of the class. Continue until you have covered all the items on the list.
- As the students compete, note down phrases that caused problems. You might ask extra language-generating checking questions for bonus points.
- A quicker (but less fun) way of doing this activity is for the teacher to provide the explanations for the competing pairs.
- Another variation is to write words on the board and tell the students to only shout out collocates rather than explanations.

Note: Due to their competitive nature and the fact they can end up being quite raucous, these particular activities often work well at the end of a course. If trying them, you may also want to ensure that you are not teaching in a room next door to a quiet class who won't appreciate the noise they may generate!

C

Teaching lexically has so far approached lessons largely from the point of view of a general English course where classroom materials are used. Teachers in different contexts may sometimes wonder whether this is relevant to their situation.

The short answer to this is that lexical teaching is fundamentally about a way of thinking about language, so the kinds of things you do in the classroom – and the techniques suggested in Part B – should predominantly stay the same; what changes is the *language* that different types of students will need.

Developing lexical teachers

However, there are certain areas, such as low-level classes, exam classes and EAP, where a 'grammar + words + skills' view has come to have a particularly strong hold. In Part C, we address some of the specific concerns about a lexical approach in these kinds of classes.

When it comes to one-to-one classes and young learners, many teachers (consciously or not) already teach quite lexically. We look at why this may be the case, and suggest some adaptations to the methodology we have so far put forward.

The rest of the sections in Part C address how lexical teaching may be encouraged through teacher training and through development in schools. Obviously, we hope that this book will play a part in this and form the basis for formal training sessions, but the emphasis here is on heightening awareness of the structures and conversations that may implicitly reinforce the 'grammar + words + skills' view of ELT. We suggest different conversations and approaches to lesson observation and training that may be more supportive of lexical teachers.

From lexical teachers to lexical writers

Central to this is, on the one hand, adopting a lexical view of published materials that may encourage a greater demand for these, but perhaps, more importantly, we suggest that teachers should start to write more material themselves. We believe there is a very positive symbiotic relationship between teaching and writing, when materials are written by teachers themselves.

We hope that you will enjoy the writing process and that you will learn as much from it as we have over the years – and we look forward to perhaps seeing the fruits of some of your labour in the future.

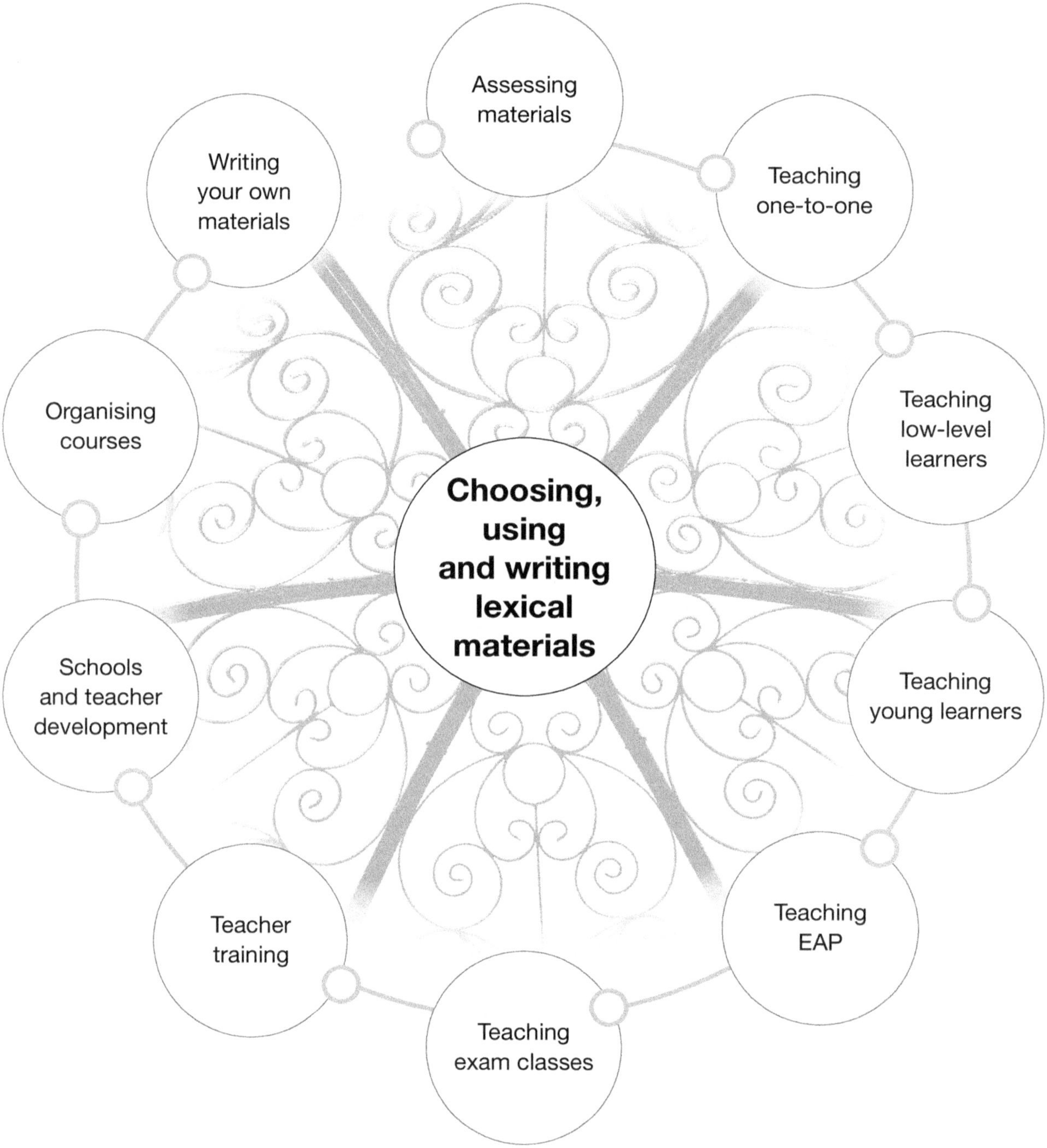
Choosing, using and writing lexical materials
Assessing materials
Teaching one-to-one
Teaching low-level learners
Teaching young learners
Teaching EAP
Teaching exam classes
Teacher training
Schools and teacher development
Organising courses
Writing your own materials

Assessing materials

In much of the discussion on how coursebooks can have a negative impact on teaching and learning, there is often an underlying assumption that coursebooks are essentially all the same. Publishers can exacerbate this by demanding that certain structures are covered at certain levels and that, at lower levels, structures should be presented in a particular order. Teachers (or whoever chooses the book) can also make the same assumption, by distinguishing books mainly on the basis of:

- the visual impact.
- the topics of the texts.
- the extras (video/website/testing pack).

While all these aspects may well have some value, we would suggest that clearer differences appear if you look in detail at the language and the activities.

Ask the following questions of your coursebook or the materials you use:

Grammar exercises

- Are the examples of structures natural-sounding, or are they unlikely to be said?
- Are they mainly spoken examples, or mainly written?
- If spoken examples, how many show exchanges, and how many are just single sentences?
- If written, are they within a text or just single sentences?
- Do they exclude other grammar structures, apart from the new structure being explicitly looked at?
- How much recycling or extra vocabulary is included?
- Do 'freer' practice activities allow the students to produce a variety of grammar (ie to integrate the new with their existing knowledge), or not?

Vocabulary exercises

- Do they mainly focus on matching single words to meaning, or do they develop deeper knowledge of a word?
- How much variety is there in the vocabulary focused on? Is it mainly based on familiar lexical sets?
- Is much of the language in texts focused on, or not? Are the students asked to do anything with this language?
- Are frequent words prioritized, or not?
- Is vocabulary practised and personalised?
- Is memorisation and varied revision encouraged? If so, in what ways?
- How much is vocabulary recycled in the texts and other exercises, both within and across units?
- Do tests and formal revision exercises deepen knowledge of words, or only look at meaning?

Speaking

- How many speaking opportunities are provided?
- How open are they? How many allow the students to push the boundaries of their language?

Listening

- How many of the listening texts are based on conversations you might hear or have? How many are interviews or monologues?
- What is driving the listening texts – the topic and discussion they generate, the kinds of conversations we want to 'teach', or a grammar presentation?
- How many exercises focus on 'hearing' language?

If you have read the rest of *Teaching Lexically*, you should now have a clear idea of what answers to these questions a lexical teacher may hope for. In doing the tasks in Part B, you may have already found limitations in some materials for more lexically-minded teachers.

These more language-focused questions about materials (you may want to think of some for reading and writing) offer new insights into coursebooks. They may also make you more aware of:

- what aspects of your coursebook to supplement.
- how you can ensure language is recycled if you replace activities or texts.
- how to approach writing your own material.

Teaching one-to-one

The lexical teaching described in this book attempts to bring some of the responsiveness and language focus of one-to-one classes into group situations. Indeed, you can see ideas from *The Lexical Approach* by Michel Lewis (1993) in Peter Wilberg's book *One to One*, published six years earlier. One-to-one classes or small groups offer a great opportunity to develop as a lexical teacher. For example, as you get to know your student, you should get better at predicting what they might say about topics; and it is easier to hear what they say and to spend time correcting and reformulating their output, especially if you know their L1.

Speaking

Being able to work directly with student language means you can be less reliant on published materials. You can repeatedly use and develop the typical conversation starters and scenarios discussed on page 80, which may in turn lead to some more intensive practice based on chunks, grammar, or lexical sets.

Similarly, you might start with activities that reflect what your student actually does in English (see also page 81). If they work in business and have to make a presentation, or are going to go out for dinner with a client, it would be best to use the lessons to do the actual presentation or to roleplay a conversation in the kind of restaurant they are going to, with you taking the role of client. Out of these activities, you might first focus on simply reformulating and producing phrases that are correct for the situation and your student's meaning, but you may then draw attention to patterns (including traditional grammar) and vocabulary. You may find it easier to do this over two or more lessons.

- In the first lesson:
  - Do the task.
  - Make initial comments about overall success.
  - Repeat the task, recording or writing it together.
- At home:
  - Analyse the language you wrote or recorded in the lesson.
  - Notice correct language to highlight and perhaps expand on (including what you said).
  - Notice errors and gaps that you can then correct and can provide additional examples for.
- In the second lesson:
  - Go through these corrections.
  - Get your student to repeat them.
  - Re-do/re-record the task.
- In later lessons:
  - Repeat the task.
  - Use the examples you highlighted/corrected, to focus on particular language areas.

Reading and listening

In one-to-one classes, it is easier to work with texts the student brings to class. If you share an L1, the best initial comprehension check may be to do a timed reading, or to listen to the text and ask your student to explain what they understood, using L1. They can then:

- read the text aloud to you, and stop where they stumble or are unclear about what they have read.
- listen and stop where they are unclear about what is said.

At these points, you obviously need to explain, exemplify and maybe ask questions. With listenings, you may want to show how the soundshapes of words change in faster speech. Finally, you can ask the student to discuss the text in more detail.

You may then use the text in a later lesson, and:

- do a revision activity such as those in Chapter 7.
- do tasks focused on vocabulary (see pages 91–93).

Published materials

This does not mean you should never use published materials. Some students won't have specific needs, and may like the comfort that a coursebook offers. You can still personalise examples of language to a greater degree, and will be able to spend more time asking questions and getting feedback. You may also bypass topics the student does not like.

Teaching low-level learners

Lexical views of language probably have most impact on the syllabus at lower levels. At Starter and Elementary levels, the traditional 'grammar plus words' syllabus primarily emphasises controlling the grammar – both receptively and productively. Most mainstream Elementary-level coursebooks have the first example of *was* around page 45, and the first example of *went* a few pages later. *Been* may not occur until page 100 or beyond, despite the fact that all these words are among the 200 most frequent words in English.

While *was* and *went* appear in all Starter courses (which begs the question of why they are then left until later units in Elementary-level books!), *been* generally does not. This means students will not encounter the questions *Have you been here before?* or *How long have you been here?* within their first 200 or so hours of study, yet are likely to be asked in many initial social exchanges.

The restrictions imposed on grammar also have an impact on the vocabulary taught, as some frequent words are commonly used with forms other than the present simple. To avoid 'unknown' grammar, these items are either presented as single words – or not taught. There is also an emphasis on lists of nouns that fit basic patterns: *There is an X, I am an X, I have an X, I play X*, etc. This may be one reason why a word like living room gets taught far earlier than a verb such as *cause*, even though it is 30 times less common in the British National Corpus (BNC).

This is not to say that frequency is everything. Students travelling abroad may want to know a range of foods, for example, some of which are infrequent in a corpus such as the BNC, but we should be *aware* of frequency and teach high-frequency words (see page 36).

Of course, all this is only true if the teacher follows the coursebook, and restricts their own input in similar ways. As lexical teachers, we may do the following:

- Introduce more grammar through chunks and phrases such as *Have you (ever) been to (Russia)? What are you doing this weekend? I didn't hear you*, etc.
- Build short dialogues starting from common conversation starters (see page 80) or common phrases in the exercises we do (page 66).
- Teach questions for receptive understanding and restricted productive answers. For example: *What time … did you / does it / shall we / will you*, etc?
- Do more interaction, and help the students to produce what they want to say – especially with the aid of L1.
- Do additional vocabulary work, particularly on high-frequency words, to rapidly develop a reading level of 500–1000 word families.
- Use and teach memory techniques, such as using mime/actions (Total Physical Response) and flashcards.
- Give full, natural examples of words, whether the students have studied the grammar in them or not.

Teacher expectations

Supporters of a more restricted 'grammar + words' syllabus tend to pose these kinds of objections:

- *Students can't just learn chunks. They will get lost.*
- *Students get confused if they see unknown grammar.*
- *Students are not ready to learn 'higher level' grammar.*
- *Students will get it wrong. They will make mistakes.*

These comments say more about teacher expectations than about low-level students:

- Students can't just learn chunks – of course. Our view is that chunks enable communication, and may help later when focusing and expanding on phrases as grammar patterns.
- Students may ask about grammar they don't know, but the answers do not have to be detailed or confusing – *'it's the past', 'it's an adjective', 'it's X in L2'*, etc, are all that is needed at this stage.
- Students may indeed not be 'ready' for any additional practice: it is the repeated noticing over time that is crucial.
- Low-level students make mistakes, with grammar and with chunks. These are steps to learning – not an excuse for more grammar practice, or for avoiding real communication.

Teaching young learners

We should make it clear that our experience of young learners is mainly based on parenting (in bilingual contexts) and reading, though we do have experience of teaching young learners from four to sixteen.

We feel that most techniques in this book are usable with teenagers – and any child who has essentially mastered their own L1, and grasps broad concepts of language such as:

- Words have different meanings in different contexts.
- Units of meaning may consist of more than one word.
- Idiomaticity – some ways of saying things are accepted in a speech community, others are not.
- Ideas such as time, hypotheticality or function can be realised using language forms and patterns.

In addition, these older learners will usually have developed cognitive abilities that enable them to:

- read and write.
- pay conscious attention to patterns.
- talk about language (not just *use* it).
- use learning strategies.
- motivate themselves.

Where this is not the case, as with many very young learners, approaches that make use of this knowledge and these skills, whether based on 'grammar + words' or a more lexical view, are constrained by this lack of knowledge. As lexical teachers, for example, we might be unable to ask some of the questions we suggested in the chapter 'Teaching vocabulary lexically' (eg *What's the noun of 'sad'?*), but could ask some others using L1 (eg *How do you know when someone is sad? / Why do people get sad?*). The answers to these questions will also be in L1, but we can translate some ideas into English.

Give plenty of exposure to language.

Because young learners may not be able to understand grammatical concepts, we must inevitably rely more on exposure to language and on teaching routines. This is one reason why – contrary to popular myth – we should expect *slower* progress for children learning in a classroom setting than for adults. As well as the ideas that follow, we may also tell stories, teach songs and rhymes – just as we would do in L1, in fact.

Start from words and collocations.

A key benefit of starting young may be the head start you get learning words. We can teach a lot through flashcards and mime/TPR. As lexical teachers, we want to move beyond single words by:

- having word combinations or phrases for the flashcards/mimes (*want an apple* – not just *apple*; *I played tennis with my friend* – not just *play tennis*).
- saying examples (perhaps with some translation) after the students remember the basic words.

Make use of routines to teach chunks and patterns.

We can ask routine questions at the beginning or end of each lesson – *What did you do at the weekend? What are you doing tomorrow?* – which the students can answer in L1 to begin with. We can then teach English answers over time. We can present class rules in English (*Don't shout, Share nicely*) or familiar routines that parents and teachers may use in L1 (*Have you washed your hands? Did you use soap? Have you brushed your teeth?*). English can be used to reinforce other learning in, say, Maths (*What's 6 times 6?*). Again, we can accept answers in L1. We may also retell stories over a term, especially where there are drill-like responses the children can learn, like *Who's been sleeping in my bed?*

Tasks and teacher–student chat

Many books and tasks that are provided for young learners involve colouring, drawing and the like. These tasks 'practise' words, but, more importantly, provide a change of pace and a way to maintain motivation. Clearly, learners are unlikely to do these tasks in English, but teachers can provide further exposure to English by making comments on what the learners are doing, or by asking simple questions (*What's this?* etc). Again, we might translate some responses into English, or encourage the students to use English words they know.

Teaching EAP

Increasingly, there are many courses aimed at preparing students for degree and master's programmes. These courses typically focus on developing academic skills – reading, writing, critical thinking, presentations, etc. As we have seen, a lexical approach emphasises word knowledge and teaching language through skills, rather than skills as strategies separate to language. It also supports programmes that focus on specific subject areas and the reading and writing that students actually do.

Understanding the vocabulary deficit

One study suggests that if you want to understand 97% of typical academic texts, you need to know around 15,000 word families. This 97% is an important figure, as it is the level at which you can deal with unknown words confidently and accurately. While non-native-speaker students may cope with a level of word knowledge below 15,000 word families, vocabulary acquisition is obviously crucial and a key reason it takes so long to advance from Upper-Intermediate level to Advanced.

What language to focus on

Many academic English courses deal with this deficit by focusing on Coxhead's (2005) Academic Word List (AWL) or something similar. Coxhead's list focuses on 570 common word families across a range of subject areas. This is a useful resource, but it is vital to recognise its limits and use it appropriately. Firstly, 600 word families are a drop in the ocean, compared to the deficit noted above. Furthermore, if students really are Upper-Intermediate, they will already know the meanings of many basic words (eg *adult*, *area*, *concentrate*, *design*, *economy*, etc). They then need to learn how to *use* these words: their collocates, co-text, opposites, synonyms, etc, within their subject areas. This is also true of other word forms within families.

Exploring the language around the items in the AWL in this way will lead to 'teaching' infrequent words. This is not a problem. Indeed, we still need to encourage students to at least remember the meaning of many infrequent words, as they will be items they lack. We can help by considering how useful words are in a subject area and training students to make choices about what vocabulary to actively remember and work on.

We may also want to spend time on how to express similar meanings in different ways – using synonyms in context more, or different word forms from the same family to paraphrase and show understanding. This is vital in academic writing and discussion.

Grammar

The main thing to note is that, in academic texts, verb phrases tend to be quite simple, while noun phrases are far more complex. One way to develop this area is to use items from the AWL and explore how information is added to these nouns in particular subject areas. You could take, for example, the word *emergence* and come up with:

the emergence of alternative finance and funding models
the emergence of a civil rights movement during WWII
You can then explore how these noun phrases might be used or might collocate with verbs and adjectives, etc.

Writing

Writing clearly plays a key role in any EAP programme and, as we saw in Chapter 6, providing models and analysing genre is key. Genre analysis has a long history in EAP, but the focus is often on professional academic writing, which differs from the writing students do. Students may need to write short paragraphs, summaries or reflective reports. Even where essays are required, these may vary wildly across subject areas.

Critical thinking

Many EAP courses also claim to develop critical thinking skills. While critical thinking is valuable, as lexical teachers, we would start by teaching the language we use to express critical judgements. That does not just mean functional phrases to express disagreement, but phrases such as *biased in favour of* or *small sample size*. Again, this kind of language may vary across subject areas.

Teaching exam classes

Rather than testing discrete items, many exams have become increasingly skills-based (listening, reading, speaking, writing). This is positive, in that there is a focus on outcomes that reflect real life: what you can do with your language, rather than just your knowledge of words and grammar rules. There may also be a washback, as teachers prepare students for exams by doing similar tasks. However, while it is good to practise skills, the primary route to better reading, listening, writing and speaking involves learning more language – particularly lexis – and, at higher levels, the lexical load increases massively.

Don't believe in shortcuts!

In the high-stakes world of testing, it is unsurprising that students and teachers believe they can beat the system and improve test scores by learning exam strategies and tricks, or by doing exam practice. To some extent, exam boards also have a vested interest in this, as they can sell past papers and preparation books.

However, by definition, proficiency exams are a reliable guide to language level. In most cases, they also use familiar task types – or ones that have been tested for transparency and effectiveness with students who do not know the exam. If this were not the case, and the exams could be 'cheated' through use of strategies, then the exam would not be fit for purpose.

The role of exam practice

We would suggest starting your course with a practice exam under timed conditions. This will:

- give you a clear idea of students' current levels.
- raise any problems in terms of how to do tasks.
- illustrate what language is tested, what is focused on, and how much needs to be learned to achieve a pass.

However, beyond this, doing past papers has limited value and is a slow way of acquiring new vocabulary – unless we use the practice texts and tasks to deliberately focus on language. In this case, we need to be aware that language items in past papers are unlikely to be directly tested again in future tests (especially at higher levels). As such, if there is a multiple-choice item, we might want to explore the vocabulary and usage related to the wrong answers as much as the correct ones! In texts, we might want to look at the language from the whole text in more detail, even where the exam task focuses on gist, or where questions only focus on narrow parts of the text. We may also discuss the texts before and after the exam task, to elicit and focus on other areas of language (see Chapters 4 and 5).

Analysing language

Where proficiency exams do have tests of discrete language items, it is also valuable for you, as a teacher, to look back over a series of previous exams and see whether there are any language areas or writing genres that are commonly tested. In exams such as the Cambridge FCE, these language areas are generally not the tenses and aspects that dominate most coursebooks, but, instead, are based on vocabulary and what it means to know a word, aspects of syntax, noun phrases and discourse such as linking words. In other words, the exam shares a more lexical view of language than you might expect! The kind of questions suggested in Chapter 1, and our approach to writing, focus attention on what is tested.

Speaking feedback that matches exam tasks

Finally, the approach to feedback suggested in Chapter 3 also allows repeated practice for the exam, via:

- provision of full examples, including grammar.
- gapped words and grammar items as they may be seen in cloze tests.
- the exploration of different words in word families, which may be needed in sentence completions.
- reformulated language and the provision of synonyms, which may appear in skills questions.

Teacher training

All trainees arrive on training courses having learned a foreign language to some degree. This can affect their beliefs about what to teach and how to do it. For many, those beliefs are based on the 'grammar + words' view of language they encountered at school. A further influence may be wider debates about young people's supposed lack of grammar. Our own experience of international training and diploma courses is that they tend to reinforce a 'grammar + words' view of language, while adding an extra layer of skills training.

Unconscious messages for trainees

The reinforcement of 'grammar + words', and the primacy of grammar, may be more or less explicit:

- Input may be divided into vocabulary and grammar, with a larger proportion of time devoted to grammar.
- Trainees have to teach specific grammar points and sets of single words, and are evaluated on completing those aims.
- Trainees are discouraged from going 'off topic' or responding to students, because their time is restricted and the completion of aims is graded highly.
- Assessors comment that trainees 'haven't done a grammar lesson yet' or 'were weak on their grammar lesson'. These become key decisions on grading, in a way that does not apply to vocabulary.
- Trainees are told to put grammar models/substitutions on one side of the board, words on the other.
- Advice on supplementing or replacing the coursebook might focus on:
  - a different/extra grammar practice.
  - a fun way to present words or grammar.
  - a more interesting or 'authentic' text.

This is instead of:

- focusing on the naturalness of the language.
- deepening word knowledge.
- thinking about the language in texts, and how it could be exploited and recycled.

Alternatives to a 'grammar + words' view are considered on higher-level teacher development courses more, but whether it is Task-Based Learning, Dogme or some kind of lexical approach, these are often presented as marginal or experimental. Through being marginalised, they are set against the 'mainstream' approach that is taught – which, in turn, can create a disconnect for teachers who align themselves with these marginal methods, especially when it comes to assessment.

This also leaves trainees short-changed in terms of how they can develop as the kinds of teacher they want to be – whether task-based, lexical or whatever. Just one example of this is the way in which teachers may be discouraged from using translation in assessed lessons, rather than learning how to integrate L1 and make use of it in consistent and principled ways.

Trainers affect change

These issues also affect trainers who may adopt some kind of lexical approach to language, but feel:

- constrained by their training syllabus.
- that a simplified version of language and teaching needs to be presented first.
- they need to prepare students for the 'real world' of coursebooks with a 'grammar + words + skills' model.

We hope that *Teaching Lexically* will already have given some ideas about how to tackle these issues. However, for those who are sympathetic to lexical teaching, there are further things that might be considered:

- Make sure you clarify your beliefs about language and learning to your trainees.
- Be aware of unconscious messages that support a 'grammar + words' view (see above) and see if you can reverse some of them.
- See how far lexical teaching fits with the existing criteria on your teacher-training programme.
- Review assessment and criteria, where possible. For example:
  - Could at least one assessment be based on teaching something new without materials?
  - Could effective L1 use be incorporated?

Schools and teacher development

Teachers and managers may find existing structures and attitudes within a school make adopting a more lexical approach difficult. As with teacher training, observations may emphasise completing narrow aims and following a tight lesson plan, which may in turn discourage freer and more student-centred approaches.

School and management observations

It may be that broad criteria such as the following would offer more scope for different approaches:

- Teach some new useful language.
- Provide the students with a chance to integrate new language with old.
- Ensure some exchange of thoughts and feelings.

Criteria such as these are more likely to lead to discussions about what is useful, how you know something is new, and the kinds of practice provided.

School structures and teacher conversations

Course structures and staffroom conversations may also covertly reinforce a 'grammar + words + skills' view, even where a manager wants to shift direction. For example, the school may sell 'grammar' courses or 'speaking' courses. They may have supplementary material on grammar, vocabulary or listening, or offer development sessions focusing on activities. Staffroom conversations may reflect and reinforce these ideas:

Have you got anything on conditionals?
We did articles, so you can do quantifiers next.
There's a crossword on family words in book X.
I need a listening.
This is a good speaking task – it took half an hour.
They seemed to enjoy it. They talked a lot.

We are not saying these conversations are bad per se, or that it is wrong to replace a coursebook or to not use one. What we are saying is that such conversations often fail to sufficiently engage with language – and how it can be integrated with what has come before and will come after.

Questions for lexical teachers

Lexically speaking, we prefer the following questions:

- *What did I learn about my students today?*
  What did they learn about each other?

These questions see the students as individuals, and may encourage more personalised practice of language and genuine interactions.

- *What new language did they learn?*
  What language did I teach that I haven't before?
  Was it useful? Will they be able to use it outside class?

These encourage teachers to push their students' language and explore areas beyond basic EFL grammar, while keeping in mind the naturalness of examples and their utility.

- *Could I write material based on that?*

It may be that you can develop new language by writing material. Writing gives you time to consider more natural examples. In turn, this can help you respond more spontaneously to students in class.

- *Were there any/better questions I could have asked?*
  What questions did my students ask?
  Did I answer them well? How could I do better?

We want to develop our ability to ask about language. This is difficult, and is an ongoing (lifelong!) process.

Teacher development within a school

Questions like those above can be asked every day and cost nothing, but can have a major impact. We also believe teacher growth develops best when teachers plan together and talk about materials they are actually using, what language is best exploited, and how.

Again, this applies to materials in their broadest sense – not just to coursebooks, but also to conversations you plan to teach (for example, see page 81) or materials you plan to write collaboratively. Obviously, we hope this book will provide a valuable guide to this process.

Organising courses

One criticism of *The Lexical Approach* (1993) by Michael Lewis is that it offered no syllabus. It might be more accurate to say that there are too many possible lexical syllabuses, compared to the one grammar syllabus we are all familiar with, especially at low levels.

We hope that you now see that even where courses are driven by grammar and lexical sets, there are still many ways of pursuing a more lexical view of language through your teaching. However, here are some alternative organising principles that have been suggested – and some additional comments.

Word frequency and word grammar

In the late 1980s, *The Cobuild English Course* organised its syllabus around the most frequent words in English. Scott Thornbury's grammar book *Natural Grammar* (2004) attempted something similar. It took high-frequency words such as *a*, *all* and *any* and explored grammatical patterns around them. Neither had great commercial success, perhaps because of the issues that arise in terms of communicative outcomes when a course is organised mainly around frequency. The most frequent words – and the most frequent collocations (eg *think that*) – form a relatively small part of any message, so, just as we limit what students can say by only teaching the present simple at Starter level, we restrict students by only teaching them the most frequent words. However, Thornbury's book may be particularly helpful for raising awareness of patterns that teachers can draw attention to, and we would see teaching frequent words as a good strand in a syllabus – perhaps introduced mainly as part of reading and listening lessons.

Keywords and word networks

Another way might be to adapt the frequency model. George Woolard's *Key Words for Fluency* (2004, 2005) selects frequent nouns at different levels and explores collocates. The nouns are mostly 'content'-based, and are sometimes organised around related themes. This approach potentially enables communication, and recycles vocabulary via collocates that recur with different nouns and examples. You might consider different choices to Woolard in terms of grading, or perhaps in using verbs or adjectives as 'keywords' – as well as nouns.

A further consideration is how much information you give about one word. You may feel Woolard's book has too much for one sitting. You might focus on fewer medium-strength collocations (see suggestions by Timmis, 2015). Another option is to explore more the networks of related words by thinking about the texts that may come out of a collocation, rather than only the collocations of the individual word (see page 42).

Texts, stories and messages

Keith Folse (2004) suggests that vocabulary might be best learnt by starting from texts and stories, rather than words and lexical sets. Stories can be about anything: losing something, going to a shop, etc. Folse argues that words in stories are less confusing, more memorable and learned more quickly. Stories may also allow you to integrate and revisit grammar more easily and lead fairly directly to students telling their own stories (see also page 75: the 'Scar' stories).

Texts don't have to be stories, though. They could be dialogues. For example, with our own coursebook *Innovations Elementary*, we based the syllabus around common conversations and questions taught with a small range of replies (including 'unmastered' grammar taught as phrases) on one spread and texts on another.

George Woolard's *Messaging* (2014) also suggests organising a course around all kinds of texts. He suggests grading them in three broad levels. From a lexical point of view, we would also argue that grading should not unnaturally restrict grammar, as many graded readers do. Start by finding or writing the texts. Compared to higher levels, lower-level texts will tend to:

- have a higher proportion of high-frequency words to low frequency.
- have a higher proportion of reuseable chunks (irrespective of grammar).
- have a lower range of grammar structures (though *not* so the text is unnatural).
- use very high-frequency words (*be*/*go*/*have*, etc) with unmastered grammar.

Writing your own materials

We were lucky enough to have been able to write two series of coursebooks while teaching regularly. A lot of ideas for lessons that we have written came out of conversations that emerged in classes we taught without materials. These classes without materials were engaging and dynamic, but they were also hard work – and it was sometimes difficult to ensure repetition of language and coherence over a number of lessons. Writing materials helped us overcome these issues.

Writing and developing as a teacher

Writing materials forces you to be more critical and considered than if you teach something on the spur of the moment. In any lesson, you can teach something that students want to say at a particular point and feel it has relevance – without considering whether such circumstances will recur, or if the language will be relevant in the future. When language is written down – when it will be kept, and might be used by other teachers and students – you have to think more carefully about long-term goals, and what others may want. You also need to be able to justify your choices about what to teach. That inevitably leads you to think about what you do in the classroom.

However, there is no doubt that, with materials, a lesson can lose some of the dynamism of no-materials teaching. This led us to think more about how to make the language on a page more dynamic and vital. In our case, that led us to develop the kind of techniques explored in *Teaching Lexically*. That, in turn, has affected the way we write material, as now we may choose some words and examples with a view to how exploitable they are.

Finally, spending time thinking how to exploit the language has often led to us being able to 'spontaneously' react to our students more, as well as generating more new language and conversation in class. So we would recommend that any teacher writes material for their class.

Process and collaboration

While writing materials may be good for development in itself, we also benefited hugely from working with a publisher. Obviously, this is not an option that will be available to everyone, but the whole process of in-house materials development can benefit from school staff taking on roles found within publishing houses:

- **The publisher**:
  This role involves deciding the overall aim of the product, or helping the writers hone their ideas. The 'publisher' writes a brief or outline for all the writers to follow. In a school, this may mean a Director of Studies setting out guidelines for specific projects or just day-to-day materials – perhaps based on the questions with which we began Part C.
- **The writers**:
  We feel writers work best in pairs – not necessarily writing side by side, but checking each others' exercises, bouncing ideas off each other or offering help. You might pair teacher-writers by level.
- **The developmental editor**:
  They are a link between publisher and writer. They check answers and ensure the work complies with the brief or discuss exceptions. They may also challenge the writers' assumptions from the point of view of other kinds of teachers.
- **The reader or pilot**:
  A teacher outside the writing team should, ideally, try out the material – and comment.
- **Teacher's book writer**:
  They check the answer key, and provide ideas on how to exploit the material.

Clearly, in a school, all this could also be done as a group.

Possible individual and group projects

To finish, here are some ideas on how you can start to turn the ideas behind lexical teaching into material of your own:

- Write revision activities (see Chapter 7).
- Rewrite a published language exercise, to include more re-usable chunks (see page 64).
- Make lists of core words to be taught at different levels. Write exercises around these words (see Chapter 1).
- Write and record meaningful drills (page 110).
- Write dialogues around situations or topics (page 81).
- Write several model texts for the writing genres your students are doing.
- Instead of finding a text or video on a topic on the internet, write your own.
- Discuss how texts (published or self-written) may be exploited, and turn them into lessons.
- Review and write teachers' notes of existing material in your staffroom.

Bibliography

Aitchison, J (1996) *The Language Web: The Power and Problem of Words* Cambridge University Press

Aitchison, J (2012). *Words in The Mind 4th Edition* Wiley-Blackwell

Alderson, J. Charles and Urquhart, A.H. (1984) *Reading in a Foreign Language* Longman Pub Group

Alderson, J. Charles (2000) *Assessing Reading* Cambridge University Press

Bilbrough, N. (2011) *Memory Activities for Language Learning* Cambridge University Press

Brazil, D. (1994) *Pronunciation for Advanced Learners of English* Cambridge University Press

Brazil, D. (1995) *A Grammar of Speech* Oxford University Press

Brown, E. and Hatch, C. (1995). *Vocabulary, Semantics and Language Education.* Cambridge University Press

Bruton, A., Garcia Lopez, Dr. M. and Esquiliche Mesa, Dr. R. *Incidental L2 Vocabulary Learning: An Impractical Term?* TESOL Quarterly Vol. 45 Issue 4: 759-768

Cauldwell, R. (2013) *Phonology for Listening* Speech in Action

Collins Cobuild Advanced Learner's Dictionary (2006) Heinle ELT

The Common European Framework of Reference is available free online: *http://www.coe.int/t/dg4/linguistic/Source/Framework_EN.pdf*

Coxhead, A. (2005) *Essentials of Teaching Academic Vocabulary* Houghton Mifflin

Coxhead, A. (2012) *A New Academic Word List* TESOL Quarterly Vol. 34 Issue 2: 213-238

Davis, P. (1989) *Dictation: New Methods, New Possibilities* Cambridge University Press

https://demandhighelt.wordpress.com

Dellar, H and Walkley, A (2004) *Innovations Student's Book Intermediate* Heinle ELT

Dellar, H and Walkley, A (2005) *Innovations Student's Book Elementary* Heinle ELT

Dellar, H and Walkley, A (2010) *Outcomes Student's Book Elementary* Heinle Cengage

Dörnyei, Z. (2001) *Motivational Strategies in the Language Classroom* Cambridge University Press

Ellis, R. (2003) *Task-based Language Learning and Teaching* Oxford University Press

Ellis, N (2013) *Usage-based Language: Investigating the Latent Structures that Underpin Acquisition https://www.youtube.com/watch?v=7cKaX57tEXc*

Field, J. (2009) *Listening in the Language Classroom* Cambridge University Press

Folse, K. (2004) *Vocabulary Myths: Applying Second Language Research to Classroom Teaching* University of Michigan Press

Grabe, W. (2008) *Reading in a Second Language: Moving from Theory to Practice* Cambridge University Press

Hanks, P. (2013) *Lexical Analysis: Norms and Exploitations* MIT Press

Hattie, J. (2011) *Visible Learning for Teachers: Maximizing Impact on Learning* Routledge

Hattie, J. and Yates, G. (2013) *Visible Learning and the Science of How We Learn* Routledge

Hoey, M. (1991) *Patterns of Lexis in Text* Oxford University Press

Hoey, M. (2005) *Lexical Priming: A New Theory of Words and Language* Routledge

Kahneman, D. (2011) *Thinking, Fast and Slow* Farrar, Straus and Giroux

Keller, E and Warner, S. T. (1988) *Conversation Gambits: Real English Conversation Practices* Language Teaching Publications

Kornell, N. (2009) *Optimizing learning using flashcards: Spacing is more effective than cramming* Applied Cognitive Psychology 23: 1297–1317

Krashen, S.D. and Terrell, T.D. (1982) *The Natural Approach: Language Acquisition in the Classroom* Elsevier

Larsen-Freeman, D. (2003) *Teaching Language: From Grammar to Grammaring* Heinle ELT

Laufer, B. (1997) 'The lexical plight in second language reading" in Coady, J. and Huckin, T. (eds.) *Second Language Vocabulary Acquisition: A Rationale for Pedagogy.* Cambridge University Press.

Lewis, M. (1993) *The Lexical Approach: The State of ELT and a Way Forward* Language Teaching Publications

Lewis, M. (1997) *Implementing the Lexical Approach: Putting Theory into Practice* Language Teaching Publications

Long, M. (1996) *The role of the linguistic environment in second language acquisition* in Ritchie, W and Bhatia, T. *Handbook of second language acquisition.* San Diego: Academic Press. pp. 413–468.

Long, M. (2006) *Problems in Second Language Acquisition* Routledge

Long, M (2014) *Second Language Acquisition and Task-Based Language Teaching* Wiley-Blackwell

http://www.macmillandictionary.com/

http://www.macmillandictionary.com/red-word-game/

Morgan, J. and Rinvolucri, M. (1986) *Vocabulary* Oxford University Press

http://www.natcorp.ox.ac.uk/

Nation, I.S.P (2001) *Learning Vocabulary in Another Language* Cambridge University Press

Nation, I.S.P (1993) *Teaching and Learning Vocabulary* Longman

Oxford, R. (1990). *Language learning strategies: What every teacher should know.* Newbury House

Pawley, A. and Syder, F.H. (1983) *Two puzzles for linguistic theory: nativelike selection and nativelike fluency* in Richards, J.C. and Schmidt, R.W., eds. *Language and Communication* Longman.

http://www.phrasesinenglish.org/searchBNC.html

Ross, C. (2002) *Tunnel Visions: Journeys of an Underground Philosopher* Fourth Estate

Swales, John M. (1990) *Genre Analysis: English in Academic and Research Settings* Cambridge University Press

Swan, M. and Smith, B. (1987) *Learner English: A Teacher's Guide to Interference and other Problems* Cambridge University Press

Swan, M. (1996) Hornby Lecture delivered at the 1996 IATEFL conference retrieved from *http://www.mikeswan.co.uk/elt-applied-linguistics/language-teaching.htm*

Thornbury, S. (2004) *Natural Grammar: The keywords of English and how they work* Oxford University Press

Thornbury, S and Meddings, L (2009) *Teaching Unplugged* Delta Publishing

Timmis, I. (2015) *The Lexical Approach and Natural Selection* [blog post] retrieved from *http://www.lexicallab.com/2015/03/the-lexical-approach-and-natural-selection/*

http://www.victoria.ac.nz/lals/resources/academicwordlist/

Walker, R. (2010) *Teaching the Pronunciation of English as a Lingua Franca* Oxford University Press

Walter, C. (2008) *Reading in a Second Language* Subject Centre for Languages, Linguistics and Area Studies Guide to Good Practice from *https://www.llas.ac.uk/resources/gpg/1420*

Wajnryb, R. and Maley, A. (1990) *Grammar Dictation* Oxford University Press

Wilberg, P. (1987) *One to One: A Teacher's Handbook* Language Teaching Publications

Wilberg, P. (1988) quoted in Lewis, M. (1993) *The Lexical Approach: The State of ELT and a Way Forward* Language Teaching Publications

Willis, J. and Willis, D. (1988) *Collins Cobuild English Course* Collins Cobuild

Woolard, G. (2004) *Key Words for Fluency Upper-Intermediate* Heinle ELT

Woolard, G. (2005) *Key Words for Fluency Pre-Intermediate* Heinle ELT

Woolard, G. (2005) *Key Words for Fluency Intermediate* Heinle ELT

Woolard, G. (2013) *Messaging: Beyond a Lexical Approach in ELT* e-book published by The Round

Wray, A. (2008) *Formulaic Language: Pushing the Boundaries* Oxford University Press

Glossary

activate schemata

Schemata are mental frameworks that help us organise and interpret information and experiences. Take, for example, these sentences: *He was miles offside. The goal should never have stood.* Without a 'football schema' these sentences will mean little or nothing. **Schema theory** claims that if we can link new information to existing schemata, the new information will be understood more easily. This led to ELT material often including activities before reading or listening texts in the hope they would **'activate'** students' schemata.

antonyms

Antonyms are words that have opposites meanings in particular contexts. For instance, we may think of *soft* and *hard* as opposites, but the antonym of *a really hard exam* is obviously not *a soft exam*. You can also think of whole phrases being antonyms, so an antonym of *I messed it up* might be *I did my best* or *I made a really good job of it.*

automaticity

Automaticity – the ability to do specific things automatically - is developed over time and allows us to perform tasks without having to focus attention on them.

backchaining

Backchaining is a technique used when drilling longer phrases or sentences. It helps students produce longer stretches of sound by starting with the last sound and then building up backwards from there. It is easier as it requires students to say the new elements first, where they are harder to forget. So if we were to **backchain** the phrase *I wouldn't do that if I were you*, we might drill:

were you; if I were you; do that if I were you; I wouldn't do that if I were you.

bottom-up processing

Bottom-up processing is a way of decoding texts that involves starting with the individual letters (when reading) or phonemes (when listening) and then combining these into syllables and words, and then clauses, etc.

chunks

A **chunk** is a group of words that often occur together. There's no universally accepted definition of what is – and isn't – a chunk, but they include collocations, fixed phrases, idioms, sentence starters and so on. All of the following are chunks: *Going back to what you were saying earlier, We'll cross that bridge when we come to it, pouring with rain, a bit of a nightmare, I'll do it later, I haven't got a clue, a pain in the neck, a bleak forecast.* We usually say chunks in a certain way, sometimes referred to as the **phonological envelope** the chunk comes in.

closed questions

Closed questions are those which can be answered with a simple yes or no response, or questions typically answered by a single word / short phrase.

co-hyponym

Co-hyponyms are words that are all examples of a particular kind of thing. For example, *coach, scooter, train, truck* and *van* are co-hyponyms as they are all kinds of vehicles.

colligation

Colligation refers to the grammatical patterns that individual words are often used with. We can say, for instance, that the verb *to fine* often colligates with the past simple passive – *I was fined £150 for speeding, They were fined £180 for littering*, etc. From these examples, you can also see that *to fine* often colligates with the preposition *for*.

collocation

Collocation refers to the way in which words often occur together with other words. For instance, certain verbs and adjectives often **collocate** with certain nouns. *Make a terrible mess, have a good time* and *have a narrow escape* are all common collocations. We can also say that *narrow* is a **collocate** of *escape* – as, of course, are *lucky, miraculous, attempted, arrange* and *bid*. In the same way, *streets, range, view* and *definition* are collocates of *narrow*.

concept checking questions

Concept checking questions (sometimes known as CCQs) are closed questions asked by teachers to check if learners understand the meaning of a new item. A teacher looking to check *I managed to pass my exam* might ask the following concept checking questions:

Was it difficult? (yes)
Did I try to do it? (yes)
Did I succeed? (yes)

connotation

The **connotation** of a word is the emotional associations connected to it. These connotations may be personal or part of a broader cultural meaning. For instance, for many people the word *liberal* has a positive connotation and they use it to describe themselves. However, for others, it may have negative connotation and suggest someone who is weak and has no morals. Many words have different connotations in different contexts.

co-text
Co-text is language that often occur around a particular item in a certain kind of text. Co-text doesn't necessarily have to come next a particular item, but may well often be found somewhere in the text. For instance, take the collocation *to be found guilty of murder*. In a written text, we might expect some of the following items to appear as co-text: *court, stabbed during a fight, considering the verdict, sentenced to life, cheers from the public gallery*, etc.

decoding
Decoding plays a central role in the way we process written and spoken texts. When we read, we decode by recognising alphabetic letters and then the words that these letters form. When we listen, we decode by recognizing the individual phonemes and the words or phrases that these make up.

discourse
Discourse is simply any piece of connected written or spoken language. Studying discourse is vital if we want to know how language is actually used beyond sentence level.

dictogloss
A **dictogloss** is a kind of dictation. Students hear a short text and then try to reconstruct the whole. Usually, they note down key words they hear and then work on their own and/or with other students before comparing their ideas with the original.

diphthong
A **diphthong** is a one-syllable vowel that involve a movement of tongue and/or lips. There are eight diphthongs in standard English – /ɪə/, /ɪə/, /ʊə/, /ɔɪ/, /əʊ/, /eə/, /ɑɪ/ and /ɑʊ/.

display questions
Display questions are questions such as *What's the past of swim?* The teacher knows the answer to these questions, but asks students to show their knowledge.

drill
If a teacher **drills** a piece of language, they say – or **model** – the item and then get students to repeat it as a group (**choral drilling**) or as individuals. You can drill everything from single words to whole sentences.

elicit
When you **elicit**, you prompt a class – or an individual student – in order to get a particular answer from them. This enables the teacher to check what students know, to encourage them to recall language, and to pool the knowledge of the whole class.

exercise
Exercises often appear in coursebooks and other classroom material and are written to allow testing, exploration and practice of particular items of language. Common types of exercises include gap-filling, matching and correct the error.

extensive reading
Extensive reading is the relaxed reading of longer texts – for pleasure, for general understanding and language development.

genre
A **genre** is a kind of spoken or written discourse recognised and used by members of a particular group. Texts produced within a genre usually share certain lexical, grammatical and structural similarities. Written genres include postcards, conference abstracts and CVs. Spoken genres include news reports and jokes.

gist
If you **get the gist** of something you've heard or read, you understand the most important points without paying attention or understanding everything. In class, we often ask **gist questions** to find out how much of the general meaning of texts students have grasped.

grammaring
Diane Larsen-Freeman (2003) came up with the idea of **grammaring** to describe the skill of 'doing grammar' – applying our knowledge of grammatical structures "accurately, meaningfully and appropriately" when speaking or writing. Grammaring is seen as a dynamic process, as opposed to grammar, which is seen as a system of rules.

homonyms
Homonyms are words that are spelled the same or that sound the same as each other, but which have different meanings. For instance, *write* and *right* are homonyms.

homophones
Homophones are words that sound the same as each other, but which have different spellings and meanings. For example, *there, their* and *they're.*

horizontal development
We can **develop** an item or sentence **horizontally** by thinking about what a writer / speaker might add next. For instance, if we wanted to develop the phrase *Sorry I'm late* horizontally, we might consider the reasons someone would add, such as *I got stuck in traffic.*

hyponym

A **hyponym** is a word which is an example of a more general type. For instance, *mango* is a hyponym of *fruit*, *cricket* is a hyponym of *sport* and *electrician* is a hyponym of *job*.

lexis

Lexis refers to what calls Michael Lewis (1993) called "socially sanctioned independent units" of meaning. These could be individual words, collocations, multi-word items or even whole sentences. We often use it interchangeably with vocabulary.

linking words

Linking words and phrases connect ideas both within and across sentences and paragraphs. They can refer backwards or forwards and express such ideas as contrasting, reinforcing and sequencing.

macro-structure

Spoken and written texts within particular genres often have a general **macro-structure**, which shapes the general form of the whole.

meta-language

Meta-language is the language such as *verb*, *adverb*, or *the present perfect* that we use to talk about language

micro-structure

Specific parts of generic written or spoken texts often have a **micro-structure**. In other words, particular sections of texts such as introductions or conclusions often pattern in similar ways and often use similar – and predictable – language to achieve particular functions.

minimal pairs

Minimal pairs are pairs of words that contain only one different phoneme, but which have two distinct meaning. Examples include: *ship / sheep*, *pair / bear*, *think / thing* and *back / bag*.

model

Teachers can **model** the pronunciation of an item by saying it loudly and clearly so the class can hear it – and try to copy it. In the same way, teaching material – or teachers – can provide **models** of particular conversations that students may want to have: they can show examples of what the conversations look and sound like.

monophthong

A **monophthong** is a single vowel sound produced while the tongue stays in one position. It does not glide up or down towards a new position of articulation. For example: /iː/ and /æ/

noun phrases

Noun phrases are made up of a main noun and additional elements that can be added to the noun. Noun phrases can be built in a range of different ways and are often used as either the subjects or objects of sentences. For example:

- *the man over there*
- *the man over there in the black suit*
- *the tall man over there standing next to the blond women with the fur coat*

open questions

Open questions are those which are likely to elicit more than single-word answers. For example, *Why is this so important to you?* is a more open question than *Is this bothering you?*

paraphrase

If you **paraphrase** something, you express it again using different words. Teachers often paraphrase in order to correct student errors or to explain new items.

phoneme

Phonemes are the smallest units of meaningful sound in a language. For example, /r/ and /l/ are both phonemes in English – and this ensures we hear the meaning of the word *rice* as separate from and distinct to the word *lice*!

priming

According to Michael Hoey, our experiences of meeting language in context **prime** – or condition – us. Our encounters – or **primings** – lead to us somehow subconsciously recording information about the way words are used and our next encounters add extra layers of information, thus deepening our understanding of the word and the way it can work. In this book, we sometimes use priming as a shorthand way of talking about typical uses of words or about our experience of language.

reformulation

If a teacher **reformulates** what a student has said or written, they present it back to the student with errors corrected – or rephrase it in a more linguistically sophisticated way in order to present new language. The teacher may explain the changes – or may not.

register

Register can refer to the degree of formality and / or politeness involved in language use. Seen like this, exchanges can be seen as more formal, neutral or informal. Register can also refer to the kind of language that's a common feature of particular areas of language use such as journalism.

sentence frames

A **sentence frame** consists of words that often occur together at the beginning and then at a subsequent point in sentences - and that can be filled in a range of different ways. For example: *One of the main causes of . . . is the fact . . .* and *I'd like to live in a place where you can . . . and where you don't have to . . . .*

sentences starters

Sentence starters are groups of words frequently used together and found at the beginning of sentences. Sentence starters can remain the same while what follows can be varied in a range of different ways. For example: *The main goal of this report is to ...*, *One thing that really annoys me is . . .* and *If you ask me, there's no point ... .*

synonyms

Synonyms are words / units of meaning that have very similar meanings. For example, *frightened* and *scared* are synonyms – and we can talk about being *really frightened* – or *scared* – at a particular point in a movie or of being *scared / frightened of the dark.* Remember, however, that two words rarely, if ever, share all the same collocations and usages.

syntax

Syntax refers to rules that govern the ways in which words can be combined to make phrases and sentences. What is possible or acceptable syntax will change from language to language. An example of English syntax is the way in which we invert subjects and verbs when we make questions.

task

In the traditional sense of the word, a **task** is a classroom activity with a communicative outcome of some sort. These kinds of tasks are generally supposed to be open-ended and completed using a range of structures and lexical items. However, there is no real consensus on what exactly a task is – or isn't – and the word is also often used to describe all manner of classroom activity: everything from pre- and post-listening tasks to practise tasks and translation tasks.

texting

In his 2013 book *Messaging: Beyond a Lexical Approach*, George Woolard introduces the idea of **texting** to describe the process of encouraging students to produce their own short texts around particular chunks such as *One of the most pressing problems facing ..... today is .....* . From such frameworks – and with assistance – students may go on to text larger messages such as *One of the most pressing problems facing major corporations today is how to motivate employees to work more productively and to increase workers' feelings of satisfaction, involvement and commitment.*

top-down processing

Top-down processing is a way of decoding texts that relies on world knowledge such as knowledge about the topic, familiarity with the speaker / writer, genre awareness, contextual clues and so on to help you make sense of what you are hearing or reading.

topic sentence

A **topic sentence** is a sentence in a paragraph – usually the opening one - that helps to organise the structure of the paragraph by summarising the main thoughts contained it in.

unit of meaning

A **unit of meaning** is word or group of words used together that form one distinct meaning. For example, the word *fire* is in itself ambiguous in meaning. However, in the collocation *friendly fire*, it forms one whole unambiguous unit of meaning – shots accidentally fired at you by members of your own army. Similarly, *a raging fire* signifies something burning out of control, while *a roaring fire* is something you might sit in front of in your living room in the winter.

vertical development

We describe **developing** an item or sentence **vertically** as thinking about the conversation: what might be said by a second person involved in the dialogue. For instance, if we wanted to develop the phrase *Sorry I'm late* vertically, we might consider typical replies: *There you are, I was starting to get worried, It's OK. I haven't been here long myself* and the reply to the reply: *Sorry, I would've rung, but my phone was dead* or *The traffic's mad, isn't it?*

word class

A **word class** is a group of words that serve a particular grammatical feature and that behave in the same way, grammatically speaking. For instance, the words *hot, cold, big, small, inedible* and *spotless* all belong to the adjective word class. Lots of words belong to more than one class. For instance, *up* can be a verb (*up your offer*), a noun (*We're on the up*), an adverb (*She looked up*) or a preposition (*He lives just up the road*).

From the editors

Teaching Lexically is essential reading for any language teacher wishing to incorporate a more lexical approach to their classes. It has been written by two authors who have extensive experience as teachers, trainers and materials writers.

Hugh Dellar and Andrew Walkley both discovered a lexical approach as language learners, and then more formally as language teachers. The materials they have written have an explicit lexical focus and they have trained teachers from all over the world in this approach.

A

The authors discuss principles of how and why people learn foreign languages and discuss choices that teachers, curriculum designers and materials writers make when they approach language and teaching.

They go on to look at two major views of language: 'Grammar plus words plus skills' and 'From words with words to grammar'. This leads to the call for a practical lexical pedagogy with a clear and concise exploration of problems and practicalities of teaching in this way; especially as language teaching operates 'in a grammar-dominated world'.

The authors provide handy and accessible definitions for many terms associated with vocabulary, and they situate grammar and the four skills firmly within this lexical view of teaching.

B

Seven chapters offer over a hundred techniques for teaching lexically through not only grammar and vocabulary but also the four skills. They also show teachers how to recycle and review their teaching with a lexical focus.

Each technique begins with a principle, followed by simple tips on how to practise this principle before finally applying the principle in different teaching situations.

C

For teachers who want to develop as a fully lexical teacher, *Teaching Lexically* encourages the exploration of this kind of approach and shows how it can be adapted and used in a variety of contexts.

Sections on teaching low-level learners, one-to-one, academic English and exam classes all give practical tips on how these circumstances needn't prove a barrier to teaching in a more lexical way.

There is valuable advice for teachers who wish to create their own, more lexically-focused, materials as well. The authors believe there is a positive relationship between teaching and writing, when teachers are writing materials themselves.

This book is much more than a simple collection of activities for vocabulary lessons, or the vocabulary focus part of a lesson. It is really a tool for development and change, based on firm principles yet rooted in the pragmatic reality of day-to-day classroom teaching.

Mike Burghall
Lindsay Clandfield

DELTA TEACHER DEVELOPMENT SERIES

A pioneering award-winning series of books for English Language Teachers with professional development in mind.

Teaching Lexically
by Hugh Dellar and
Andrew Walkley
ISBN 978-1-909-78322-5

Teaching children
how to learn
by Gail Ellis and Nayr Ibrahim
ISBN 978-1-905085-86-6

Film in Action
by Kieran Donaghy
ISBN 978-1-909783-07-2

Going Mobile
by Nicky Hockly and
Gavin Dudeney
ISBN 978-1-909783-06-5

Storytelling
With Our Students
by David Heathfield
ISBN 978-1-905085-87-3

The Autonomy Approach
by Brian Morrison and
Diego Navarro
ISBN 978-1-909783-05-8

Spotlight on Learning Styles
by Marjorie Rosenberg
ISBN 978-1-905085-71-2

The Book of Pronunciation
by Jonathan Marks and
Tim Bowen
ISBN 978-1-905085-70-5

The Company Words Keep
by Paul Davis and
Hanna Kryszewska
ISBN 978-1-905085-20-0

Digital Play
by Kyle Mawer and
Graham Stanley
ISBN 978-1-905085-55-2

Teaching Online
by Nicky Hockly with
Lindsay Clandfield
ISBN 978-1-905085-35-4

Teaching Unplugged
by Luke Meddings and
Scott Thornbury
ISBN 978-1-905085-19-4

Culture in our Classrooms
by Gill Johnson and
Mario Rinvolucri
ISBN 978-1-905085-21-7

The Developing Teacher
by Duncan Foord
ISBN 978-1-905085-22-4

Being Creative
by Chaz Pugliese
ISBN 978-1-905085-33-0

The Business English Teacher
by Debbie Barton,
Jennifer Burkart and
Caireen Sever
ISBN 978-1-905085-34-7

For details of these and future titles in the series, please contact the publisher: *E-mail* info@deltapublishing.co.uk
Or visit the DTDS website at www.deltapublishing.co.uk/titles/methodology